Local Government Institutionalization in Hungary

Gábor Soós

Local Government Institutionalization in Hungary

PL ACADEMIC RESEARCH

Bibliographic Information published by the Deutsche Nationalbibliothek
The Deutsche Nationalbibliothek lists this publication in the Deutsche Nationalbibliografie; detailed bibliographic data is available in the internet at http://dnb.d-nb.de.

Library of Congress Cataloging-in-Publication Data
Soós, Gábor.
Local government institutionalization in Hungary / Gábor Soós.
pages cm
Includes bibliographical references and index.
ISBN 978-3-631-65734-8
1. Local government—Hungary. 2. Political parties—Hungary. I. Title.
JS4673.S66 2015
320.809439—dc23
2015003711

In cooperation with Ad Librum Publishing, Budapest

ad LiBRUM

ISBN 978-3-631-65734-8 (Print)
E-ISBN 978-3-653-05128-5 (E-Book)
DOI 10.3726/978-3-653-05128-5

PL Academic Research is an Imprint of Peter Lang GmbH.

Peter Lang – Frankfurt am Main · Bern · Bruxelles · New York · Oxford · Warszawa · Wien

This publication has been peer reviewed.

www.peterlang.com

Contents

Introduction

This book investigates the institutionalization of a specific organization, the local political party, and explores the factors that influence the level of local party institutionalization.

Three questions can be raised concerning local party institutionalization. The first is normative: does a high level of local party institutionalization contribute to democracy? Shall we promote the institutionalization of local politics through party organizations? The second question is empirical: what determines the level of local party institutionalization? What conditions make local party institutionalization possible and what conditions make it thrive? Finally, the third question is related to policy: How can the level of local party institutionalization be influenced? What kind of legal measures can alter the institutionalization of local parties?

I will focus on the second question in this book: What explains the different levels of institutionalization? In a more technical way, my research question is: What are the systematic factors that shape the degree of local party institutionalization and how strong are their effects? Thus, the aim of the research is to identify variables that statistically explain the variance in the level of local party institutionalization.

The Research Question:

What explains the level of local party institutionalization?

While the majority of the book focuses on the empirical problem, it is not possible to avoid the discussion of the two other questions. Therefore, a part of the first chapter deals with the normative question. It places local party institutionalization in the context of other forms of institutionalization and points to the benefits of party-based local political systems. The concluding chapter returns to the basic questions and provides policy advice on the means by which the level of local party institutionalization can be increased.

The first three chapters of the book outline the research design. In addition to the normative justification of the subject matter, Chapter 1 also defines the basic concepts of this research. Local party institutionalization is conceptualized as a multidimensional notion with four components. The definition of a local party involves not only the local chapters of national parties, but also the civil society organizations that act as local parties by nominating candidates. The last section sheds some light on the endogenous logic of party formation from the viewpoint of national party centers and local politicians. Chapter 2 identifies the independent variables that potentially explain the variance in the level of local party institutionalization. It surveys three bodies of literature to put forward hypotheses about the legal, demographic, socioeconomic, geographical, historical, and typological factors that may influence local party institutionalization. The multidimensional concept of local party institutionalization and the explanatory variables are operationalized in Chapter 3. It also presents the main features of the local government system in Hungary and the sources of data to be used throughout in the research. The clear requirements of data exclude some variables, proposed in the previous chapter, and reduce the number of hypotheses.

The next four chapters discuss the available evidence. Chapters 4 and 5 examine the two most measurable indicators of the *explanandum*, Local Party Government and Local Party Loyalty. Both follow the same pattern: first the overall picture, then bivariate relationships, and finally the multivariate analysis. Chapter 6 builds causal models with several variables to explain the variance in the above mentioned indicators of local party institutionalization by means of indirect paths. Chapter 7 relies on three surveys to provide additional evidence for the evaluation of all dimensions of the central concept of the research and to test the remaining hypotheses.

The last chapter concludes with an assessment of the four dimensions of party institutionalization in the local governments in Hungary and an overview of the tested hypotheses. As already mentioned, it also offers policy advice that could inform analysts and decision-makers regarding the problem of amalgamation from the point of view of political institutionalization. The chapters of this thesis are not of equal length simply because the issues to be discussed required discussion of different breadth and theoretical discussion cannot be as concise as the presentation of statistical findings.

The case that the research project covers is Hungary. As a new democracy, this country can serve as a test case, especially for the region of Central and Eastern European. Moreover, Hungary has a fragmented local government system that may provide interesting findings for other countries of similar territorial organization.

A few words about the terminology of this research are needed to avoid confusion and make the reading of this report simpler. As all localities have the right to form a local government in Hungary, I use the terms of 'municipality', 'local government' and 'local community' interchangeably, and 'settlement' and 'locality' interchangeably if not indicated otherwise. That is fully possible in the Hungarian context. By 'national party', I mean party organizations that are organized on the country level. The term would be 'country-level parties' in Hungarian (and never 'national parties'). As Chapter 1 defines, the term 'local party' or 'local party organization' refers to both the local sections of national parties and civil society organizations. I occasionally call civil society organizations 'social organizations', which is the standard legal term in Hungarian. I distinguish in this research between population size and functional size. The more encompassing category of 'municipality size' includes both of them. Other definitions, which are more related to the conceptual framework of this research, can be found in Chapter 1. Operational definitions appear in Chapter 3. The two main indicators of local party institutionalization, local party government and local party loyalty are also defined and operationalized in Chapter 3. Finally, the electoral systems of the local government tier play a major role in this research. I briefly refer to them as 'short ticket system' (or 'short list system') and 'mixed system'.

Chapter 1: Local Party Institutionalization

The first task of the project is to present a conceptual framework that can be the basis of the research design. Therefore, the following chapter defines the concept of local party, institutionalization and local party institutionalization. It also explains why local parties matter for both local democracy and national parties, and why parties are formed and maintained.

1.1. The Importance of Local Party Institutionalization

Well-established political systems function differently from weakly institutionalized ones. The level of institutionalization of political actors and processes shapes the perception of political reality, calculation, and behavior, influences the durability of governments and their policy performance, and defines the common interests. In Huntington's (1968: 24) words:

> Political institutions have moral as well as structural dimensions. A society with weak political institutions lacks the ability to curb the excesses of the personal and parochial desires. Politics is a Hobbesian world of unrelenting competition among social forces – between man and man, family and family, clan and clan, region and region, class and class – a competition unmediated by more comprehensive political organizations. The "amoral familism" of Banfield's backward society has its counterparts in amoral clanism, amoral groupism, amoral classism. Morality requires trust; trust involves predictability; and predictability requires regularized and institutionalized patterns of behavior. Without strong political institutions, society lacks the means to define and to realize its common interests. The capacity to create political institutions is the capacity to create public interests.

Local communities in Europe in general, and in Hungary in particular, are obviously provided with governing institutions. The institutions of local governments and elections supply a framework with the potential to "curb the excesses of the personal and parochial desires," and define and realize the common interests. The extent to which this potential is realized, however, depends on the existence and nature of the institutions that mediate between the local society and local government. The way in which societal demands are channeled makes a difference between opaque, unstable political systems with uncontrolled notables, on the one hand, and transparent, predictable political systems in which leaders' excesses are curbed, on the other hand. In the following pages, I make an attempt to show why the specific type of institutionalization based on party organizations is, from a democratic point of view, superior to the available alternatives of mediating institutions on the local level.

1.1.1. Potential Forms of Institutionalization

This book focuses on the institutionalization of a particular form, the political party. Party institutionalization is not the only form of political institutionalization. To take a broad view, parties are new-born babies in human history. The party as an institution is less than 200 years old and gained a prominent role only in the late 19th century. Lots of well-institutionalized political systems emerged and passed away before the age of party politics. To take a more contemporary view, no political system is totally party-based. Parties always have institutional alternatives. Established parties are not the only form of political institutionalization. The politics of local governments are particularly based on clans and personal (non-organized) patronage quite often. Alternative institutionalized forms exist even in the most party-dominated polities. Accordingly, the degree to which local political parties and the local party system are institutionalized is not necessarily a good indicator of the overall level of institutionalization of a local polity. In my view, the following institutionalized models are the usual rivals of parties in contemporary democracies:

- Personal connections, built on kinship and friendship, are still important. Horizontal and vertical links may form a strong informal institutional system even in seemingly monolithic, authoritarian polities (see e.g. Peng 2004). In local politics, personal networks and patronage links often play an important role due to the small scale of the political unit.
- Institutionalized direct democracy is also a rival to parties (see Katz 1987: 20). In principle, as communities are small enough, local governments especially offer good opportunities to directly involve citizens. In spite of many challenges, Switzerland is still a prime example of institutionalized direct democracy (Bützer 2004; Ladner 2002).
- While individual movements are *per definitionem* not institutionalized, the political use (and abuse) of social and political movements and single-issue organizations can be a well-established, legitimate, i.e. institutionalized, component of political systems. Movements indeed have an institutionalized position in Southern Europe.
- The activities of organized pressure groups are also of a non-party character, even if parties are often the targets of lobbying. The system of lobby groups can also be an alternative to party rule (see Katz 1978: 19), as the example of the US politics, both on the national and state level, demonstrate.
- Governance has been one of the key words of political and administrative sciences for the last ten years or so (see e.g. John 2001; Marcusen and Torfing 2003; Sørensen 2003; Sørensen and Torfing 2004; Klijn 2004). In a wide

sense, it includes neo-corporatism (also listed by Katz 1987:18 as an alternative to party rule). In a more strict sense, governance in the recent literature refers to an integrative institution whose member organizations reach (at least rough) consensus on policy issues through deliberation. This institution bypasses parties and makes policy directly. This is not only prescriptive theory: governance on the local level is actually emerging, though some argue that its scope is more limited than it is generally supposed (Damgaard 2004).

This previous list of alternative political institutionalization does not mean to be comprehensive. My aim is to show that (local) party institutionalization happens in a competitive institutional environment and not in an institutional vacuum or tabula rasa.

Not all of these alternatives are feasible in the case analyzed in this research. In Section 7.4, I will show the weakness of direct democracy on the local level. Although the legal rules would allow the establishment of a system in which the means of direct democracy are regularly used, both the weaknesses of civil society and the relative strength of representative institutions make the institutionalization of a direct democracy-centered local political systems unlikely.

Local single-issue movements do occur in Hungary. Still, their frequency is low and, what is even more important from the perspective of this research, they do not occur in a concentrated manner.

Pressure group politics are also unlikely in Hungary. The local government system does not allow interest groups much access to policy-making. Instead, the system encourages attempts to influence local representatives, which makes interest groups partners rather than rivals of the parties. The overall strength, or rather weakness, of the local civil society does not make institutionalized pluralism likely.

Institutionalized governance, most probably in the form of policy communities, may exist in Hungary. Still, its rare occurrence may be proved by the total lack of scientific literature and news reports on local governance institutions. Given the under-institutionalized nature of the local interest groups and their apparent organizational weakness, the lack of governance is quite understandable.

Apart from the general under-institutionalization of Hungary, the main rival of party-centered local politics are personal networks. The well-established power of extended families, friendly networks, and clientelistic hierarchies have characterized communities since the earliest times of history. Solving collective problems by means of family, clan or clientelistic ties is more ancient than any kind of organizational politics. Thus, I compare the main characteristics of institutionalized local party systems to those of uninstitutionalized and family-based systems in the following section.

1.1.2. Local Party Institutionalization in Comparison

In my view, institutionalized party politics contribute more to local democracy than either atomistic, unorganized politics or institutionalized personal networks. A comparison follows along the dimensions of local democracy.

The most important contribution of parties to local democracy is the popular control of local politicians in various ways. One major form is transparency in two senses. Party organizations structure politics by providing informational cues. Their names act as trademarks that orient citizens, who may not follow politics day by day, but can remember party labels. Obviously, more institutionalized parties fulfill this function better. Without those labels, voters face lots of candidates and incumbents from whom they choose by chance. Even if some notables are more or less known by many, the rest of the candidates, the potential alternatives to notables, remain a list of indistinguishable names. Citizens have weaker informational cues without parties.

In another sense, transparency prevails in council politics too. In order to win votes (and donations that allow them to court voters), parties formulate policy programs and make them understandable for voters in the form of slogans and other informational cues. That reduces complexity and extends transparency in the same way as party labels do (see the first point). Parties prioritize different, often conflicting policies and construct more or less coherent packages. Policy packages can be implemented as (local) government programs. Thus interest aggregation contributes to governmentability as well. Individuals, *ad hoc* organizations and family-based groups have much less capacity to do this job for lack of established procedures and expertise. Moreover, an effective majority in local councils can be reached much more easily if the number of players is limited and players are predefined. Parties make the coalition formation more effective and this kind of transparency also enhances the governability of the political system.

Predictability is another issue. Institutions are by definition stable. Thus, the continuous functioning of parties tends to secure predictability. The rules of personal networks also make the behavior of members predictable for the members. However, those networks are opaque institutions for outsiders, who see only personalized, non-predictable behavior. Private predictability has much less value than public predictability.

The transparency of party organizations also makes party rule more accountable. Party 'trademarks' enhance the accountability of the political system. The responsibility for implemented policies cannot effectively be linked to concrete actors if the number of independent, uncoordinated representatives is large. Bergman and Strom (2004) point out that in a principal-agent framework the decline in political party cohesion leads to a decline in citizens' capability to exercise accountability through the chain of political delegation. Again, ever changing, unstable party organizations or personal networks are less able to carry out this function.

Institutionalized parties directly "curb the excesses of the personal and parochial desires" of individual politicians by imposing discipline on them. The rules of party organizations structure the behavior of members and leaders. If the normative and cognitive constraints would not be enough, institutionalized parties are effectively able to sanction the deviation from those rules. It is quite likely that those who claim parties are undesirable in their respective communities, or in general in local governments, are the local winners of the political transition, whose power, built on their personal networks, kinship connections and economic and social resources, is threatened by the control of institutionalized organizations.[1]

In addition to control-related arguments, there are other considerations that justify the importance of parties. Parties select and train politicians. By their selection, they accredit and audit candidates by giving proof of their capabilities. Career paths within parties play an important role in the recruitment of councilors and local leaders as well. More institutionalized parties with better-defined roles, selection and training techniques are more appropriate to meet this requirement than new, weakly patterned parties. While the established kin networks also select and train the new generation of leaders, their 'recruitment' is limited to the family circle. Community leadership cannot be inherited so easily nowadays, while parties have a wider selection and more legitimate methods.

In terms of inclusion, parties are clearly superior to family-based institutions. If a citizen accepts the goals and ideology of a party, he or she may join it. Should parties be closed, a group of citizens can form a new party organization. Nothing similar is possible in extended families or networks based on strong ties.

A frequent argument against the existence of local parties is that they bring conflicts into the life of communities. Parties are said to generate conflict even if a consensus can be achieved. I believe this is true: the competitive environment forces parties to continuously look for ways in which they can emphasize their differences and gain an advantage over other parties. Without parties, there are much less open conflicts. Behind this idyllic facade, the actual relationships are often laden with hidden conflicts among individuals, families, and groups. Since

1 For a similar argument about the lack of party institutionalization in Russian regions see Stoner-Weiss (2001).

the basis of cooperation is informal and personal connections, the disagreements rarely become overt. When the tension reaches a high level, the conflicts become highly dangerous and break up the community for a long time (see Dahl and Tufte 1973: 91–94). True, parties generate overt conflicts; however, they are able to channel them. If there are no institutionalized relationships or only personal networks that coordinate collective action, conflicts tend to be more personal and bitter. Such polarizing hostilities are less likely to be resolved through compromise in the absence of formal institutions of conflict management.

Parties contribute to the mobilization of citizens. Parties want voters, so they make much effort to offer incentives of political participation. As a by-product, the general level of participation, an important prerequisite of democracy, is increased. However, the competing families and the clienteles of local moguls seem to be even more effective in mobilizing local voters. Parties (and media) are successful mobilizers only in large cities (see Swianiewicz 2002b: 310–312).

By training their politicians and mobilizing citizens, parties that are willing to participate in the electoral competition are likely to inculcate certain values, including democratic ones. This socialization process covers not only politicians, but also citizens. Political education is a by-product of party activities. Since socialization requires organizations that are infused with values and externally legitimate, more institutionalized parties perform better in this respect too. In contrast, such political education does not take place in anomic local societies. Familism inculcates the value of loyalty to intimate and familiar groups, and distrust toward any other political forms. Parties tend to teach more democratic values than personal networks.

Through democratic socialization and mobilization, parties legitimize democracy at both the national and local levels. Legitimate, taken-for-granted parties contribute more to the legitimation process than *ad hoc* political organizations or notables.

Parties also articulate the interests of certain groups. This kind of problem identification can be especially important on the local level where the organizational density is lower and not all groups are able to form interest organizations. Even if parties take up the representation of certain groups, they do it in a less narrow sense than interest organizations. In all probability, older, more established and socially embedded parties are in a better position to identify needs than flash parties or individual politicians.

Political parties contribute to the integration of communities (Lipset and Rokkan 1967). Again, this is not one of their explicit goals, rather a functional by-product of their activities. Local communities are strengthened by local party organizations. This function is especially important where the local political units have been formed in a non-organic way (usually as a consequence of territorial reform). Naturally, older, more stable and embedded party organizations can contribute more than young organizations or independent politicians.

A specific function of local party organizations is the representation of local interests on the supra-local level. They can do that through their parties' senior-levels to which they have better access than any powerful, but nonpartisan, local politician or association. Parties with a well-institutionalized hierarchical structure show a better performance in the representation of local interests than weakly institutionalized ones or personal networks, which have, at best, only a limited number of vulnerable links with the world outside their community. This function may become especially prominent in local governments, e.g. suburbs, which are integrated in a web of municipalities and, consequently, largely depend on the outside world.

One should not have illusions about parties. They are more likely to curb the excesses of local notables and integrate the parochial interests into a wider perspective. Nonetheless, institutionalized party systems may also have a dark side. Here is a list of dangers:

- Voters can choose among closed packages only. Aggregated programs of parties are inflexible. Voters may like only one or two elements of them, but they cannot signal that to parties.
- Local politics may be excessively nationalized. Ladner (1999: 219) illustrates this dilemma with the example of Switzerland. If a local politician becomes a member of the cantonal parliament, the local chapter gains prestige and opportunities. Nonetheless, party consensus is often disturbed and the party organization may lose votes because of a conflict between cantonal commitments and local interests.
- The leadership of well-established parties may become closed, as in Michels' (1968) iron law of oligarchy. In such a situation, municipality politics are controlled by a handful of powerful party leaders acting behind closed doors. A high level of party institutionalization increases the likelihood of such an oligarchic outcome.
- Party failure may result in the de-legitimation of local democracy. If parties are dominant, local democracy is associated with party activity. The breakdown of party representation disillusions citizens of democracy.

Nevertheless, none of these potential drawbacks can be avoided by ceding the local communities to the personal rule of powerful notables. Closed packages are better than the lack of transparent programs. In all probability, the endogenous mechanism of party competition rules out the rivals that are not committed enough to local problems. The rule of personal networks and their bosses more likely results in oligarchies than party government and the break-up of organizational oligarchies is more probable than a subversion of the rule of notables. The difficulties stemming from under-institutionalization or the dominance of big families may lead to democratic disillusionment in the same way as party rule. The potential advantages of local party institutionalization outweigh its potential dangers.

1.2. The Concept of Local Party Institutionalization

1.2.1. Institutionalization of Organizations

Institutions and organizations are not the same. Certain institutions are not organizations and organizations can be more or less institutionalized. (For more discussion of the distinction, see Scott 2001.) Organizations are pools of resources under centralized control. As Kuper and Kuper (1985) define, organizations "come into existence when individuals place the resources available to them (such as skills, money or prestige) under some sort of central control, rather than using them individualistically." To give a preliminary definition by contrast, institutions refer to routinized, stable behavior implying some kind of rule.

There is no more consensus regarding the concept of an institution than there is for other concepts in the social sciences. I follow Scott's (2001: 48) conceptualization as it is one of the most comprehensive ones (though not the most parsimonious). His "omnibus" concept of institution, which is actually a summary of his full argument, is as follows:

- Institutions are social structures that have attained a high degree of resilience.
- Institutions are composed of cultured-cognitive, normative and regulative elements that, together with associated activities and resources, provide stability and meaning to social life.
- Institutions are transmitted by various types of carriers, including symbolic systems, relational systems, routines and artifacts.
- Institutions operate at multiple levels of jurisdiction, from the world system to localized interpersonal relationships.
- Institutions by definition connote stability but are subject to change processes, both incremental and discontinuous.

The first point of this definition points to the stability of institutions. The second contains the three "pillars" of the concept of institution, which summarizes a complete literature on institutions. The three pillars are as follows.

1. The regulative pillar. Many authors regard institutions as regulative systems that constrain and regularize behavior. Institutions establish rules, monitor activities, and sanction behavior. Institutional economists like Douglass North (e.g. 1990) and rational choice political scientists like Weingast (e.g. 1996) offer good examples of this.
2. The normative pillar. That includes both values and norms. Values are "conceptions of the preferred and the desirable, together with the construction of standards to which existing structures or behavior can be compared and assessed." Norms, by contrast, "specify how things should be done; they define legitimate means to pursue valued ends" (Scott 2001: 54–55). Certain norms and values are attributed to certain specific actors: these institutionalized positions are roles.
3. The cultural-cognitive pillar. This element of institutions implies "the shared conceptions that constitute the nature of social reality and the frames through which meaning is made" (Scott 2001: 57). Actors are social as long as they attach meaning to their action. The internally attributed meaning is shaped by external cultural frameworks: myths and ceremonies (Meyer and Rowan 1992). Institutions are often taken-for-granted schemas, which are applied unconsciously.

From the perspective of this research, Scott's (2001) conceptualization portrays institutions as highly complex social entities: they imply rules, sanctions, values, norms, roles, scripts, and schemes. Not only does he confront the "logic of consequence" (the regulative pillar) and the "logic of appropriateness" (the other two), following March and Olsen (1989), but he also makes a distinction between institutions' normative and cultural-cognitive content. An account for the level of institutionalization must reckon with these dimensions.

As it might become obvious, institutions can be formal as well informal. The legal or other formal recognition of rules, roles and procedures are not needed. Norms and widely shared conceptions are rarely formalized.

Institutions constrain and empower at the same time. For example, being a party official involves several responsibilities and duties. An official must follow rules, norms and widely shared scripts. However, such a role provides rights and privileges as well. The official is entitled to do certain things others are not allowed to do and enjoys a respect others do not.

The institutionalization of organizations is the process by which organizations become stable and legitimate both internally (for their members) and externally (voters, supporters and sponsors).

Institutionalization is not identical to rigidity. "Institutionalization does not preclude change, but it limits it" (Mainwaring 1998: 6). As Schedler (1995) argues, the relationship between democracy and institutionalization is not linear. Both under- and over-institutionalization is dangerous to the party system. Extreme fluidity often leads to political collapse. However, hyper-institutionalization also implies a mortal danger to the system. Rigidity caused by over-institutionalization makes the system unresponsive and the lack of adaptability to the changing circumstances can result in the emergence of new forces, which demolish the system as such. As over-institutionalization is not a likely danger in new democracies and Schedler (1995) also presents it as a more exceptional case, this research will not examine it in a deeper manner.

This process is not teleological. There is no historical inevitability of progressing toward ever more institutionalized systems. In fact, parties and party system sometimes de-institutionalize, as happened with the Congress Party in India or the Italian party system in the first half of the 1990s.

Institutionalization is not a dummy variable, but a matter of degree. Even the loosest group has a formally or informally recognized leader. The institutionalization of the group starts by the establishment of roles. At the other extreme of the institutionalization scale, one finds the old, highly bureaucratized, taken-for-granted organizations. The aim of the book is to measure and explain the *level* of institutionalization.

1.2.2. Local Party Institutionalization

As Huntington defines in his classical work (*Political Order in Changing Societies*, 1968), institutions are "stable, valued, recurring patterns of behavior" and institutionalization is "the process by which organizations and procedures acquire value and stability" (1968: 12). Mainwaring has a similar notion: "a process by which a practice and organization becomes well established and widely known, if not universally accepted" Mainwaring (1998: 5). Therefore, an institutionalized party system "is one in which actors develop expectations and behavior based on the premise that the fundamental contours and rules of party competition and behavior will prevail into the foreseeable future. In an institutionalized party system there is stability in the identity of the main parties and the ways in which they behave" (Mainwaring 1998: 6).

Parties can also be more or less institutionalized. For example, parties in the US are much less organized most parties in Europe. Still, US parties are in many ways highly institutionalized (see the process of the selection of presidential candidates).

Party institutionalization has a huge literature – without a widely shared definition.[2] Authors emphasize different aspects of party institutionalization and

2 Actually, a large part of the literature on part institutionalization has been written by Latin Americanists. This is probably not an accident. The importance of the concept

often suggest more than one dimension along which it can vary. In fact, the common denominator of conceptualizations is the perception of party institutionalization as a multi-dimensional phenomenon. The most frequently mentioned aspects are as follows.

1. *Adaptability*. The capability of adapting to environmental challenges is a prominent element of the conceptualization of Huntington (1968), measured by organizational age, the number of generational changes of leadership, and the number of functional changes.
2. *Systemness*. Panebianco (1988: 55) defines this dimension as "the degree of interdependence of its different sectors." Actually, the concept covers what Huntington (1968: 17–20, 22–23) calls complexity (differentiation of subunits) and coherence (consensus on the functional boundaries and conflict-solving mechanisms). The conceptual opposite of systemness is factionalism, i.e. a situation in which groups within the party "autonomously control (independently of the organization's center) the resources necessary to their functioning" (Panebianco 1988: 56).
3. *Value infusion*. An organization is infused with value when its members and leaders identify themselves with it and their commitment is beyond their instrumental considerations (Randall and Svåsand 2002:13).
4. *Autonomy*. Panebianco's other criterion of institutionalization is the autonomy of organization vis-a-vis its environment. An organization is not autonomous when its "indispensable resources are in part controlled by other organizations," for instance the dependence of certain social democratic parties on trade unions (Panebianco 1988: 55).
5. *Reification*. Janda (1980: 167) defines party institutionalization "as the extent to which a party is reified in the public mind so that it exists as a social organization apart from its momentary leaders while regularly engaging in valued patterns of behavior." Randall and Svåsand (2002: 14) interpret this concept as the external legitimacy of parties and party systems. Parties are reified when the public takes them for granted and this assumption structures other expectations.

Randall and Svåsand (2002) made an interesting attempt to tidy up this inconveniently complex and differentiated picture. The assessment of the institutionalization in their approach focuses on two dimensions: organizational capacity

---

of party institutionalization becomes manifest in an environment where adequate political institutionalization is lacking.

and legitimacy. Both dimensions can be analyzed from an internal as well as an external viewpoint. Thus, the systemness (i.e. the routinization of internal processes) and decisional autonomy (i.e. independence from sponsor organizations and national or other bodies of the organization) are internal and external aspects of organizational capacity. Value infusion (i.e. members' and supporters' identification with, and commitment to, the organization) and external reification (i.e. the taken-for-grantedness in the public imagination) are two aspects of legitimacy.

Table 1.1. Dimensions of party institutionalization

Institutionalization of political organizations	Internal	External
Structural	Systemness	Autonomy
Attitudinal	Value infusion	Reification

Source: Randall and Svåsand (2002: 13)

This research follows Randall and Svåsand's conceptualization and defines local party institutionalization in the following manner.

Definition 1

Local party institutionalization is the process through which political groupings on the local government level acquire value and stability both internally and externally. It has four dimensions: systemness, decisional autonomy, value infusion and reification.

The frequent problem of multidimensional concepts is that the conceptual components do not always 'hang together'. The dimensions of local parties also form different aspects. Thus, there is a good probability that those dimensions will not correlate. Morlino (1998: 23) criticizes Huntington (1968) precisely because the measures of institutionalization are incompatible. Empirically, Levitsky (1998), analyzing the Peronist party in Argentine, points out that 'value infusion' and 'behavioral routinization' (systemness) do not necessarily go together. This is the reason why I will examine the four dimensions separately as far as the available data allows.

Finally, an important distinction must be made. Party institutionalization is often linked to democratic consolidation. Sometimes the two concepts are identified (taking party institutionalization as a dimension of democratic consolidation), sometimes party institutionalization is presented as a prerequisite of the consolidation of democracies. Indeed, the literature on Russia and Latin America portrays a strong link between party institutionalization and democratic consolidation (see Mainwaring and Scully 1994; Evans and Gel'man 2004; Colton and McFaul 2004). Nevertheless, this supposed link has been subject to much criticism. Morlino (1988: 205–212) rejects the idea that party institutionalization is a prerequisite of democratic consolidation. Referring to Spain and Greece, he argues that "There are other 'anchors of consolidation' that may be added or alternatives to party institutionalization" (1988: 212). Tóka (1997) also contends that democracy was consolidated in Central Europe without a visible link between party institutionalization and consolidation. Bae (2003) draws the same conclusion in the case of South Korea. On the other hand, Stoner-Weiss (2001) clearly demonstrates how detrimental the under-institutionalization of parties in Russian regions is to democracy. The point here is that party institutionalization and democratic consolidation are distinct concepts both theoretically and empirically.

1.3. The Formation of Institutionalized Local Parties

1.3.1. Local Parties

This paper focuses on a specific form of organization, the political party. As usual in social sciences, there is no consensus over the concept of the political party. Nonetheless, summarizing the classical definitions, one may not make a big mistake by defining the political party as an organization running for office at elections. Duverger (1964: xxiii) claims that "The role of all these institutions is to win political power and exercise it." Sartori (1976: 64) defines the political party as "any political group that presents at elections, and is capable of placing through elections, candidates for public office."

Such a definition is close to Panebianco's (1988: 3–6) concept. He rejects two kinds of "prejudice". The sociological prejudice regards parties as the political manifestations of social groups. This overlooks the inequalities within an organization, the parties' relative autonomy from societal inequalities and their capability to produce new societal inequalities. The representatives of the teleological prejudice define parties in terms of their supposed goals. The first version of this approach claims that parties have the goal of reaching their ideological aims. However, the assumption that parties are goal-oriented groups constitutes a problem to be examined. There are many examples of parties that do not further their self-proclaimed ideological aims or do not really want to win elections. As a conclusion, Panebianco advises parties be defined in terms of their activities: "parties are the only organizations which operate in the electoral area, which compete for votes. This allows us to distinguish them by an *activity* (tied to a specific environment) foreign to all other types of organizations, allows us to leave open the question of their possible goals (given that the same activity can be motivated by different goals)" (1988: 6, emphasis in the original).

Following these authors, parties are regarded as candidate-nominating organizations in this research. Since my specific focus is on *local* parties, the definition must be completed with a reference to the local character. The definition of party is obviously of a functional, not legal character. Although parties are defined by a legal act (official nomination of candidates), the definition does not imply a legal recognition as parties. The distinction is important in many countries, including the case studied here, where the Local Government Act allows 'social organizations' (to use the language of the Hungarian law) such as associations or trade unions to nominate candidates at local elections. Consequently, those civic organizations may have factions in the local government council and are active political players in their municipalities. Thus, the category of 'local political party' implies the local chapters of national parties as well as 'civic parties', i.e. political groupings registered as 'social organizations'.

Definition 2

The local political party is an organization independent of its form of legal registration that nominates candidates at local government elections.

1.3.2. National and Local Parties

Why do national political parties make efforts to form local chapters? The question has more than academic relevance, as party strategies play a major role in every democratic polity. In the age of mass communication, many authors regard local party organizations as irrelevant. Proponents of the electoral-professional party model (e.g. Panebianco 1988) believe that parties tend to centralize and use campaign specialists and the electronic media, which have the potential to reach each citizen, and have a higher publicity than any extensive party organization. The theorists of the cartel party model (Katz and Mair 1995) argue that parties are intertwined with the state and government their main source of support, which makes local chapters unnecessary. (For a more detailed literature survey, see Clark 2004: 35–36.) Nevertheless, some authors have doubts. Yishai (2001) offers evidence about how parties re-socialize themselves by building local organizations and contacts with civic organizations in Israel, one of the most 'cartelized' countries. Clark (2004) presents theoretical considerations about the importance of local party chapters. He claims that parties need local chapters to enhance their legitimacy by making the image of a big, omnipresent party, effective at the local level, raising funds for party activities and offering solidarity incentives to members.

The most extensive list of reasons why parties need local organizations can be found in Hans Geser's work (1999: 4). He argues that "most institutions, organizations, and collectivities are segmented into smaller local subsystems where spatial proximity of members (and adherents) allows for more intensive and informal social interaction." He identifies eight basic functions that local subunits of political parties may perform for the party as a whole:

1. Local subunits are training sites for both would-be politicians and adherents. National parties can build up a large reservoir of potential candidates for local and supra-local public offices and party positions. On the other hand, citizens can be socialized into democratic norms in general, and the values of the party in specific.
2. Local chapters are often the laboratories of party innovations. For example, new forms of campaigning tactics, party slogans or new types of coalitions can be tested on the subnational level without risking the position of the country-level party organization.
3. Local party organizations offer incentives for membership that national party organs cannot provide. Parties on the local level like to organize social activities for their own members and supporters because this is cheaper than any kind of material incentive and attracts individuals who are not sufficiently moved by ideological commitments. "Solidary motivations", i.e. social gratification, maintains the cohesion of the party even in difficult times and allows the rebuilding of the party from below after the collapse of the national party. So, nationally weak parties profit the most from motivating adherents socially. By contrast, parties that are powerful on the higher level attract more careerists who often destroy local solidarity and use professional campaign tools, which lead to the alienation of local members.
4. Organizing the party on the communal level generates volunteers who are willing to contribute with their free time and their own facilities (home office, mobile phone, etc.). Thus, local members and supporters subsidize the party with unpaid work and private infrastructure. Professional campaigns decrease the importance of local adherents' contributions.
5. Even in the age of highly sophisticated professional campaigns, personal contacts are still powerful ways of influencing citizens (see e.g. Gerber and Green 2000; Farrell and Webb 2000; Frendreis, Gibson and Vertz 1990). In fact, there are voters who cannot be reached in any other way. Other voters simply disregard media messages and mostly decide based on personal information. Local party

chapters are very good at diffuse interpersonal communication. Therefore, parties with extensive local infrastructure have an advantage in electoral campaigns.

6. Local party organizations can translate the general values, programs and policy proposals of the party into specific local actions and local government decisions. Local chapters make influence in local politics possible.
7. Local organizations make the party more flexible. The innovative small-scale organizations are able to quickly react to the changes of socioeconomic and political environments, which gives leverage to the encompassing party organization.
8. Finally, community-level party organizations are less elitist than the supra-local levels. Thus, they can involve individuals from more marginal social groups. That increases the sensitivity of the party to the needs and wants of less visible societal segments.

The objective of this section was to justify the significance of local party organizations by showing the many ways in which they may affect, both positively and negatively, the quality and form of local and national democracy. The conclusion is that local parties and the level of their institutionalization are important for both local democracy and national parties. The rest of the book focuses on the determinants of local party institutionalization, treating it as a dependent variable.

1.3.3. Party Formation

'New institutionalisms' became an important trend in the scholarly literature of the 1990s. Their main message is that pure self-interest cannot explain human behavior and institutions also must be taken into account (Hall and Taylor 1996; Immergut 1998; Koeble 1995; Peters 1999). They have often been successful in explaining social and political actions by explaining how institutions structure behavior. Nonetheless, they showed a disappointing performance in accounting for institutional change. New institutionalism concentrates on the effect of institutions (as independent variables) and neglects (or has difficulties with) the question of the emergence and transformation of institutions (as dependent variables). For example, sociological institutionalism (see e.g. Powell and DiMaggio 1991) focuses on the normative dimension of institutions. It claims that the logic of appropriateness is often more important than the logic of consequentiality (March and Olsen 1989). However, this Parsonsian approach portrays institutions as social entities that maintain themselves forever. Only one of these new institutionalisms, the rational choice approach, has something to say about institutional change (Knight and Sened 1998).

The most extensive discussion of the emergence of political parties was written by John Aldrich. Why would local politicians establish parties? Aldrich (1995: 28–61) assumes that politicians are office-seeking individuals, who calculate their political steps rationally. He relies on three bodies of literature: public choice, collective action and motivation theory. First, he claims that party formation resolves public choice and social choice problems that arise in the legislature. Those who form parties can have a better payoff than those who remain independents. Second, parties solve the problem of collective action of voting. Parties can mobilize potential voters more effectively by offering selective incentives to the voters. They lower the 'costs' of voting by giving information in readily available form and increase the rewards of voting by arguing that each vote matters. For candidates, parties offer a brand name, a source of reputation and economies of scale in the campaign. Finally, joining a party increases the chances of a long and successful political career, which is the dream of the rational, office-seeking politician.

There are three problems with Aldrich's theory. First, it is over-individualized. He focuses only on selective incentives; however, parties often offer a very limited amount of selective incentive to most of their members, activists, and supporters.

Second, the theory is clearly under-socialized and under-cultured. Aldrich's politicians do not feel loyalty to their party. If they calculate that they have better opportunities for a reasonable political cost in another party, they simply change their affiliation. He simply neglects socialization. If someone brought up in Social Democratic family and was socialized in a Social Democrat youth organization, he or she is unlikely to easily choose any other party than the Social Democrats. Aldrich also overlooks the importance of the diffusion of organizational models, scripts, and innovations. Imitation is not a rational process either. In other words, the normative and cognitive-cultural pillars of institutions must be considered in addition to the regulative one.

Third, Aldrich's theory is over-rational. Neither politicians, nor voters are political calculators. They often have no idea about the payoffs of their legislative acts or the costs of voting and do not assume that others know their utility functions better and act rationally. Politicians simply guess in many situations and expect others to do that too. Especially at the local level, where actors are less professional and information is not available, trial-and-error decision-making is much more common than the precise calculation of not easily definable payoffs. Political agents are rational in the sense that they try to adapt to the changing circumstances. Local party formation and institutionalization happens when the circumstances are appropriate for that. However, it may take time to find it, as it is not the product of omniscient calculators. Party formation and institutionalization is a social innovation, which may be selected in some situations, but not in others. The task of this research project is to find the conditions under which local party institutionalization is the winning formula for local political agents.

My conclusion is that a theory of local party institutionalization must (1) take into account both selective and collective incentives, (2) seek the logic of appropriateness, not only the logic of consequence, and (3) find the conditions to which both individual and collective agents adapt themselves by creating and maintaining local political parties. This is the task of the next chapter.

1.4. Summary

This research focuses on local party institutionalization, defined as the process by which organizations become stable and legitimate both internally (for their members) and externally (voters, supporters and sponsors). The four dimensions of the concept (systemness, autonomy, loyalty and legitimacy) will be treated separately. The importance of institutionalized local parties has been justified by their functions: local parties make local politics more transparent and accountable; control their members and leaders; enhance government with competing policy programs; promote the formation of ruling coalitions; channel conflicts and integrate the interests of local communities in wider frameworks. Local parties are defined as organizations that nominate candidates at local elections. No distinction is made between legal forms: the local chapters of registered parties and of civic organizations can both be regarded as local political parties. The discussion of party formation will rely on both the selective and collective incentives, and the normative and cognitive circumstances that influence political agents' decisions.

Chapter 2: Explaining Local Party Institutionalization

This chapter aims to put forward hypotheses concerning the causal relationship of local party institutionalization with its potential determinants. I first review the size and democracy literature and propose 'functional' size as an alternative conceptualization of municipality size. In the second section, I formulate several hypotheses about the potential effect of socioeconomic factors on the level of local party institutionalization. The third section constructs further hypotheses concerning legal, geographic, historical and typological factors. Finally, I change the perspective and approach the problem from the viewpoint of the dependent variable. The concluding section presents all the discussed variables in an organized manner.

2.1. Size and Local Democracy

This section first presents the literature on size and democracy. I focus only on the works that are relevant to my research. Then, I propose an alternative concept of size, functional size. I conclude with two general hypotheses concerning the relationship between size and local party institutionalization.

2.1.1. Size and Democracy

The classical piece of the size and democracy literature is Robert A. Dahl and Edward R. Tufte' *Size and Democracy*, published in 1973. Not only did the authors gather the relevant evidence of their time on their subject matter, but they also outlined several theoretical propositions, which still influence the research agenda of the students of the size and democracy field.

One of the important points in Dahl and Tufte's book is the distinction between the various potential interpretations of size. They distinguish among five forms of size: (1) size as population, i.e. the number of persons (inhabitants, adults, voters, etc.); (2) size as area, i.e. the territory of political units; (3) size as population density, i.e. the number of people per unit of territory; (4) size as the distribution of the population, both in terms of geography (e.g. dispersion among small islands vs. compactness) and of settlements (small settlements in Sweden vs. large urban centers in England); (5) relative size, i.e. the size of political units compared to other, especially neighboring units and (6) size as economic development (referring to modernization theory I discuss in a later section). In addition, the authors point in very briefly to the importance of the change in size, quoting the example of Austria after the First World War (and they could refer to Hungary in the same time period). In the rest of the book, Dahl and Tufte usually identify population with size to explore the empirical relationships between size and two dimensions of democracy (citizen effectiveness and system capacity).

There are a few other propositions in *Size and Democracy* that are also important for my research. The authors examine the relationship between size and diversity. They claim that there is a positive association between size and heterogeneity, referring to both cultural diversity (variation in language, religion, race or region; ethnicity is probably understood under the category of language) and socioeconomic heterogeneity (variation in occupation, education, income, wealth, etc.). They find some (but not very firm) evidence for the correlation between population size and heterogeneity among subnational units, but not among countries. Size as economic development, however, seems to have a positive influence on diversity among, as well as within, countries.

Dahl and Tufte also argue that size is positively related to the number of organizations. The larger the territory and the more people they have to contact, the more the organizations tend to develop subunits. The decentralization rule applies to governmental and nongovernmental organizations in the same way. Following this logic, the number of interest groups also increases with the size of the political unit. Dahl and Tufte (1973: 39) formulate (though without empirical support) The Plumber's Law:

> If there is approximately one plumber to every 1,000 people, then a community of 1,000 inhabitants is likely to have only one plumber – and no specific organization of plumbers. A town of 10,000 will have about 10 plumbers, and a better chance of a plumber's union. A city of 100,000 will have 100 plumbers or so, and very likely an organization of plumbers. A city of a million, with 1,000 plumbers, will probably have a plumber's organization with a number of subunits and some specialized services.

Dahl and Tufte also examine the relationship between size and participation. They begin with two contradictory hypotheses, which are still at the center of debates on this issue. (A) The larger the political system, the less effective the individual citizens feel themselves, which leads to lower participation in larger units than in smaller ones. (B) Larger systems are more competitive, thus citizens feel their votes are more important, which, in turn, results in higher participation in large units. The authors find no association between the size of countries and their level of participation. Nonetheless, there are countries within which there is a correlation between size and participation. However, it is positive in some countries, while negative in others. Thus, Dahl and Tufte's findings are inconclusive.

The two scholars make an attempt to theorize the impact of size on the communication among citizens and between citizens and leaders. They argue that the larger the size of the political unit, the more likely it is that citizens cannot communicate directly with each other and their leaders. Consequently, the role of mediating organizations and media increases, and communication between voters and decision-makers becomes asymmetric with size. In contrast, in smaller political systems communication is more direct and reciprocal among citizens and between leaders and citizens, and the role of intermediate organizations and the media is more limited.

In terms of competition and conflict, Dahl and Tufte weigh the chances of dissent. Their proposition is that the larger the scale of the society, the more likely a dissenter can find enough allies to reach the minimum number and proportion for dissent. Accordingly, as size increases the likelihood of an overt and permanent opposition to the views of the majority is greater. As smaller units are more homogeneous, the pressure for conformity decreases with size. Thus, group conflicts are predicted to be frequent in larger polities. On the other hand, the conflicts in smaller units, while less frequent, are more devastating. As the relations between leaders and groups are less institutionalized and more personal, conflicts polarize small communities much more than large ones.

From the perspective of this research, Dahl and Tufte's remarks on the relationship of size with the degree of party competition are very interesting. The authors claim that the greater the population the higher the political diversity: the specialization and differentiation, on the one hand, and urbanization and density, on the other hand, increase with the size of the political unit. More political diversity, then, leads to more party competition; manifested in a greater number of parties and a lower proportion of votes for the leading party. The overall strength of political organizations tends to be higher in large political units.

Since the publication of Dahl and Tufte's classic, two debates deserve attention from the point of view of the present research: the often heated debate on the correct policy concerning the amalgamation of small municipalities into larger ones and the more academic discussion of the relationship of size to participation.

The appropriate size of local governments has been the subject of long debates in countries facing public administration reform. This practical problem has inspired an important body of theoretical and empirical research. As regards the relationship of size with local democracy, two entirely opposite sets of arguments have emerged.

The first claims that the larger the local community, the better the democratic performance is. Three intervening variables are used when explaining the mechanism between size and performance. The most conventional argument points at the existence of economies of scale. In larger units, more institutional services are available (since there is a threshold for the provision of services) and services are more efficient (since there is a negative relationship between the amount and the unit cost of production). Another variable is heterogeneity. While majority preferences are more likely to be dominant in smaller communities, larger units are more heterogeneous and local politicians are more constrained to take minority preferences into account. The third variable is participation in local affairs. Larger local units control more aspects of citizens' life; they, therefore, have more incentives to participate. Furthermore, collective and more effective forms of political participation (e.g. political parties or trade unions) are more likely to be organized in larger communities. The conclusion of this logic is that more efficient services, greater attention to minority preferences and greater participation lead to greater satisfaction in local society (and satisfaction is identified with institutional performance in this approach).

The second set of arguments has an opposite claim. It maintains that citizens are more satisfied in smaller communities (and performance is equal to people's satisfaction). The intervening variables are the same, but the argument is totally different. This approach argues that smaller political systems are more efficient. Even if the production of services is cheaper in larger units, their provision gives more satisfaction for people in smaller communities. Public services are offered in a less bureaucratic way in smaller units, because the number and size of offices are smaller, leaders and ordinary people are closer to each other, and local government is less dominated by professional interests. Participation is also greater in smaller communities. Citizens are more aware of the fact that bureaucracies can be controlled and, hence, their personal responsibility is higher. Finally, homogeneity is also claimed to lead to more satisfaction in smaller units. In greater settlements, preferences are more divergent and it is more difficult to reconcile them. In smaller communities, the more homogeneous population is more likely to achieve legitimate agreements. In sum, this perspective asserts that citizens are more satisfied in smaller units because services are more efficient, participation is higher and demands are less divergent.

Diagram 2.1. Mouritzen's (1989) model

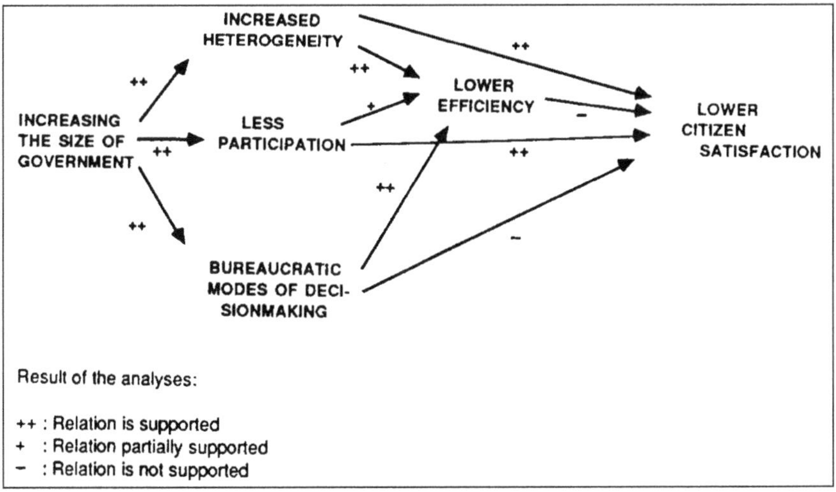

Mouritzen (1989), who, following Ostrom (1972), outlined these competing theories, tested the propositions of both approaches against evidence, stemming from the Danish reform of local governments. Figure 2.1 shows his results. Mouritzen concludes that "small is beautiful" and most propositions of the second approach have been confirmed.

It is essential to take into account Lijphart's (1977: 65–70) propositions as well. Exploring the factors favorable to consociational democracy, Lijphart analyzes the consequence of internal and external characteristics of small states regarding the direct and indirect effects on the probability of a consociational democracy. The direct internal effect of smallness is the enhancement of the spirit of cooperativeness and accommodation within the elite. In small states, the elite are more likely to know each other frequently and personally, which decreases the likeliness of zero-sum games. The direct external aspect of smallness is the increased unity and solidarity under the threat of other countries. The hostility between segments has an external limit beyond which all of them will be losers. The indirect internal effect of the small size is that the decision-making process is less complex in small countries. Where the number of groups with divergent interests and values is fewer making a decision is easier. Finally, the indirect external aspect of smallness is the high probability of a foreign policy of neutrality, which also reduces the load on the decision-making system.

Although the last point can be questioned (neutrality may require even more work from the foreign policy bureaucracy), it does not matter in the case of local governments. The other external effect is important not because local governments are threatened by foreign invasion, but because small communities are more vulnerable to relatively small changes in their economic and infrastructural position. In terms of survival and prosperity, small units depend more on their environment. It may encourage the internal unity and solidarity of the community, which, in turn, may have an effect of the role of parties.

Table 2.1. Lijphart's argument on the effect of small size on consociational democracy

	direct	**Indirect**
internal	elite closeness	complexity of decision-making
external	external threat	Imposed neutrality

The other debate on size and democracy in the recent literature focuses on the impact of size on the level of local political participation. To a certain degree, this body of literature also attempts to provide evidence to the proponents and opponents of municipal amalgamation. Still, it also contributes to the wider discussion on the determinants of the quality of democracy. Several studies have been a reaction to the general decline in electoral turnout in some countries, a phenomenon that appears on the local level too. I cannot give a full overview of this literature as it is part of the huge field of voting studies.

A prominent model is the rational voting theory. Downs (1957) argues that investing in the cost of voting is more 'profitable' in small local governments where a vote has more chance to be decisive. The social-psychology theory, well represented by Verba et al. (1978), call attention to the importance of group-related motivations. In this argument, small places are more likely to have high turnout because the deeper feeling of identity involve a civic duty of participation in local life. Oliver (2000) brings this argument closer to the social capital theory by claiming that the level of civic engagement, including turnout, is higher in suburbs (independent from the size of the metropolitan area) than in large cities. Nonetheless, Verba et al. (1978) have another model, which predicts a higher turnout in large municipalities. The mobilization model is based on the idea that the higher significance of issues and greater competition in large municipalities result in more efforts to convince citizens of the importance of voting. Almost all empirical studies have found a positive correlation between size and turnout, which supports the first model, called the 'decline-of-community' model' by Verba et al. (1978). The actual causal mechanism, however, has been less investigated. It is unclear whether the higher turnout in small municipalities is due to civic duty (and more anomie in large municipalities) or to the organization of the local society, e.g., the higher mobilizing capacity of families and clienteles.

Before moving on to other potentially useful bodies of literature, I present a concept of size that can be an alternative to the commonly used population-based indicators.

2.1.2. A New Concept of Size

Dahl and Tufte (1973: 17–19) enumerate a few potential concepts of size such as population, area, and population density. As many other scholars, they also use population as the main indicator of size. Still, the idea that size is not necessarily population is intriguing in itself. In an unreflective manner, size is too often identified with the number of people living in an administrative unit.

In many quantitative researches, especially in local government studies, the variable size is the logarithm of the population. The explanation for that is technical. The difference between the smallest and the largest units is too large and the distribution is often very uneven (there are usually many small and relatively few large cases); linear regression analysis requires a transformed measure. While the conformity to the assumptions of statistical analysis is an important improvement of quantitative studies, it does not imply any interpretation of the new variable. Actually, the creation of a new variable is not even explicitly recognized. It is treated as the same variable indicating size. The cost of the transformation is not discussed. Moreover, it is unclear why the transformation technique is used. The size distribution may vary from country to country (for example, it is more lognormal in China, while closer to Pareto distribution in the US; see Anderson and Ge 2003). In most cases, one may suppose a simple, not very conscious conformity to conventional methods.

On a more conceptual level, one may also argue that one unit's increase has a radically different meaning in small cases. There may not be a big difference between a city of 100,000 and 101,000 inhabitants. However, the difference may be quite significant between a village of 100 and 1,100 citizens. The logarithmic transformation expresses this nonlinear relationship. But again, the actual mechanism behind nonlinearity is not discussed.

When municipality data are aggregated by population groups, equal categories (such as 0–10,000, 10,000–20,000, 20,000–30,000, etc.) are rarely used. Instead, unequal but more meaningful categories are often published (e.g. 0–2,000, 2,000–5,000, 5,000–10,000, 10,000–50,000, etc.). In a sense, such a taxonomy is quite strange, as categories are very different in terms of size (for example, the 10,000–50,000 category has a range of 40,000, while the 2,000–5,000 category only 3,000). Still, this is supposed to be meaningful; 'meaningful classification' refers to the nonlinear character of the change in significance. Nevertheless, the basis of categorization is never reflected on.

I believe that functional size, that is, functional centrality and complexity, is the underlying factor of the nonlinearity of size. Indeed, the same difference of size has different 'meaning' for small and large municipalities. The reason is that new functions are taken up according to categories and the population range of those categories is rather different in the case of small and large units. The population categories, widely used in social science research, and the logarithmic transformation represent correct methodological tools if the measurement of functional size is not available. In this research, the correlation between municipality significance and the natural logarithm of population size is quite high (0.91), which points to the usefulness of the log population as proxy of functional size. However, this may not be the case in other countries or in other periods in Hungary. Thus, functional size must be measured whenever possible and the use of transformed population indicators as a proxy must be justified by prior research on the actual level of correlation.

It is also very important to point out that the use of population categories and logarithmic transformations may be correct in measuring functional size, but it is incorrect to say that the variable measured is population size. These transformations and categorizations refer to another form of size that must be made explicit in any research using the nonlinear transformations of population size.

What makes the question more complicated and interesting is the fact that functional size can be interpreted both as centrality and complexity. Certain functions are not needed in each local government. The municipality that provides services to other municipalities increases its centrality. In addition to this external view, the internal view focuses on functional complexity. More significant municipalities by definition have more administrative, social and economic institutions. This dense functional network makes local governance more complex. Consequently, further research could rely on the conceptual and methodological advancements of two types of literatures. In terms of centrality, the rapidly expanding network analysis field provides various concepts of centrality and techniques to actually capture them in a relation-based dataset. In terms of complexity, governance studies may offer measures that can grasp the interaction of local institutions.

Is functional size simply a consequence of population? Is it a new name for the same phenomenon? Certainly not, there is a clear association between population size and functional size (0.5 in my measurement), which corresponds to the expectations that larger communities play a more central role in their milieu and face more institutional complexity. Nonetheless, the variance in significance is only partially ($R^2 = 0.25$) explained by the size of the population. There are at least six other factors that may account for the level of significance. First, the legal status of local government obviously has a large impact. Formal administrative centers by definition have certain competency others do not. Cities of the same size but of different administrative status have different level of centrality and complexity. To take an example from Hungary, Szekszárd, a county capital, is more significant than Cegléd, a town close to the capital, although both have roughly the same number of inhabitants. Formal administrative status brings extra functions to the municipality, which may extract other ones (for instance, the regional headquarters of companies).

Second, history matters. Certain administrative functions are retained even when the previous administrative position is already lost for a long time. Economic institutions do not move even after a de-industrialization and regional shift of economic power. Economic history, especially the developments of industrialization and industrial policy, as well as the history of public administration play a certain role.

Third, geographical position may add to, or subtract from, the significance of municipalities. Transportation is of great importance. Centrality in the transportation network add to the general level of centrality. Specific location may also increase or decrease functional size. An island municipality has more function simply due to the distance and specific transportation circumstances. Remote, isolated towns have more functions than municipalities of the same size but of different location.

Fourth, the distribution of population also affects the level of importance. Dahl and Tufte (1973: 18) call this relative size. A small town can become very significant among small villages, while it would be insignificant in the shadow of a large central city of a metropolitan agglomeration. The central cities of metropolitan areas gain their importance partly from the uneven distribution of settlements. Relative size and administrative position often interact and overlap. The most importance municipality in an area is usually designated as administrative center, and the evaluation of importance is often based on the relative size of the communities in the region.

Sixth, economic power and structure greatly contribute to the level of significance. Powerful local economies build up lots of functions and provide their local governments with resources to attract others. Moreover, certain economic sectors, especially services like tourism, establish many institutions.

Summing up, functional centrality and significance are not necessarily related to size. It is also a matter of administrative status, administrative and economic history, geographical position (especially the location in the transportation system), the relative size in the local distribution of population, and economic power and structure.

If so many factors may influence the level of significance in addition to the size of population, the question is inevitably raised: is it really a form of size? I believe the answer is affirmative. Everyday perception is one argument. A city is called 'large' if it provides many types of administrative, social, economic, etc. services. The perception of 'large' is not based on the latest census data, but the perception of political (in terms of administrative institutions) and economic (in terms of job market and commercial sector) power. Cities of the same population may be (and often are) perceived as being of different size. The everyday language often implies those perceived differences. (For example, Hungarians 'go up' from a smaller municipality to a larger city.) Another, more conceptual, argument refers back to Dahl and Tufte (1973). As they point out, size can be conceptualized in more than one way. The notion of functional size certainly conveys the concept of magnitude as much as other measures such as density or area. The significant correlation with other indicators of size also underlines its belonging to the same family. Still, its correlation with other measures is not so high that one could simply identify it with something else.

I believe that functional size is a separate and legitimate concept of size. The empirical part is to prove the usefulness of this new concept.

2.1.3. Hypotheses About Size

The discussion so far has led to important general hypotheses:

Hypotheses

The larger the municipality's population, the higher the level of local party institutionalization.

The larger the municipality's functional size, the higher the level of local party institutionalization.

2.2. Socioeconomic Factors

The survey of the size and democracy literature already pointed to a number of potential factors that may intervene between size and indicators of local democracy such as the level of local party institutionalization. Some of them were related to socioeconomic variables and the societal organization. Thus, I review the literature focusing on the relationship between modernization and democracy, and social capital and democracy. Then, I conclude by putting forward hypotheses about the factors that may account for the variation in local party institutionalization and intervene between size and local party institutionalization.

2.2.1. Further Literature Survey

2.2.1.1. Development and Democracy

The largest school of empirical democratic research has up to now been the modernization theory. The basic tenet of this perspective is that an overall transformation in which economic, social, and political changes (e.g. industrialization, urbanization, migration, and democratization) coherently go together is the master process of our age. This transformation is basically the same everywhere and occurs through evolutionary stages. Consequently, societies can be placed on a development scale and their futures can to some degree be predicted. Not surprisingly, the modernization school had its heyday in the optimistic 1960s, when many former colonies seemed to adopt the Western economic, social, and political model. It became discredited in the 1970s under the heavy pressure of both the scientific critiques and the changes in world political patterns. Still, one can argue that the inclusion of the development factor as an independent variable in a multivariate analysis is both theoretically and empirically well supported in the literature.

The idea of modernization goes back to the classical writers of social sciences. Marx emphasized commodification, i.e. the process whereby goods and services increasingly became merchandises in the market. Durkheim conceptualized modernization as social differentiation, i.e. the process by which institutional activities became divided, separated and more specialized. Weber portrayed the transformation of pre-modern societies as increasing rationalization, which, from a political point of view, mainly means bureaucratization. After WWII, the structural-functionalist vogue stressed the changes in norms and value systems and interpreted modernization as the replacement of traditional values with motivational patterns more favorable to economic growth and social change. Since then, the idea of modernization has appeared in several forms. In this section, the writings analyzing the relationship between democratization and economic development will be discussed. This means a neglect of the functionalist ideas of modernization school.

Empirically, the evidence to which the proponents of this approach most frequently refer is a high and significant correlation between the level of democracy and the level of socioeconomic development. Lipset's paper on "Some Social Requisites of Democracy", originally published in 1959, was a breakthrough in this respect. Based on Lerner's *The Passing of Traditional Society* (1958), Lipset claimed in this paper that the level of economic development and the level of democracy are related issues. "The more well-to-do a nation, the greater the chances that it will sustain democracy" (Lipset 1981: 31). To support this claim, he analyzed data from 51 countries, divided into two categories: European and English-speaking countries vs. Latin America. In both sets, he distinguished between democracies and dictatorships. Then, Lipset related the means of the two groups within each regional set to five indicators of socioeconomic development (wealth, industrialization, education, urbanization). He claimed that these "aspects of economic development [...] are so closely related as to form one major factor which has the political correlate of democracy" (1981: 41). The results showed that democratic countries are more developed on average than non-democratic countries. In the Postscript of his *Political Man* Lipset reasserted the basic claims of this train of thought.

Lipset's findings were criticized by many (e.g. it was argued that European dictatorships had had a higher mean of development than Latin American democracies), but it generated a long line of research. Coleman (1960), on a much more functionalist ground, examined 75 Third World countries and classified them in three categories according to their respective level of democracy. He then compared the categories on 11 indicators of modernization. The results of 10 variables demonstrated the same order: competitive, semi-competitive and authoritarian regimes. Cutright (1963) opened a long series of papers based on correlational analysis. He replaced Lipset's crude, two-value (democratic/non-democratic) scoring system with a scale of political development (measuring competition and stability by scoring the years when competitive parliament and elected chief executive existed). Cutright, then, related this index to socioeconomic indicators such as urbanization, communication, education and industrialization. The multiple correlation explained 67 percent of the variance around the mean. If taken alone, however, one component, the communications development index, accounted for 65 percent. Cutright called attention to the high correlation among the explanatory variables as an explanation and argued for the single dimension of development. As a good functionalist, he claimed that "if a nation has departed from its predicted values, we can view it as being under some pressure to move toward the predicted score" (1963: 262). In order to find their equilibrium, poor democracies would become less democratic, and relatively more wealthy nations would come closer to democracy.

The association between economic development and political democracy has been supported by recent studies as well. Powell (1982) reported a moderate association of various modernization indicators with participation, no correlation with executive durability and a curvilinear relationship with violent acts. Diamond (1992) cross-tabulated six regime-types and four income groups (based on per capita GNP) for 142 countries. The data demonstrated a clear positive association between economic development and democracy at the.0001 level (Chi square). Hadenius (1992) also found correlations with socioeconomic variables (GNP level, daily newspapers, infant mortality, primary-, secondary- and higher education, literacy, radio sets, telephones, employment in services, etc.) in the right direction. However, only one component of modernization survived when regressed with other variables. This central factor of the modernization process is not an economic variable, but literacy. (For a very informative summary of the quantitative studies on socioeconomic determinants of democracy, see Diamond 1992: 111–113.)

Where is the level of economic development that leads to democratic transformation? Several authors tried to identify a certain level above which democratization takes off. Dahl (1971) claimed that the relationship is not linear but curvilinear. There is an upper threshold ($700–800 per capita, 1957) "above which the chances of polyarchy (and hence of competitive politics) are so high that any further increases in per capita GNP (and variables associated with such an increase) cannot affect the outcome in any significant way" (67–68). Similarly, there is a lower limit ($100–200) below which there is only a slight chance for democracy. Recently, Huntington also pointed to "a zone of transition or choice, in which [...] new types of political institutions are required to aggregate the demands of an increasingly complex society and to implement public policies in such a society" (1984: 201). Thus, democratic transformation occurs at the middle level of economic development. The events of 1990 do not refute Huntington's findings.

To explain the well-established correlation between the levels of democratic and economic developments, students of empirical democratic theory attempted to identify specific causal mechanisms and theoretically explain the correlation by several intervening variables. Lipset mentioned (without much systematic evidence) some mechanisms through which economic development had an effect on democratization. All of these variables seem to refer to a central prerequisite of democracy, tolerance and moderation. For example, he summarized the effect of education this way: "Education broadens man's outlook, enables him to understand the need for norms of tolerance, restrains him from adhering to extremist doctrines, and increases his capacity to make rational electoral choices" (1981: 39). Education makes people sophisticated, informed and tolerant. A high level of education is, for Lipset, a necessary condition for democracy. Economic development also affects the distribution of wealth. Great inequality leads to extremities in the poor, who regard the established political system as the enemy, and to anti-democratic feelings and arrogance in the wealthy, who see a danger in the inclusion of the poor. Socioeconomic development, however, strengthens the middle classes, which are the more moderate and, thus, the most pro-democratic social force. More educated and less-poor lower classes are more exposed to cross-pressures that reduce the influence of extremist ideologies. (This will be discussed in the subsection 3.2.2 on cleavages.) Lipset also contributed a great role to intermediary organizations that prevent the state from domination, communicate ideas among citizens, create new ideas, socialize political skills and increase participation. More wealthy nations have stronger intermediary organizations, which, in turn, contribute to a more tolerant, sophisticated, informed, and, thus, a more democratic citizenry.

Subsequent authors developed and elaborated on the ideas that appeared in Lipset's analysis, but did not disclose why development tends to generate democracy. While the study on the relationship between economic and political development became more and more sophisticated concerning methodology, it was not further supported theoretically. The phenomenon that was more emphasized in later works was communication. Economic and social development leads to the expansion of newspapers, radio and TV. According to this argument, increasing media exposure makes people more interested in politics and more familiar with political phenomena. More sophisticated citizens, then, take part in democratic policy-making, in the form of both electoral turnout and participation in political organizations (mainly in mass parties). This is also the logic of Karl Deutsch's (1961) social mobilization scheme. McCrone and Cnudde (1967) used time-series analysis to infer causal patterns. They found that the first step in modernization and democratization was urbanization, which had a certain effect on democratization and increased the level of education. Better education, they claimed, amplified media, which, in turn, had a large impact on democratization. They concluded with a communications theory of democratic development. Dahl (1971) also stressed the role of communication and literacy. He accounted for the deviant cases, i.e. the countries where democracy exists (India) or existed (ancient Greece, 19th century US) at a lower level of development, with the fact that a relatively high level of education, literacy and mass media can be achieved even in poor or pre-industrial countries. The other explanation for deviant cases lies in the equality of resources (see subsection 1.3).

Diagram 2.2. The scheme of the modernization school

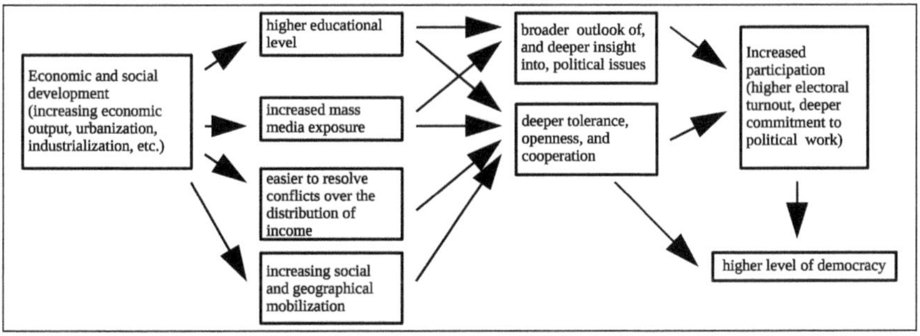

The study of the modernization effects on democracy received many criticisms. Inglehart, who attempted to rejuvenate modernization theory, acknowledged five points to be revised. (1) Socioeconomic change does not move in one direction, in a linear way. History "reaches points of diminishing returns" and begins "to move in a fundamentally new direction" (1997: 10). (2) The supposed relationships tended toward an oversimplified determinism. Economic determinism (like Marxism) and cultural determinism (like Weberian theories) are both mistakes, because these systems are mutually supportive and the causal linkages are reciprocal. (3) The modernization school was often accused of ethnocentrism. This Western-oriented view hinders the understanding of modernization. (4) Modernization does not necessarily lead to democracy. Fascism and communism are also alternatives in the modernization phase.

Some of the above critiques (especially ethnocentrism) were supported by the non-functionalist proponents, who emphasized only the relationship between economic and democratic development. Another critique, the problem of causality, is not unusual in quantitative studies. It is, however, particularly effective against the economic development perspective because of the poverty of a convincing specification of causality. What this branch of the empirical democratic theory found are no more than correlations, which do not tell us the direction of causality nor the causal mechanism. The causal mechanisms were not at the center of discussion. Some pointed to problems with the dependent variable, especially Cutright's index that is used by many. The next subsection summarizes the critique of dependency theorists.

In spite of the many criticisms, one must face up to the empirical relationship between socioeconomic development and the level of democracy. This association was demonstrated in so many studies with so many cases that the propositions, which can be unfolded from the modernization approach, must be tested in a multivariate analysis against evidence.

Research on the relationship between socioeconomic development and the degree of democracy has brought some variables to the front. Not all of these variables can usefully be interpreted in the case of local communities nowadays. For example, the rate of literacy or mobility does not express much in a within-country comparison in the beginning of the 21th century. From the perspective of this research, the supposed intervening variables are the most relevant factors. There are three variables which can be well theorized with regard to the degree of democracy in local governments: the level of education, citizens' standard of living and the strength of the media.

2.2.1.2. Civil Society

Theorizing civil society has a long and venerable tradition from Aristotle's *politike koinonia* to Hegel's *bürgerliche Gesellschaft*. As a consequence, there are many conceptualizations of civil society. This project uses a common and easily operationalizable definition. Civil society here refers to the realm of voluntary, self-initiated, and self-organized intermediary groups that are independent of the family, the market and the state. It is operationalized as the domain of non-governmental, legally accepted organizations.

A special and currently fashionable branch of the civil society literature focuses on the connectedness of individuals. The social capital school (see e.g. Putnam 1993; Putnam 2001; Field 2003; Edwards et al. 2001; Edwards and Foley 1998) interprets this connectedness either structurally (e.g. Lin 2001) or culturally, focusing mainly on trust (e.g. Uslaner 2002). Several studies have dealt with the role of social capital in local politics (e.g. Cusack 1997; Milner and Ersson 2000; Soós 2004).

Civic groups give shape to various efforts and initiatives of citizens that address different public issues. Local civic associations, organized around single or complex issues, address locally relevant policy issues, express specific opinions and interests between two elections and often provide services for the local communities. Civil society organizations are crucial actors in the local policy making process in several ways. Based on Diamond, Linz and Lipset (1995), Schmitter (1997), Post and Rosenblum (2002) and Soós (2001), I identify seven mechanisms through which civil society may affect local democracy.

The first approach deals with civil society as a social force limiting and monitoring the state. Civil society is presented in this perspective as a societal sphere that is capable of resisting the state, exploiting its independence from the state.

Making (local) government actions public, civic organizations hold public officials accountable. The tyrannical actions by rulers are potentially impeded by an opposing civil society. This train of thought was quite common in Central Europe in the 1980s. Democratic dissidents of the communist regime like Kuroń, Michnik or Konrád drew up a strategy for the opposition to form a counterweight to the communist state. As Smolar (1996) points out, this Central European "society-first" approach was fully anti-political (György Konrád has a collection of essays under the title "Antipolitics"), seeking remedy for political problems outside the official sphere. The philosophical basis, based on Hegel, was later summarized by Cohen and Arató (1992). In the 1990s, when the elite which had initiated the "antipolitics" went to the new official political life the idea of civil society as a limiting force became less popular in political theory (see Lomax 1997 and Miszlivetz 1997).

A second positive impact of civil society organizations on local democracy is the furthering of information-flow. Civil organizations provide information on many aspects of the state of the municipality, from the opportunities of project funding to the technical difficulties in implementing policy decisions. A good flow of information helps policy-making as well as implementation.

Thirdly, civil society provides channels to articulate and aggregate societal interests. Political parties and other political organizations fulfill the same function, but it has turned out that in the democratic practice civil associations are indispensable in the expression of a wide variety of interests that cannot be channeled by parties. This stabilizes social and political expectations. The literature of corporatism especially focuses on the mediating institutions through which certain civil organizations take part in the officially recognized aggregation of societal interests: well-articulated interests make policy-making easier and improve responsiveness. Putnam's studies (1993, 1995) are the most influential formulation of this idea in the recent literature.

The fourth hypothesized effect of civil society is the stimulation of political participation. People taking part in civic activities gain a feeling of political efficacy, i.e. an attitude that one can influence political life. Social participation leads, as the argument claims, to political participation. Where people are engaged in civic associations, interest in elections, electoral campaigns, street demonstrations, single-issue movements etc. is higher. High-level political participation, then, results in better-performing governments.

The fifth contribution of civil society to democracy is the inculcation of civicness. Tolerance, moderation, trust and accommodation of difference are the building blocks of democratic political life. These norms and attitudes help to resolve conflicts peacefully.

Schmitter (1997) calls attention to a sixth contribution of civil society to democracy. A sixth, indirect contribution of civil society to political performance is the promotion of the sense of community. Civil society is a channel not only for the expression of interests, but also of sentiments and identities. People participating in civic activities are less likely to be alienated from the system because they tend to be more integrated through self-expression in civic groups. Identification with the community can lead, in a democracy, to a more legitimate status of the political system.

A seventh way in which civil society indirectly influences the level of democracy is the training of new leaders who have roots in certain social spheres. Those who learn how to manage a civic organization are much more prepared to run political organizations. In addition to this competence, these persons also tend to have stronger democratic commitments and a larger social capital in the sense of Bourdieu's theory. Leaders coming from civil society bring many connections with them, which is highly important in political recruitment.

After enumerating seven potentially positive effects found in the optimistic literature, one must admit that civil society may also have a negative influence on democracy. The same organizational capacity can be used to siphon-off public resources and undermine the delivery of public goods. To explain the actual effects, other characteristics of civil society should be taken into consideration. One of them, cleavages, will be discussed later.

The structure of local civil society influences the actual role it plays. Where a big and well-organized social organization dominates the field, one cannot expect an equal access of all organizations to local government. The biggest organization will, in all probability, put forward its claim to be the voice of the local society and distort the allocation of public resources and the above-listed positive effects will, at best, not come true, or, at worst, hinder local democracy.

Another important feature of local civic organizations is their inclusiveness. The same ties that promote the interests of the civil organization allow the exclusion of outsiders from a certain sphere of local life. Such an organization does not produce civic values, weakens the sense of community, hinders interest-formation and the flow of correct information. What is expected public good in the case of inclusive organizations becomes a public bad in the case of organizations based on exclusion.

Finally, a direct effect of civil society is executed by civil organizations purposefully designed to improve local democracy. Human rights groups or tax reform movements provide information and opinion independent of governmental information and opinion. Local development groups or the associations that provide public services also have more direct influence on local governments. Although all civil society activities may produce civic values and skilled leaders, political actions especially make the contributions described as the seven mechanisms above. One should consider the political activity of local civil organizations in a separate variable.

2.2.2. Hypotheses Concerning Intervening Factors

In the rest of this section, I put forward hypotheses concerning the variables that potentially intervene between municipality size and local party institutionalization.

2.2.2.1. Political Distance

A possible link is related to social distance. Increasing size means increasing distance between voters and representatives (see also Dahl and Tufte 1973). The size of the local council cannot be proportionate to the size of the local government. To take an example, a Hungarian village of 100 inhabitants elects three representatives. In other words, three percent of the population serves in the council. In a fully proportionate system, a city of 100,000 (e.g. Kecskemét) would elect a council of 3,000. The Soviet Union or the PRC might sport such huge representative bodies, but an effective (local) government requires a smaller council (e.g. Kecskemét has 32 councilors). The increased disproportion results in an increased voter/representative ratio (in the previous example, from about 28 to 2682 voters per representative). As size increases, it is increasingly difficult to reach voters through inexpensive personal contacts. Therefore, candidates have to use more costly campaign strategies. The larger the local government is the more campaign money is spent, the more specialists are involved, the more significant media is and the less personal the persuasion methods are. Campaigns are both quantitatively and qualitatively different in small and large municipalities. The need for indirect communication does not stop to exist on election night. Gaining popular support for policy initiatives also requires concentrated resources. Social distance between voters and representatives (which is often a physical distance too) leads to more professional and mediated political communication with higher costs. This, in turn, favors political organization as campaign money and influence-making resources must be pooled, and the salience of candidates and proposed policies in media must be increased. Continuously functioning organizations for nominating candidates are especially beneficial in large municipalities as they can maintain a permanent presence in local citizens' minds.

Geser (1999: 27) suggests a similar, but not completely identical hypothesis. He argues that the smaller the community the more likely that the character and even survival of local political organizations hinges on certain core individuals. In smaller places, the number of politically capable persons is more limited and their families, clans and followers take a larger share of the local population. As a result, a personal turnover often leads to the breakdown or weakening of local parties (especially political associations). A manifest sign of party institutionalization is the survival of the leaving of leaders or generational change (Huntington 1968:14–15). The raw number of individuals with the right amount of human capital (leadership and organizational skills, political talent) and personal social capital (connections, support) is expected to have a significant effect on the level of local party institutionalization.

Hypotheses

The distance between representatives and voters positively influences the level of local party institutionalization.

The distance between representatives and voters is an intervening variable between population size and local party institutionalization.

2.2.2.2. Municipality Significance and Complexity

National parties are more attracted by large local governments. While issues are often rather trivial in small communities, cities decide on more relevant problems. Important problems involve more money and appointments, which gives not only more prestige, but also a great opportunity for distributing selective incentives. Solving more important issues may also increase the support for the parties governing the city, which may be transformed into seats on the supra-local levels too. The need for more expertise to resolve complex issues makes political activity for some talented people more meaningful and rewarding. Thus, the significance of the municipality shapes the degree of local party institutionalization and the level of the penetration of national parties.

The complexity of local public affairs also can be conceptualized as an intervening variable. The more people who live in a local government the more diverse the issues that emerge and the more various those issues are. Dahl and Tufte (1973: 30) define complexity as "the number of variables that have to be taken into account in order to understand, explain, or predict the behavior of the system" and "the variation of the relationships among these variables". The municipal complexity is well indicated by the size and organizational complexity of local government offices and the number and variety of functions they perform. The Local Government Act also gives more responsibilities to city governments, especially to regional centers. This complexity needs more diverse expertise from local politicians, which easily exceeds the knowledge and experience of individuals. Their cooperation is more and more rewarded as the population size of the local government grows. Thus, complexity has a grouping effect on political entrepreneurs. Political groups or local parties attract more skilled and motivated politicians to take part in local politics as specialists.

As I proposed in the previous section, municipality significance and complexity can be conceptually unified in one variable: functional size. This leads to the following hypothesis.

Hypothesis

The larger the size of the local population, the larger the functional size of the municipality.

Functional size intervenes between population size and local party institutionalization.

2.2.2.3. Media

As Dahl and Tufte (1973: 68–88) claim, the form of communication changes with the size of the political community. The larger the political system, the more mediated the political communication. Thus, the media is an important component of politics. The number, diversity and importance of media outlets grow with municipality size in both senses. Larger population as well as more centrality and complexity create a functional need for the media. More extensive media presence makes political competition more expensive, which, as mentioned before, increases the likeliness of party institutionalization. The effective existence of media also changes the way in which politics are done. Political leaders and candidates have to appear in the local press, which can be done more effectively if political activists join their efforts. Media communication also requires specialists both in public administration and political representation (Dahl and Tufte 1973: 76–77). The relationship between party institutionalization and media strength is not one way, as they are parts of the general institutionalization process. Media makes parties more viable, but media outlets are often sponsored by parties, are (or used to be) satellites or belong to a wider political network.

Hypothesis

The more important the local media, the more institutionalized the local parties.

The importance of the local media acts as an intervening variable between municipality size and local party institutionalization.

Two other types of intervening variables are supposed to mediate the effect of size on local party institutionalization: social heterogeneity (and cleavages) and social and political participation.

2.2.2.4. *Social Heterogeneity Hypotheses*

Party institutionalization may be promoted by the existence of easily definable societal groups. Such groups have different interests and/or values. The candidates who espouse those interests and values face a social pressure to, and have a vested interest in, forming a joint organization since a common label can catch loyal voters, campaign resources, and inter-election support for policy initiatives. The availability of socioeconomic, linguistic, ethnic or religious groups, i.e. societal heterogeneity, is expected to correlate with the level of local party institutionalization. Not all types of groups have the same relationship with size. The presence of socioeconomic groups are more likely to have a more or less linear relationship with the size of the population. The larger the number of people living together, the more likely that the local economy and society become more complex (richer variety of jobs, industries, services, etc.). One can expect some general association between size and the existence of identity groups based on ethnicity, religion, language or even sexual orientation. Still, ethnic or religious divisions may and do exist in the smallest villages. To sum up, the general hypothesis is that societal heterogeneity increases the chances of local party institutionalization and that there is a correlation between the size of the local population and the existence of social divisions (especially the socioeconomic ones).

Societal heterogeneity reaches such an extent that each group organizes its own social institutions, forming 'consociational democracies' (Lijphart 1977; Luther and Deschouwer 1999). Organizational 'pillars' or subcultures in the (local) society include a representative organization too. Therefore, one may hypothesize that the level of general pillarization in the municipality is strongly related to the level of institutionalization of local parties.

Large cities are often characterized by a high turnover of their population. Immigrants from the countryside and abroad primarily go to cities where they can finds jobs more effectively and can be integrated into the local society more easily. In contrast, villages are often more closed. Small communities do not encourage immigrants and their turnover is usually small. Population change increases the heterogeneity of the local society, as newcomers often have different jobs, values, religion or ethnicity. Therefore, one may hypothesize a positive relationship between population size and turnover and a negative one between population change and societal homogeneity.

It is unclear whether societal heterogeneity and pillarization increase or decrease the costs of political communication, an important factor of party institutionalization. On the one hand, the more diverse the local society, the more difficult to reach potential supporters and the more expensive political networking. On the other hand, parties with a societal niche such as the working class or the catholic subculture have to spend less on political communication as they have a direct contact with their constituency.

Hypotheses

Population stability positively influences the level of local party institutionalization.

The degree of societal diversity positively influences the level of local party institutionalization.

The strength of societal (socioeconomic and ethnic) diversity intervenes between municipality size and local party institutionalization.

The degree of political diversity intervenes between municipality size and local party institutionalization.

Population stability intervenes between municipality size and local party institutionalization.

Both social and political participation may be intervening variables between size and institutionalization. They will later be discussed in detail.

2.2.2.5. Standard of Living

The literature on socioeconomic development calls attention to two important factors: the standard of living of citizens and the level of education. Communities with a better standard of living differ from poorer ones in many respects relevant to this research. Middle-class people have more spare time to deal with public issues. They often have more experience in voicing their claims. That results, on the one hand, in a higher level of social and political participation and, on the other hand, a larger pool of potential leaders and supporters, decreasing the importance of the political gurus and increasing the chance of local party institutionalization. More wealthy citizens also have more time and money for newspapers and electronic media, which makes the local media market wider, more diverse and independent.

Hypotheses

The standard of living of the local society positively influences local party institutionalization.

The standard of living intervenes between municipality size and local party institutionalization.

2.2.2.6. Education

The level of education also has an indirect effect on local party institutionalization. More educated citizens have a need for, and actually consume, more media, which increases the importance of the local press. A higher proportion of people with better education enlarges the pool of potential leaders and activists, giving party institutionalization a higher chance. A larger number of potential leaders also means a larger sub-elite and potential rivals for leaders, which decreases the power of core individuals in community and makes local politics less personalistic. More educated people are more likely to participate in civic organizations, partly to safeguard their narrow or wide interests, and partly to express themselves. It is difficult to put forward an a priori hypothesis about the effect of education on electoral participation. On the one hand, educated citizens may realize the importance of politics better; have better articulated interests to defend and attribute more symbolic value to voting. On the other hand, educated citizens have access to more channels to make their voice heard, so they are less encouraged to turn out to vote.

Hypotheses

The education level of the local society positively influences the degree of local party institutionalization.

The education level of the local society intervenes between municipality size and local party institutionalization.

2.2.2.7. Social Participation

Both size and socioeconomic development influence the level of social participation. By social participation, I mean here the level of organization and institutionalization of civic groups. A vibrant civil society with many well-organized groups may help the organization of local parties in more than one way. First, successful groups provide a model of organization. Second, they also provide skilled leaders, who are able to organize a political organization. Third, civic groups, especially interest organizations, can be powerful partners in reaching the local society. If civic organizations are not only well-organized, but also well-institutionalized, they offer party organizations an incentive to maintain a continuity. The incentive is the possibility of a long-term cooperation with institutionalized (and, therefore, in all probability well-known and respected) players of the local civil society. Breaking up, or leaving a party with many institutionalized ties with other influential organizations costs more than liquidating, or defecting from, a weakly embedded organization.

Another channel of social participation would be through network-like social connections. While informal networks are poorly organized, they can be very well-institutionalized. Actually, as Chapter 1 mentioned, networks can be powerful rivals of party organizations. Nonetheless, they can also strengthen party institutionalization by providing local politicians with already institutionalized social structures. The effect of networks on political institutionalization is largely undertheorized and the amount and significance of networks has never been surveyed. So this type of social participation will not be included in the research design.

Hypotheses

The social participation of local citizens positively influences local party institutionalization.

The social participation of local citizens intervenes between municipality size and local party institutionalization.

2.2.2.8. Political Participation

In addition to social participation, the level of political participation is also predicted to influence the degree of local party institutionalization. A distinction must be made between electoral and non-electoral participation. Electoral participation refers to the act of voting and the turnout rate at local elections. Non-electoral participation includes any kind of commitment to local political activities, ranging from simple information processing (when citizens keep an eye on what happens in the local public life) to hard-core political activism such as the organization of, or participation in, street demonstrations. Both types of participation may have positive or negative consequences for local party institutionalization. Elections with large turnouts also mobilize people with weaker or nonexistent political preferences and information. One may argue that that improves the opportunities for challengers, as they can get votes from the larger pool of voters. However, one may also argue that well-established trademarks have an advantage to attract less-informed voters while low turnout favors those who leave the party, and can take a part of the electorate with them. Non-electoral participation may also have positive and negative effects. Institutionalization can be impeded by a high level of local activism; political movements and protests may stop the routinization of organizations. On the other hand, many politically committed people means many potential party members and voluntary work, which can be channeled by the usual methods of parties.

Thus, the effect of political participation is unclear. What is more, this relationship can be reversed. Well-organized and institutionalized parties may increase participation by mobilizing voters. On the other hand, established parties may make elections and political life boring or unattractive, as outcomes can easily be predicted.

The level of social and political participation may be influenced by the social and political heterogeneity of the local community. Social diversity, i.e. the existence of various societal groups, implies the defense of different interests that clearly contribute to the emergence of parties. As far as political diversity is concerned, an obvious consequence of the formation of political subcultures is the establishment of party organizations. As pillarization is a permanent societal feature, the parties that represent subcultures have a good chance to become institutionalized.

Hypotheses

The political participation of local citizens positively influences local party institutionalization.

The political participation of local citizens intervenes between municipality size and local party institutionalization.

2.2.3. Factors Intervening Between Municipality Size and Local Party Institutionalization

Although the prior research on the relationship between population size and local party institutionalization is very limited, the available literature and simple deductions suggest some mechanisms and intervening variables that may explain the link between population size and local party institutionalization. In Chapter 3, this model will be further reduced to meet measurement requirements.

2.3. Other Effects

In addition to size, there are some other exogenous variables that may influence the level of local party institutionalization. These are control variables from the viewpoint of the size and institutionalization approach. This section focuses on the potential consequences of electoral rules, geography, history, and organizational features.

2.3.1. Electoral Rules

Probably the most obvious factor that may influence the level of local party institutionalization is the electoral system. Electoral rules provide very direct incentives to those who would like public office. Supposing that local politicians, for whatever motivation, really want to get elected, one may predict with a high probability that the electoral system shapes the behavior of both the individual and organizational actors.

Mayors of municipalities, capital districts and the capital are directly elected in Hungary.[3] Mayors are *ex officio* members of the local council, if they are not elected as representatives. The electoral system differs between large and small municipalities. In municipalities of less than 10,000 inhabitants voters may choose from a single list as many candidates as there are number of seats in the local council. In larger municipalities, there are ten or more individual constituencies and citizens may vote for one of the candidates in their respective constituencies. About forty percent of the seats are distributed among compensation lists of organizations (parties and NGOs) that run candidates; this mechanism makes the composition of local councils more proportionate. The councils of the capital and counties are also directly elected via party lists. So, for instance, Budapest voters receive a minimum of four ballots, with candidates for constituency representative, district mayor, capital mayor and lists for the capital city council.

On the one hand, First-Past-the-Post systems favor those candidates who are able to concentrate both human and material campaign resources. This encourages organizational nominations and the cooperation of nominating organizations. On the other hand, the opportunity of running party lists obviously acts as an incentive for local politicians to join forces. Winning extra places is certainly attractive in the local electoral system in Hungary too, as the defeated candidates' votes are aggregated and approximately 40 percent of the council positions are distributed among the nominating organizations. (For a more detailed presentation of the local electoral system see Chapter 4.) Even independents have an incentive to run a joint electoral list, since they can get the chance to gain extra places. However, it must be very difficult for independent individuals to agree on the list, as typically only one or two of them may obtain mandate this way. A certain level of longer-term cooperation and, in all probability, institutionalization

3 Between 1990 and 1994 only mayors of small municipalities were directly elected.

is consequently necessary. Thus, the existence of "compensation lists" encourages both the formation of nominating organizations and their institutionalization.

Generally, the hypothesis is that electoral systems have an effect on the level of local party institutionalization. Specifically, the mixed electoral system with First-Past-the-Post districts *and* compensatory party lists is predicted to encourage local party institutionalization in Hungarian local governments.

Hypotheses

The level of local party institutionalization is higher in the mixed electoral system than in the short ticket system.

2.3.2. Social Geography Hypotheses

Social geography can be theorized as relevant in two ways. First, the internal morphology of local government must be taken into account. Many local governments are compact units with a continuously populated territory. However, some have a more fragmented structure, composed of more than one locality. In countries where local governments are large (England is the major example in Europe), the fragmented nature is the rule, not the exception. Still, even in countries where each locality has the right to form a local government (Hungary is a typical case in this category), there are municipalities which are divided due to historical or geographical reasons. There is also a difference between densely populated and loosely populated municipalities. Municipalities of low population density, characterized by districts and suburbs with smaller houses have a different social and communication relationship from densely populated municipalities with high, multi-storied buildings. The distance between citizens and groups of citizens shapes the degree of complexity of public affairs, which, in turn, has an effect on local party institutionalization. Fragmented topography also tends to result in more diversity. As it is discussed in the section on size, heterogeneity probably affects the level of party institutionalization.

Second, diffusion is tied to the geographical position of municipalities. As a model, political party is an innovation. Kopstein and Reilly (2000) point to the importance of neighborhood in the Post-Communist democratization process. A similar democratic 'contagion' may happen on the local level too. Municipalities in a central position take up social innovation first, then local governments close to the centers adapt them. Municipalities far from cultural, administrative and political centers learn innovations at the lower speed. The position in the structure of municipalities may also influence the level of local party institutionalization, as the administrative position is a kind of expression of centrality. A major form of closeness is the integration in a metropolitan area. By definition, suburbs have many contacts with the central city in a metropolitan area, which is likely to affect the capacities of local party formation.

Hypotheses

The closer to political and cultural centers the local government, the more institutionalized its parties.

The more fragmented the populated territory of the local government, the more institutionalized its parties.

2.3.3. Path Dependency Hypotheses

The development or evolution of institutions is not continuous. While even institutionalized organizations may change incrementally, their transformation by formative moments is more likely (Rothstein 1996). When political institutions are unable to handle the changing situation, they transform relatively suddenly. Then, the transformed structure (in the case of a successful adaptation) characterizes the institution for a long time. Such a formative event is the penetration of rivals.

The analysis of the local development of parties led Schneider (1999) to the conclusion that the penetration of national and regional parties into the local scene, a consequence of the territorial reform in the 1970s, transformed local association that had long dominated local governments. The formerly loose groups of notables became more professional and institutionalized. (Actually, parties also changed as they had to offer more collective incentive by organizing social and political events for their local activists and supporters.)

Before 1989, there was only one party in Hungarian localities for more than four decades. The success of the reformed Communist party (called the Socialist Party since the end of 1989) was uneven in the country. In many new local governments, the ex-Communists were able to maintain their presence and coherence, and gained many seats on local councils at the second local election (1994). In other communities, however, the local party organization fell apart, its former activists joined other parties or, more typically, stood as independent candidates. This probably had a consequence for the institutionalization of other parties. Facing a strong Socialist-Party local chapter may have encouraged other candidates to form formal organizations or make them more disciplined and routinized. Those local politicians may become the local basis of right-wing parties, even if they had no ideological affiliation in the beginning or perceived their belonging to a right-wing party somewhat cynically. By contrast, an atomized local competition did not encourage deeper institutionalization. There may be an interaction between size and electoral systems here; the First-Past-the-Post system in the local government of 10,000 or more inhabitants gives a huge advantage to the well-organized party if other candidates are independents. Thus, institutionalization was predictably faster where the ex-Communist party could preserve its organizational strength after the collapse of Communism and, in general, parties have become more institutionalized since then. In the electoral system used in municipalities of 10,000 or less inhabitants the profit of preserving the party cell might have been more limited. Therefore, the survival of a strong ex-Communist local party organization was less likely, as former Communists could be successful as independents. That limited the chances of the institutionalization of other parties as well.

The previous logic can be extended to any kind of situation in which a well-organized group of candidates has electoral success due to the formation of a party in an independent dominated local government. The success helps to stabilize the winning party and others are compelled to imitate the politically profitable model. This is one form of the mimetic processes.

Finally, one may formulate a hypothesis concerning the effect of overall democratic consolidation on local political institutionalization. For many, the consolidation of democracy implies, or is identical with, political institutionalization. More consolidated democracies are expected to have more institutionalized political institutions. Following this logic, one may claim that local political parties become more institutionalized as the consolidation process goes on. With time, viable party organizations are naturally selected and stabilized. In the long run, institutionalized organizations with their centralized pool of resources are more likely to obtain a more central role even in smaller municipalities. Moreover, the party building process has progressed in a top-down way in Hungary. Thus, one may expect national parties to penetrate into more and more localities and less and less populous ones. In sum, more than one causal mechanism can be presented to support the hypothesis on the association of the age of democracy with local political institutionalization. This continuity hypothesis does not contradict the hypotheses on formative events, as it refers to aggregate changes. While the political history may be discontinuous in certain localities, the aggregate level may show a smooth development.

Hypotheses

The older the democracy, the higher the overall level of the institutionalization of the local political parties.

The penetration of national parties makes all local parties (especially associations) more institutionalized.

The more successful the transformation of the former Communist cell, the quicker the institutionalization process and the more institutionalized the local parties.

If a party achieves electoral success in a previously independent-dominated local community, the party becomes more institutionalized and other local parties are also formed.

2.3.4. Party Typology Hypotheses

I forward less hypotheses on the organizational characteristics of individual parties than on the community-level environmental factors. Nonetheless, that does not mean that organizational features are less important; they are just more idiosyncratic and less systematic. Therefore, theorizing organizational characteristics is simply more difficult and results in less testable hypotheses. In a sense, this section focusing on the second face of Janus is theoretically as important as all the hypotheses presented so far.

First a distinction should be made between the local sections of national parties and local associations functioning as local parties. Their average level of institutionalization may be different. Supra-local levels are well-institutionalized and have a vested interest in the continuity and success of their local anchors. Therefore, they keep their organizations alive even if core individuals leave the local party organization. Local chapters are reorganized if they break up. National parties have more professional politicians who also are present in municipal politics. Not only do those individuals maintain a personal continuity, they also provide resources through their offices and provide local activists with collective incentives like access to the latest ideological statements or first-hand gossips (thus giving an insider feeling). The well-established socialization process of the party and the promises of political careers make the defection to other parties more difficult. Finally, the missionaries of the supra-local levels come to the municipality with well-prepared scripts of how to organize and maintain a local party chapter.

In contrast, civic groups are more often than not organized from below. This grassroots character makes them more personalized, which exposes them to the danger of falling apart when the founders retire or disagree among themselves. As civic groups are largely free from ideology, they can offer a limited amount of ideological incentives. The truly local character does not hold out the best hopes of a political career that would be a major selective incentive. Summing up, civic groups are hypothesized to be more vulnerable and less stable than the local chapters of national political parties.

The local sections of national parties have to face another challenge. As the last section of Chapter 1 discussed, the development of local party chapters is nested in the evolution of national parties. The dynamic on the national level has an effect on local party developments. When the mother party fails and the 'brand name' weakens, the local party organization may also lose votes, sometimes drastically (see the local history of the Smallholders' Party in Hungary). Conversely, a successful national party may greatly contribute to the electoral performance of its local chapters.

The most successful national parties are those that obtain seats in the parliament. One may expect that the local chapters of parliamentary parties are more institutionalized than other local parties as they, in all probability, have a more continuous overall functioning, are embedded in more stabilizing relationships, and simply have more resources to maintain the uninterrupted operation of their local sections.

Hypotheses

The local chapters of national parties are more institutionalized than grassroots civic associations functioning as local parties.

The developments of supra-local levels of parties influence the level of institutionalization of their local chapters.

The local chapters of parliamentary parties are more institutionalized than other local party organizations.

2.4. An Explanandum-Oriented Summary

The discussion has so far focused on the causal model from the viewpoint of the exogenous variables, particularly the size factor of municipalities. The following section shifts the perspective by beginning with the *explanandum*, local party institutionalization, and extending the inquiry to the closest explanatory variables first and the more distant ones later. By 'closeness' I mean the causal distance between the *explanandum* and *explanans*. The closest variables are the factors that explain the variance of the dependent variable directly, i.e. without intervening variables. The more variables intervene, the wider the distance between the independent and dependent variables.

What are the closest variables that account for local party institutionalization? I identify seven theoretically important factors that are expected to be direct explanans:

1. the advantage with which the electoral rules provide the organizations vis-a-vis independents;
2. the municipality's importance to national parties;

3. the role of core individuals and their networks;
4. the availability of potential political activists;
5. the degree to which group preferences exist;
6. the costs of local political mobilization;
7. the culture of cooperation.

Diagram 2.3. Factors directly affecting local party institutionalization

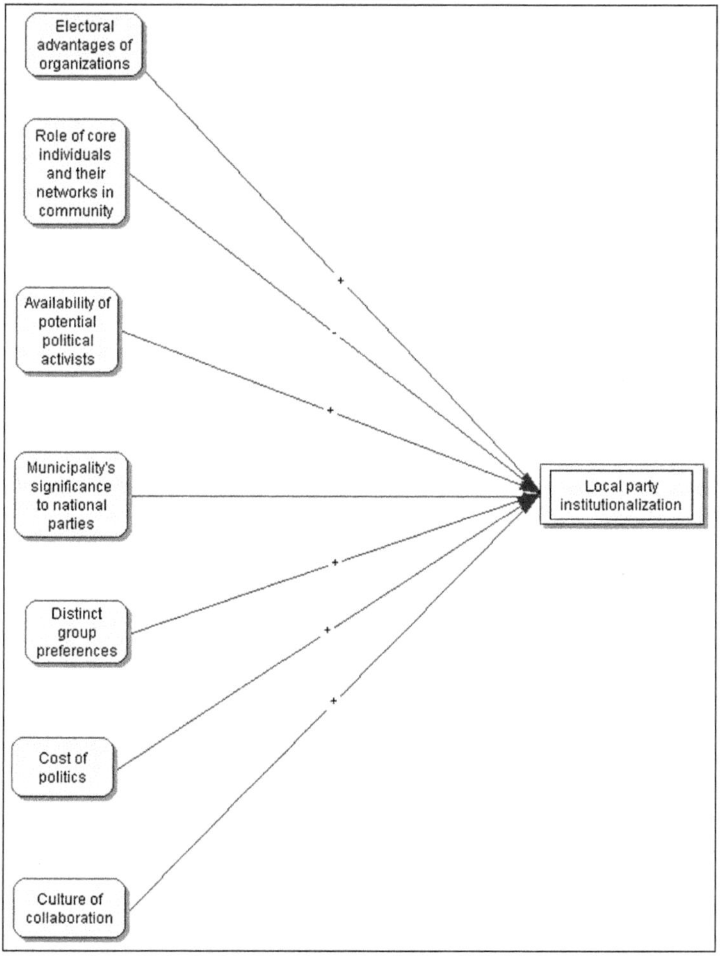

2.4.1. Electoral Incentives

To begin with the electoral system, the concept of electoral advantage refers to the degree to which certain elected positions are more accessible to organizations or are not accessible to independents at all. As it was mentioned above, the short list system, functioning in the municipalities of less than 10,000 inhabitants, is quite neutral in terms of electoral incentives to organizations. Candidates belonging to organizations may enjoy certain advantages as a consequence of their joined resources, but they may be viewed as 'partisan' persons, who divide the community and make trouble by bringing partisan tensions into the municipality. The electoral system of short lists does not provide any specific incentive or disincentive to the formation of local parties. By contrast, the mixed system involves the strategically crucial element of compensation lists that makes the opportunity structure absolutely different from that in short list system. Approximately 40 percent of council positions are accessible exclusively to candidates running under the umbrella of an organization, which provide a strong and very direct incentive to form representative organizations and make them permanent. That has an important effect on the campaigning in the individual districts. The First-Past-the-Post system potentially has a double effect: it presses for coalitions, but, at the same time, it gives a major role to well-established candidates and, consequently, personalizes politics. Thus, it encourages and discourages local party institutionalization at the same time. In the case of the mixed electoral system on the local level in Hungary, the First-Past-the-Post interacts with the compensation lists. Individual candidates in electoral districts have the incentive to run as organizational candidates. All candidates are to a certain degree interested in helping the election of one or two candidates of their organizations from the compensation list because they may get an extra influence on the policy-making in the council. Leaders and candidates who can collect many votes have a special interest in compensation lists because they can get a prominent position on them, which gives an extra chance for them in the competition.

Diagram 2.4. Electoral rules and local party institutionalization

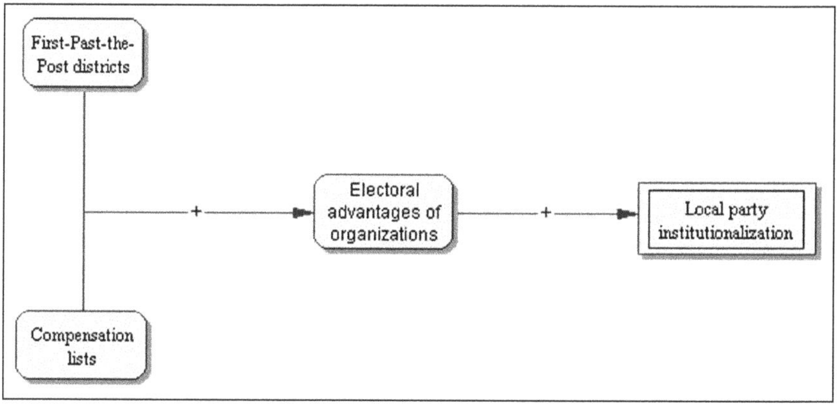

2.4.2. Municipality's Significance to National Parties

Municipalities attract national parties, major contributors of party building on the local level, to a very different degree. The variable of the importance of municipalities to national parties refers to the extent to which parties organized on a larger, usually country level, evaluate the significance of individual municipalities from their specific point of view. Communities that attract the attention of national parties are more likely to have well-established local parties, since national parties send or train party organizers and provide them with the necessary resources, including political information and ideology.

When are parties attracted? First of all, when they can gain many positions and votes. Cities that hold out promises of rich spoil certainly seem more noteworthy for the parties. The bigger the cake, the more parties—hungry for the largest possible piece—band together. Every party needs positions in which their would-be politicians can be trained, their temporarily or permanently failed leaders (especially the middle-level ones) parachuted, and important activists compensated with prestige and money. The resources that can be distributed in municipalities also play a role. They can be extracted and exploited to satisfy party supporters from the simplest activists to powerful businesspersons.

In addition to the potentially available prey, national parties may be attracted by the number of available voters in a municipality. The more voters they can gain, the more profitable the efforts of establishing a local chapter may be. A local party section may mobilize voters at election times and win over lots of citizens to the position represented by the party on the national level between elections. What is more, successful local representatives of the party in all probability contribute to the success of the whole party. (For a longer discussion of the potential advantages of local sections for national parties see Chapter 1.)

The functional size of municipalities may also influence the degree to which national parties are interested in the building of a local section. Functionally larger local governments usually have more voters and positions, and are more prestigious in the eyes of voters and opinion-makers in the country. This effect may be especially important in a region where the municipality has a central place.

The size of the pool of potential local activists matters too. The more possible agents available, the easier the organization of the local chapter is and the more important it is to snatch away talented young politicians from rival parties. However, this effect can be reciprocal. The more active the national parties in a local government, the more likely that they attract political activists and spread the culture of activism, which also widens the pool. As it was presented above, recursive models do not allow reciprocity, so the more likely direction of causality is included in the model.

Finally, the distance of municipality from political centers may also influence the level of interest of national parties. Country-level parties usually have a top-down organizational history. Most of them were originally organized in the capital and a few regional centers. This organization was extended to cities, then towns. This top-down organizational process is still taking place in Hungary, as the highly competitive political market forces the two big parties to penetrate into smaller and smaller communities. Geographic distance matters here, it is easier to start the organization in a suburb than in a distant municipality. The closer the local government to a political center, the more likely the representatives of national parties show up and try to sell their merchandise.

Diagram 2.5. Municipality's significance to national parties and local party institutionalization

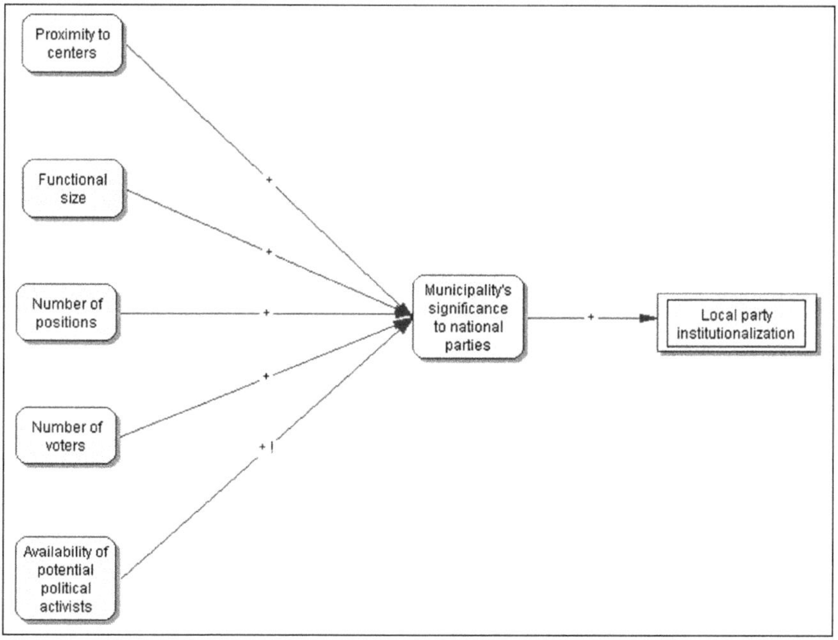

2.4.3. Importance of Core Individuals

The main rival institution of local parties, especially in smaller municipalities, are family ties and network relationships based on personal contact. Personal clientelism, built in these relationships, is a powerful way to establish a linkage between voters and representatives. The variable of the importance of core individuals and their networks refers to the significance of the role notables and their circles play in the local community. Those notables may be the leaders of important families or groups, or may rely on a network of friends and clients in a web of exchange relationships. If certain core individuals and their networks are important it is less likely that local party organizations exist and are stabilized in an institutionalized form.

The role notables play may be affected by three variables. The most important one is municipality size. Clientelism can effectively function in large cities, as the machine politics of 19th–20th century US cities clearly demonstrate. Nonetheless, the same example also shows that clientelist relationships must take an organizational form in a large polity. The wider and more complex the community, the less likely that notables can rule it based on their personal connections. No personal network can penetrate into every segment of a large and complex local society. The other important factor is the availability of rivals. The larger the pool of individuals who are capable and wish to influence the developments of local politics, the less likely a few core individuals can play a significant role.

Diagram 2.6. Importance of core individuals and local party institutionalization

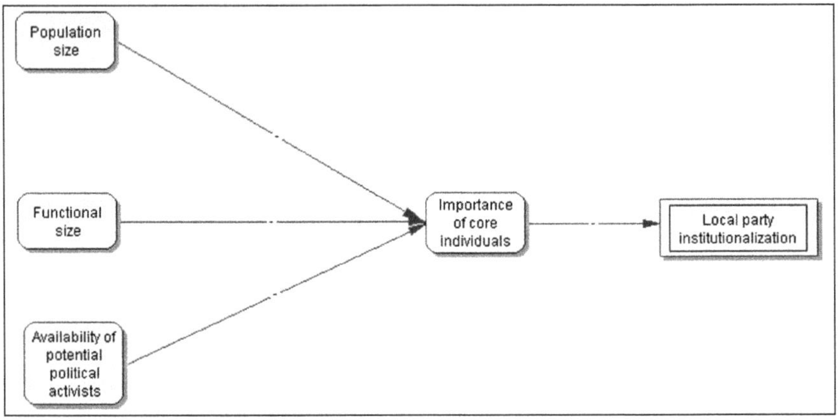

2.4.4. Availability of Activists

The availability of potential political activists deserves careful discussion, as it may affect local political life to a large degree. As has been presented, it has an influence on two other variables of the first block, the importance of core individuals and the attractiveness of municipalities to national parties. The size of the pool of activists can be predicted to have a large effect on the establishment of local political parties. Structural potentials and opportunity structures cannot become realities if there are no agents who activate them. The variable of the availability of potential political activists refers to the size of the pool of individuals who have both the capability and motivation to actively form community politics. The level of actual capability, motivation, and involvement obviously varies from individual to individual. The variable refers to the aggregated amount of agent potential in municipality.

The size of the pool of activists may be influenced by several factors. Municipality size is an obvious potential determinant. The larger the pool of citizens, the larger the pool of activists. If, on average, every 50th citizen is ready to join a party, the number of party members will be higher in large municipalities.

Educated people with regular income are more likely to participate. A decent standard of living provides citizens both with the free time necessary for political activities and the financial independence that give the confidence needed in public life. The age structure of the community may have a similar effect. Retired people with independent, regular (though not necessarily large) income and plenty of free time are more likely to become activists (until they become too old) than young people with small children.

The functional size of the municipality and its closeness to central cities may also make a difference. Functional size attracts talent; central places and communities close to centers are more likely to have a larger pool of motivated activists. Nevertheless, activists can be trained within the municipality too. Civil society organizations often fulfill that function. Well-organized, stable associations often produce leaders who are capable to act on the political scene.

Diagram 2.7. Availability of activists and local party institutionalization

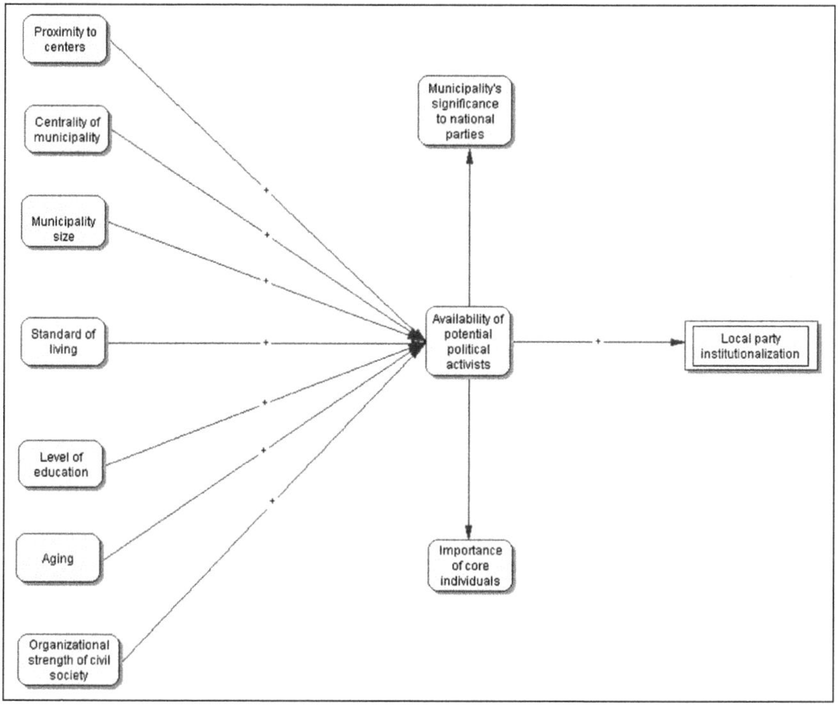

2.4.5. Distinct Group Preferences

Group preferences may influence local party institutionalization by offering ready-made societal groups with specific interests and needs for representation. Where distinct group preferences can be aggregated into political programs, more parties have a chance for both an initial establishment and subsequent institutionalization. The variable of group preferences refers to the extent to which societal groups articulate their perceived interests and values within the local community. The term 'distinct group' refers to a social entity with a certain degree of self-consciousness.

The existence of different life situations is a prerequisite for the emergence of distinct groups. No group consciousness can emerge in a fully homogeneous local society. Some kind of differentiation is needed for the emergence of societal groups. While the existence of societal complexity is a necessary condition for distinct group preferences, it is not a sufficient condition. There are many cleavages in modern society. Still, only a few of them become important. Even if a cleavage exists, it may not lead to the formation of distinct groups. In other cases, group formation takes place only on one side of the cleavage (e.g. employers tend to think of themselves as a separate group with distinct values and interests, while workers do not articulate themselves in the same way). Developing a theory of group formation is well beyond the ambitions of this study. Still, one probable rule can be hypothesized; a well-organized civil society is not only a sign of group preferences (as interest organizations usually defend the interests of specific groups), but it also contributes to the articulation of new interests and values. Thus, the organizational strength of civic groups may account for the degree to which well-articulated, conscious societal groups exist in the community. The functional differentiation of the municipality, indicated by the variable of functional size, has a similar effect.

Diagram 2.8. Group preferences and local party institutionalization

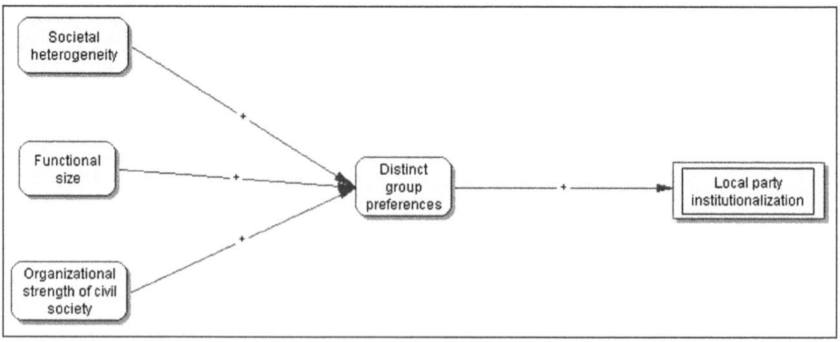

2.4.6. Costs of Mobilization

The costs of local political mobilization likely play a major role in the decision to form a local political party organization. If voters cannot be reached without the use of expensive advertisements, mass events, and media presence, the candidates who join their resources have a better chance to reach voters. The variable of local political mobilization costs refers to the amount of monetary and non-monetary expenses that are needed to inform and influence local voters.

The most likely determinant of local mobilization costs is the distance between politicians and voters, a political aspect of municipality size. The higher the ratio of voters to elected positions, the less likely candidates are able to reach citizens personally. The larger the constituency, the more the candidates have to resort to indirect communication. The costs of indirect communication both in the campaign and between elections tend to be much higher than personal persuasion.

The cost of political mobilization is influenced by other factors than political distance. However, their effect is much less predictable a priori. The presence, extensiveness and significance of political press may lower costs by providing a ready-made infrastructure of political communication. Nonetheless, not all political forces have the same access to local media. Those without such access have to mobilize from a standstill and spend more on communication activities. Similarly, socioeconomic fragmentation and the development of civil society organizations may make reaching of certain social groups easier and allow cheap representation of societal niches. But it also may make the communication more costly, as the sociopolitical market is more fragmented and politicians have to spend more on specific communication activities.

Diagram 2.9. Political costs and local party institutionalization

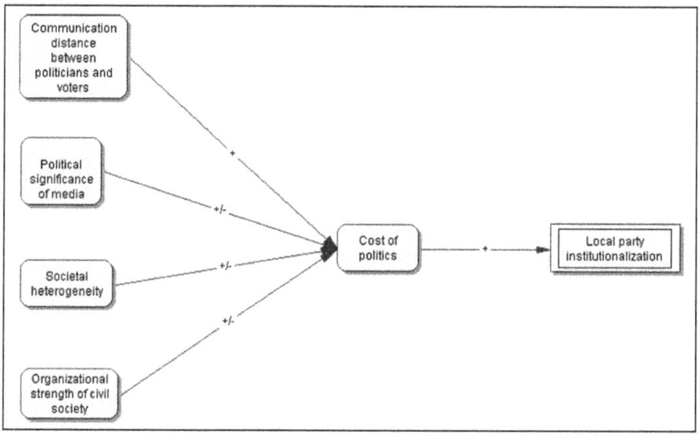

2.4.7. Collaborative Culture

The social capital literature calls attention to the importance of collective action problems and the role of trust and cooperative attitudes in resolving them. The variable culture of cooperation refers to the degree to which cooperation is a legitimate as well as a known and practiced social technique.

The level of collaborative culture depends on previous experience. Successful cooperations in the past encourage actors to apply the method again or imitate it. Civil society is the terrain where such cooperative experience can be gained. The relationship between culture and structure may be reciprocal here. The strengthening of civil society and the culture of collaboration can be (and probably often are) parallel processes. In political centers, collaborative solutions are likely to be more frequent, which may also give patterns to be imitated in neighboring municipalities. It is often shown that educated people are more tolerant and ready to associate with others.

Diagram 2.10. Collaborative culture and local party institutionalization

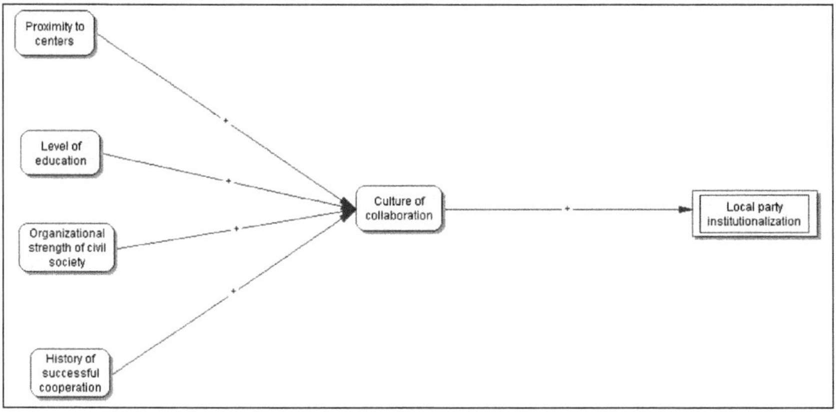

2.5. Summary

This chapter aimed to generate hypotheses concerning the factors that potentially influence the level of local party institutionalization. Based on a literature survey and deduction, I formulated several propositions about the causal connections. The main exogenous variable of the causal model was population size. I also suggested the importance of an alternative concept of size, the functional size. The following table summarizes the factors that were discussed in this chapter. The table makes a distinction between exogenous and two types of endogenous factors: intervening and dependent variables. The important endogenous relationships among the intervening variables are not shown in this table format.

Exogenous variables	Distant intervening variables	Proximate intervening variables	Dependent variable
• Population size • Proximity to centers • Electoral system	• Functional size • Number of political positions • Number of voters • Education • Standard of living • Urbanization • Age • Societal heterogeneity • The organizational strength of civil society • Political (electoral) participation	• Electoral advantages of organizations • Municipality's importance to national parties • Importance of core individuals and their networks • Availability of potential political activists • Distinct group preferences • Political mobilization costs • Cooperation culture	• Local party institutionalization

Obviously, the variables included as endogenous variables may have other determinants as well. For example, the level of urbanization is influenced not only by the size of population or the municipality's proximity to urban centers, but also by historical and economic factors that are not involved in the model. Technically speaking, the variables included in the model will not explain the full variance in the level of urbanization. One cannot expect a total model in the social sciences.

In addition to the causal model, I also formulated a few specific hypotheses about historical development and organizational features; the following table lists those.

Exogenous variables	Dependent variable
• Age of democracy • Snowballing of party formation • Survival of the former Communist party cell • Institutionalization of senior party levels • Penetration of national parties • Parliamentary representation • Registration form (party vs. social organization)	• Local party institutionalization

The next chapter attempts to operationalize the variables listed above. It will not be feasible to indicate all of them in a valid and reliable manner. That leads to a more simplified model and a reduced list of hypotheses.

Chapter 3: Methods and Indicators

The aim of this chapter is to identify the variables that can be included in the empirical investigation and to operationalize both the dependent and explanatory variables. The first section provides a short overview of the local government system in Hungary. Next, the two main indicators of local party institutionalization are discussed. The second half of the chapter focuses on the independent variables. The variables that conform to the requirements of the multivariate and causal analyses are specified, and, thus, the list of hypotheses that are to be tested is finalized. Finally, the independent variables are operationalized and characterized.

3.1. The Local Government System in Hungary

The present system of Hungarian local government was established in two subsequent waves of qualified majority legislation in 1990 and 1994. Act No. LXV of 1990 and Act No. LXIII of 1994 recognized the rights of municipalities to self-government and transformed the system of public administration from the centrally directed local councils of the Communist times to autonomous, democratically elected municipal self-governments. The new system followed the principles of the European Charter of Local Self-Government of the Council of Europe and the historical traditions of Hungarian public administration.

Within the framework of local governments, consecutive pieces of legislation established a two-tiered system – based on historical traditions – where municipalities (villages, towns/cities) represent the basic unit of the system, while counties form the middle tier. There is no hierarchy between these two levels, as they have different responsibilities. Certain cities have county rights and act both as municipalities and counties. The capital, which is nine times larger than the second largest city, has a special legal status with its own two-tiered local government system. This system consists of the local government of Budapest itself and the local governments of the twenty-three districts of the capital. In this system, the district governments fulfill the role and functions of municipal governments independent from the Budapest city government.

The requirements of EU structural funds prompted the creation of seven statistical regions, which have neither organizational form such as elected or appointed leaders, nor administrative staff. A new level between municipalities and counties was also planned, but has not yet been created.

Municipal governments have mandatory and optional responsibilities in service provision, as enumerated in the Act on Local Government and determined by Parliament. Mandatory responsibilities can be further divided into two categories: basic tasks, mandatory for every settlement in Hungary regardless of the size of the municipality, and functions delegated through legislation as mandatory for larger settlements. The Act lists the mandatory tasks of local governments: municipalities are obliged to provide pre-school and primary school education, basic health care and welfare services, public lighting, cemeteries, healthy drinking water and the protection of ethnic and national minorities. Legally delegated mandatory functions for cities with greater capabilities are identified as the maintenance of fire brigades, technical rescue service and a wider range of social welfare services. The Act also allows for optional duties, giving local governments the right to voluntarily undertake other duties if these tasks have not already been assigned to other administrative bodies by law and if local governments have enough of their own resources to carry them out.

The most important actors of local decision-making consist of the council of representatives, the committees, the mayor and the chief administration officer (CAO) or notary. Basic rights and powers reside with the body of representatives. It may delegate competence to the committees, the mayor, local minority self-governments and district governments. It also establishes and organizes the procedures of operation through decrees.

The mayor represents the body of representatives and exercises authority with its assistance. He or she is also responsible for local policy implementation and performs local and state administrative tasks. The mayor exercises employer's rights over the vice mayor, the CAO and heads of local government institutions. The CAO is appointed by the body of representatives through open competition. The CAO manages the day to day affairs of the office of the local government and exercises employer's rights over civil servants employed in the office.

A special Hungarian institution is minority self-government. Minorities in Hungary live dispersed in the country, so the system of minority local representation cannot be based on territorial units. Ethnic and national minority groups have the right to form minority self-governments through a special electoral procedure. Municipal councils must obtain the consent of minority self-governments for decisions that affect interests in minority education, culture, etc. The law on minority self-government recognizes the right of individuals to choose identities and, therefore, the choice of identity is absolutely free and confidential. Candidates can run and voters can vote in minority elections without needing to prove membership in the ethnic or national minority that they represent and vote for. (For more information on minority self-governments see Csefkó – Pálné 1999.)

This overview of the local government system in Hungary focused on those points that directly affect the analysis in this project. For a longer discussion of the history, characteristics and challenges of the local government system, see Temesi (2000), Marelyin et al. (2001) and Soós and Kálmán (2002).

3.2. Measuring Local Party Institutionalization

What criteria should an indicator of local party institutionalization meet? The measures indicating the dependent variable must fulfill the requirements of context, validity, reliability, extensiveness, and timeliness.

1. First of all, the measures of local party institutionalization must fit in to the realities of the legal-institutional and political context in Hungary. Indicators used in prior research must be adapted very cautiously, as the same indicator may measure different phenomena in different contexts.
2. Local party institutionalization is a multidimensional concept. The indicators should capture as many dimensions as possible. Those indicators have a relative advantage which make it possible to clearly determine which dimensions they actually cover.
3. Causal models can be qualitative, but this is a quantitative research. The regressions on which the empirical part builds needs indicators measured on interval-level and with low noise.
4. The indicators should cover as many cases as possible. Preferably, the indicators should extend to all local governments in Hungary.
5. In addition to geographical extensiveness, the indicators should cover a longer time, i.e. more than one electoral periods. On the one hand, certain hypotheses are time-related. On the other hand, the mean values of more than one electoral period filter out fluctuation and idiosyncratic components of the measured values.

Data from case studies are excluded by Criterion 3 (though strongly favored by Criterion 2). Criterion 4 and 5 make the use of survey data impossible. The natural choice that can meet all the requirements is the analysis of electoral data. Electoral results are very precisely measured, are available for all local governments, and are collected periodically. The real challenge is to find measures that can be computed from the official electoral data and clearly cover at least one dimension of the definition of local party institutionalization. I believe that two indicators fulfill the criteria listed above.

1. The first indicator, which I labeled '**party government**', is measured as the proportion of votes cast on the candidates of local parties (i.e. non-independents). In my view, it predominantly covers the dimension of reification, i.e. the external legitimacy or taken-for-grantedness of parties as dominant players in local politics.
2. The second indicator is **party loyalty**. It measures the degree to which party-nominated candidates remain loyal to their organization. This indicator primarily covers the dimensions of value infusion, but also reification (when party candidates become independents), systemness and autonomy.

Finally, to increase the validity of this research, I will analyze a number of other indicators from surveys of local representative organizations, local councilors and local administrative leaders. These data do not meet Criteria 3, 4 and 5, but provide additional evidence on the determinants of local party institutionalization.

3.2.1. Party Government

Richard S. Katz (1987: 7) defines party government by five characteristics:

> 1. Decisions are made by elected party officials or by those under their control;
> 2a. Policy is decided within parties which
> 2b. then act cohesively to enact it.
> 3a. Officials are recruited and
> 3b. held accountable through party.

This study focuses more on the level of institutionalization than the way in which decisions are made. Thus, in my narrower conceptualization, party government is a form of the democratic political system in which party organizations play a prominent role. In party government, parties are regarded the main legitimate actors of politics. A corollary of this perception may be their prominent place in decision-making, as Katz describes.

The widely recognized special role of parties does not necessarily mean that they are popular. Legitimacy is not always associated with a high reputation or effectiveness in citizens' perception. The concept of party government does not presuppose more than that parties are central in local politics. In such governance, it is perceived that political decisions are born of the interaction of party organizations.

The degree to which party government becomes stable and accepted refers to the level of local party institutionalization. As the definition suggests, party government, as an indicator of local party institutionalization, is mainly related to the reification dimension. The prominent role parties play in local party government implies the taken-for-grantedness of their rule and that parties structure the perceptions of other actors. Indirectly, party government may capture other dimensions too. Internally weak institutionalized party organizations lacking autonomy are less likely to be able to maintain a dominant position in the local polity.

As Katz (1987) argues, party government is an ideal type and its realization is a matter of degree in reality. "Party governmentness", as he calls it, actually has various levels. This makes an interval-level measurement possible; in fact, it requires such an assessment. Here, the degree of party government is measured by the proportion of votes that organization-nominated candidates gained at local elections. In other words, this aspect of local party institutionalization is indicated by the votes cast on non-independent candidates. It is simply computed by adding up all the votes gained by organization-nominated candidates and divided by the total number of votes.

To make an analysis by type possible I also broke down the organizational votes into two categories, associations and the local chapters of national parties. The votes of national parties were also grouped along the parliamentary/extra-parliamentary divide. The parliamentary parties in 1998 were: FIDESZ-MPP, MSZP, FKGP, SZDSZ, MDF, MIÉP. The parliamentary parties in 2002 were: MSZP, FIDESZ-MPP, SZDSZ, MDF.

What are the limitations of this measure of local party government? First of all, the vote-gaining capacity of parties does not necessarily refer to their actual institutionalization. In other words, the measure is not weighted by the qualities of local political party organizations. Charismatic parties, to take a classical example, may attract a large number of votes without contributing to the overall level of institutionalization of the local political system. The leveling-off of the electoral results may help in some cases (as personalized parties are more prone to large fluctuations), but charismatic leaders may survive more than one or two electoral periods. The validity of the index of local party government is limited by this fact.

A second problem is related precisely to the computation that levels out the proportion of votes gained by organizations. The mechanism makes the measurement more reliable if the oscillation is not high, but may hide extreme changes, which certainly indicate a low level of institutionalization. Therefore, I also examine the size of fluctuations in the chapter of local party government in Hungary, between 1998 and 2002. This extra dependent variable may shed more light on the level of the institutionalization of party rule on the local level.

3.2.2. Party Loyalty

The empirical basis of the Party Loyalty variable is a special electoral dataset of the local elections in 1998 and 2002 in Hungary.

The database created for this research is a comparison between the two latest local elections in Hungary. The task was to identify those who run at both elections and find out whether or not they were nominated by the same organization. The first major problem was the identification of organizations. Since 511 organizations nominated candidates in 1998 and 787 in 2002, some kind of automatic comparison was needed. Several technical difficulties cropped up. The Electoral Office used different coding at the two elections, based on the order of registration. While it was easy to identify the well-known national parties, the smaller, less-known organizations caused more problems and lessened the reliability of the dataset. Some candidates might remain loyal to their organization, but it might run under the umbrella of a coalition, unite with other organizations or simply change its name. Errors in the registration process also seem to have altered the name of certain organizations, e.g., by using a shorter name or abbreviation instead of the full name. In some cases, the registrars simply misspelled names. The comparison of the two lists of nominating organizations required a thorough one-by-one check. The overall conclusion is that the stability of nominations may be somewhat underestimated due to the aforementioned technical problems. Nevertheless, there is no reason why this underestimation is in all probability unsystematic and is restricted to the less significant organizations. Organizations were categorized primarily by their legal type (party vs. civil society organization) and secondarily within their legal type (left and right-wing parties; minority and non-minority organizations).

The second and even tougher challenge was the comparison of the 63,160 candidate names in 1998[4] with the 66,510 names in 2002[5]. The large number of cases did not allow a one-by-one comparison, but automatic identification was hindered by name changes. Many people's names change between elections. One reason is women's marriage and divorce. An even more frequent cause is the similarity of the names of two candidates. For this reason, one of the candidates must change their name (using a middle name or an additional initial), which may not be required at the next election when such a similarity does not occur. Sometimes, candidates are inconsistent in using their middle names or administrators leave them out or add them at will. All these problems result in a – hopefully small, but actually unknown – underestimation of how many candidates contested at both elections. The reverse problem is that the same name may cover different people, but my counting identified them as one person running

4 47839 on short lists and 15321 in the mixed electoral system.

5 52207 on short lists and 14303 in the mixed electoral system.

again for local office. This may lead to another type of error. There is no reason, however, to believe that loyalty rates are systematically under- or overestimated in some types of localities due to these known problems. The only municipality type in which a single error may make a relatively large difference is the category of very small local governments with a small number of candidates. Fortunately, this category includes many municipalities: more than 1,000 local governments have less than 500 inhabitants, and hence coding errors are likely to cancel out each other. In all probability, the statistical analysis and the conclusions drawn from those analyses are not affected by the problem of name identification.

The level of institutionalization was measured by candidates' loyalty in 2002 to *at least one* of the organizations that nominated them in 1998. Local parties form different electoral coalitions, which are beyond the will of individual candidates. Thus, a full loyalty would be too demanding a request. The assumption is that the candidate belongs to the organization that nominated him or her both in 1998 and 2002. Nonetheless, that is not necessarily true, as it may cover a change of loyalty from one nominating organization of a 1998 coalition to another one, maybe in another coalition. This cannot be controlled, but it is certainly not a frequent case.

In the mixed electoral system, the names appearing on the tickets of electoral districts in 2002 were compared to the candidates' names running in districts in 1998. This rule neglected those who were mayoral candidates or ran only on a compensation list. Both cases are quite unlikely. Mayoral candidates who have only a limited chance usually run for council seats too. That is better for them personally and for the party. In all probability, the number of those politicians aspiring for mayorship in one election and then accepting a less prestigious position at the next is small. As the number of places on the compensation lists is lower than the number of districts, it is unlikely that candidates other than those running in the district would appear on party lists. Compensation lists do not have a high profile, as citizens cannot vote for them directly. So putting prominent persons on the list does not make much sense. Parties do not have so many able candidates, so they cannot afford to spare certain candidates (usually specialists or senior leaders) from the actual fight in one of the electoral districts. In sum, the likeliness that the method presented here missing candidates running again in 2002 is low and the missing cases are not likely to be systematic.

3.3. Cases and Data Sources

Three extensive and high quality datasets comply with the requirements of the research design.

(1) The local electoral data. They obviously cover all the local governments as needed. They are of a very high quality due to the seriousness of the stakeholders of elections. The results of local elections are available from three elections (1994, 1998, and 2002), which is enough for the purpose of the research. The data were provided by the Electoral Office in a format structured by the official minutes. I converted the text files to database tables in the MySQL program (see Appendix B). The coding system changed from election to election, which caused some problems. Although the data are generally of a high quality, several small mistakes had to be corrected (e.g. "Dr." appeared both with and without dot) to make the results comparable across electoral periods. A further challenge was the management of the large number of tables. The raw data were the text files (minutes of elections) provided by the Electoral Office. Three to four tables were used per electoral system and election. In addition to the six to eight tables per election, the tables containing the aggregations and comparisons made the task even more complex. The tables were therefore merged and converted into spreadsheet files by election.
(2) The statistical data of municipalities (T-STAR). The Central Statistical Office (KSH) collects a large number of indicators on every local government each year. The data are considered by Hungarian academics as reliable. In a very traditional way, the Statistical Office treats those local governments that have a higher legal status (towns/cities vs. villages) in a different way by gathering more data on them than on the municipalities of the same size, but of lower status. Since the city indicators do not cover the same population as the general indicators, only the latter ones are used. I had access to the database of the indicators in 2001; as the census data are from the same year and the date is between the local elections I analyzed (1998 and 2002), the 2001 dataset seems absolutely acceptable from the viewpoint of data requirements.
(3) The census conducted in 2001. The census data were also aggregated on the municipality level. The census dataset provids lots of information on the population and employment of local societies. The source of the non-electoral indicators of this study is mostly the census data.

Electoral, census and socioeconomic data were merged in a single dataset. The final database is the product of more than 30 transformations of previous databases in three different softwares.

The scope of the cases covers all the local governments in Hungary, except for the 23 districts of the capital, Budapest, because those district governments function within a single city and under very different political conditions. Moreover, four of the local governments became larger than 10,000 inhabitants between the two elections (all of them are Budapest suburbs). Since they had a different electoral system in 1998, they were also left out. Thus, the dataset of the mixed electoral system consists of comparative data from 138 local governments. As data are not available for one of the electoral periods, the municipalities founded between elections are excluded. The population was occasionally limited to the local governments of 1,000 or more inhabitants for measurement reasons. These reasons will be presented in the next chapter.

In addition to the statistical and electoral datasets, Chapter 7 provides an overview of survey data to give further evidence. Three surveys are used in the analysis.

(1) The Local Party Survey was conducted by the Tocqueville Research Center in 2004–2005. It focused on the organizational characteristics and institutionalized connections of local party organizations (both the local chapters of national parties and civil society organizations). The survey covered 271 organizations from 147 local governments.
(2) The Local Representative Survey surveyed the social background, political culture, activities and contacts of councilors and mayors in 2002. The database contains the answers of 983 respondents from 193 local governments.
(3) The Local Government Survey was carried out by the Tocqueville Research Center in 2002. It collected information from chief administrative officials in 647 local governments. Both the Local Government Survey and the Local Representative Survey was financed by the Local Government and Public Service Reform Initiative (Open Society Institute, Budapest) in the framework of the Indicators of Local Democratic Governance Project.

Chapter 7 also uses some legal documents like party charters and referendum statistics.

3.4. Causal Modeling

This research project is partly based on causal models. *Causal models* involve a set of variables, embedded in a system of effects. A causal model is a multivariate way of thinking. It presents the variables considered theoretically important for the research problem and specifies the direction of effect among them. The basic idea behind such models is that a variable can influence another variable not only directly, but also indirectly, i.e. through one or more *intervening variables*. One-step effects are *direct*, while *indirect* effects involve more than one step. In more complex models, there is more than one indirect way through which a variable affects another one. The direct and indirect routes between variables are called *paths*. In fact, the most popular specific form of causal modeling is called *path analysis* or path model.

Diagram 3.1. Examples of recursive and nonrecursive causal models

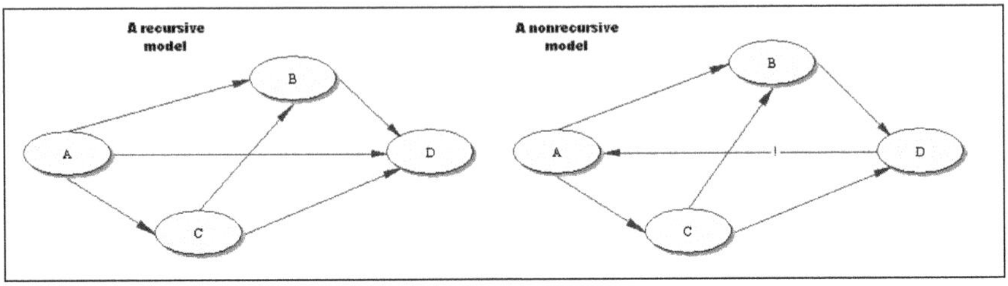

Causal models can be recursive and nonrecursive. In *recursive* models, the causal argument flows from one or more prior variables toward one or more other variables. Every variable is either cause or effect in each separate relationship. The example on the left of the diagram shows an example for recursive models. In *nonrecursive* models, a variable can be both cause and effect at the same time. As a result, nonrecursive models contain loops. In Davies' (1985: 18) formulation: "If there is a path starting from X and returning to it without retracing any steps, X and all the variables on the path form a loop. Variables in a loop have no order." There is no logical order of the variables in nonrecursive models. The diagram on the right, above, shows a nonrecursive model. It actually differs from the left one by reversing the arrow from A to D. While recursive path models can be analyzed by means of extended multivariate regression techniques, nonrecursive models require highly sophisticated statistical methods and are more restricted. "[L]ooped variables cannot be analyzed except by very sophisticated techniques *and* by invoking strong empirical assumptions about causal effects of outside variables feeding into the loop" (Davies 1985: 18; emphasis in the original). The statistical techniques using time-series data in nonrecursive models are especially complicated.

This research project has a clearly defined dependent variable. Thus, it needs an ordered model without loops. That makes recursive modeling a more natural approach for the design. Still, as the forthcoming discussion of relationships will demonstrate, there are causal links which can not easily be conceptualized as one-way effects. For instance, the relationship between the degree of local political participation and the level of local party institutionalization may be reciprocal.

After all, parties can (and do) shape their environment; they do not simply react to changes. In such cases, I acknowledge the potential two-way or reciprocal relationship, but make a decision about the direction of the link at the outset on theoretical and substantive grounds (see Asher 1983: 11). All research designs simplify reality to keep the theoretical argument manageable. The use of nonrecursive models would have made the research design, which is very complex anyway, even more difficult to handle. The discussion of under-identification and over-identification problems (see Asher 1983: 53–73), for example, would be a major concern without really advancing an answer to the original research problem. The simplification of recursive models will be added to the acknowledged limits of the present research project in the concluding chapter.

An important distinction is made between exogenous and endogenous variables. *Exogenous* variables are those variables whose variation is explained by factors outside the causal model. By contrast, the variance of *endogenous* variables is accounted for (at least partially) by one or more variables included in the model. The dependent variable is by definition endogenous. In standard regression analysis, which can be regarded as the simplest form of causal models, the dependent variable is the only endogenous variable, while all the other variables are exogenous.

The exogenous-endogenous labels are relative to the model. For instance, size is treated as an exogenous variable throughout this project. Municipality size, indicated by the number of inhabitants, correlates with some of the other exogenous variables, e.g. citizens' standard of living. These relationships are spurious, not causal. The modernization process, especially the forced industrialization of the communist period, and the centralization of the country resulted in a better standard of living in cities than villages. A new exogenous variable, a historical factor, would make both size and living standards endogenous. So the exogenous character of municipality size is relative to the model.

The central problem of causal systems is how certain variables control other variables. That makes the distinction between causal and spurious effects relevant. Not all correlations imply causal effects. Brothers often look similar. However, that does not imply a causal relationship between their look, as the common real cause is the look of their common ancestors. The spurious effect between two variables is a correlation generated by a third variable. Causal effects, by contrast, imply a genuine causal link between the variables.

As all other quantitative approaches, causal models also involve probabilistic rules, not deterministic laws. Thus, causal models are about trends and allow individual exceptions. Causal models also belong to the quantitative family in the sense that the usual caveat about association and causality applies. Correlation alone is not a proof of causation. Without a convincing presentation of the causal mechanisms through which the effect is brought about, the statistical findings do not satisfy the needs of scientific research.

Causal models include propositions; the propositions are always built on both theoretical and statistical logic and are empirically supported by data. All causal explanations go back to the simple principle of time sequence. What was prior may have an effect on what happened later, but the past cannot be changed. For instance one may predict population size according to the size prior to electoral results because the voters in the municipality lived together before the election day. The underlying idea of causality is almost always a temporal sequence.

Technically speaking, the causal or path analysis is an extension of regression analysis. As such, the usual requirements of the regression analysis technique apply to causal models. Path coefficients are computed as the multiplication of the partial correlations of individual links.

Recursive causal models rely on a certain number of assumptions. Those assumptions have a great effect on the design of this research.

(1) As it was discussed earlier, recursive models imply only one-way causal flow. No feedback loops or reciprocal effects are allowed.
(2) All relationships in the model are linear and additive. This is handy since the partial effects of nonlinear relations cannot be computed in an additive way. Total effects cannot be broken down into direct and indirect ones if compound relationships are included.
(3) The variables in causal models must be measured on an interval scale or else be dichotomized.
(4) Residuals are uncorrelated with all other variables and residuals in the model. This is a general assumption of multivariate linear regression.
(5) The variables in path analysis are measured without error. This assumption requires data of very good quality.

These assumptions become important in the selection of testable variables, which is the objective of the next section.

3.5. Variables and Hypotheses

The measured independent variables must fulfill the same requirements as the indicators of the dependent variable.

1. The indicators should have a high validity in the legal-institutional and political context in Hungary.

2. The indicators should be valid in the sense that they should cover the concept of the indicated variables as much as possible.
3. The indicators should be measured on interval-level or be dummy variables. The reliability requirement also implies a low level of measurement error.
4. The indicators should preferably be available for all local governments that have a value on the indicators of local party institutionalization.
5. They must be available for the electoral periods that are covered by the party institutionalization indicators.

In addition to the above-mentioned requirements, the independent variables must conform with the demands of causal analysis. Unfortunately, it is not possible to find indicators that meet these criteria for all variables listed as potential determinants of local party institutionalization in the previous chapter. Thus, not all variables will be included into the specific path model to actually be tested. Two types of variables will be left out for measurement reasons.

(1) Some of the variables cannot be measured in the way in which the high data quality requirements could be satisfied. Unfortunately, none of the variables that are predicted to directly affect the level of local party institutionalization (see section 2.5) can be explained by indicators, and hence they all be removed from the analysis.

It is possible to measure the degree of municipalities' importance to national political parties are. The analysis of internal party documents and the observation of party builders' activities would help to evaluate the relative importance which parties attribute to the individual municipalities. Based on content analysis or activity statistics, a quantitative indicator might even be prepared. Unfortunately, no one has carried out such an investigation. Moreover, even if studies on certain parties would be available, it is very unlikely that anyone could reliably cover all the parties. In addition to the party coverage, the coverage of municipalities also would be problematic. In any studied period, not all local governments are dealt with by party managers. Thus, a value cannot be attributed to each municipality, which would be a data quality requirement.

Some other variables in the same block seem to require either qualitative case studies or public opinion surveys. The importance of certain core individuals in local politics, the availability of the pool of potential political activists, the existence of distinct group preferences and the collaborative character of the local political culture all belong to this category. While case studies would not generate quantitative data necessary for this research design, they may result in methodological advancements by pointing to certain proxy measures. Even proxy measures like the number of party members (a potential proxy of the availability of political activists) would need surveys.

In addition to the variables identified in Section 2.5, one other variable, media significance, also is left out for the same reason. It seems to be difficult to find a satisfactory indicator of this variable for most municipalities. While survey data are available for the existence and impact of local media outlets, they only cover a fraction of the cases to be analyzed in this research.

(2) Some other variables can be measured, but the measured values are too close to other variables. One of those variables is the ratio of voters to local representatives. This can be computed in a quite straightforward manner. Still, it correlates so well with population size that it cannot be simultaneously included in any regression model. The following variables are left out for the same reason: number of voters, number of local political positions and the organizational strength of local civil society indicated by the number of nonprofit organizations.

To conclude, the following independent variables will be included in the causal models:

1. Population size
2. Functional size
3. Urbanization
4. Population instability
5. Age composition
6. Socioeconomic heterogeneity
7. Ethnic heterogeneity
8. Citizens' resources
9. Civil society's organizational strength
10. Political participation
11. Proximity to urban centers
12. Electoral system

The availability of testable variables also limits the list of testable hypotheses. The final list of hypotheses can be found in Appendix A.

3.6. Measuring Explanatory Variables

3.6.1. Population Size

Population size is interpreted as the number of people living in the municipality. There are two types of data that can be used to measure size perceived this way.

First, the T-STAR dataset contains data on municipalities' permanent population, i.e. the number of people who registered their main address in the municipality. As most people vote where registered, this measure is closer to the voting body of municipalities. The second indicator includes not only permanent, but also temporarily registered inhabitants. This measure indicates the number of people who actually participate in the everyday life of the municipality. I chose the second option for reasons of data quality. The 2001 census found much more people in Hungary than the previous administrative data, based on citizens' registration, had suggested. After the socially turbulent years of the 1990s, census data are widely considered to be more reliable than the incrementally updated data collected by the police and public administration. The census gathered data on the people found in a certain place on a certain data, disregarding their officially registered address. To keep consistency, certain other data, e. g. the occupational structure of local societies, has also been taken from the census database.

As I mentioned, the local government system is highly fragmented in Hungary. That means that the range between very small villages and relatively large cities is huge: the largest local government analyzed here (Debrecen, 211,034 inhabitants) has more than 16,000 times more inhabitants than the smallest one (Tornakápolna, 12 inhabitants). In other words, the standard deviation around the mean (2,686 inhabitants) is very large (9,468). Such an enormous difference may cause a problem in multivariate statistical analyses, as the independent variables must meet certain conditions. To overcome this problem of skewedness, I often break down the analysis into population categories (usually by electoral systems, which form two distinct population categories).

3.6.2. Functional Size

The functional size variable is a single measure with a double interpretation. On the one hand, it attempts to measure the level of governmental complexity as an indicator of the degree to which the items on the local political agenda are likely to be numerous and conflicting. The idea is that the more functions the local government performs, the more complex the governance of the municipality. That also expresses the importance of the municipality. The more functions the municipality has, the more likely it is perceived to be important among the many other municipalities.

The municipality centrality/significance variable is operationalized by the number of institutions existing in the local government. The T-STAR database contains a long set of dummy variables about the existence of specific institutions. This list includes locally important economic and social institutions such as schools, hospital, railway station, library, gas station, bank office, pharmacy or museum (see Appendix C). The centrality/significance index was first computed by simply adding up the number of institution types that existed in municipality. To emphasize the additional centrality and complexity stemming from a senior role in the public administration system, the central municipalities of small regions ('kistérség'), county capitals (counties are the only functioning middle level in administration) and regional centers (usually university centers with an important cultural role) obtained one extra point. While the composition of the list and the weighting of its items are arbitrary from a methodological point of view, they largely reflect the importance of the administrative levels and the educational-cultural role of regional centers. The index ranges from 1 to 38 with a mean of 11.8 institutions and a relatively large standard deviation (7.4). This indicator effectively differentiates between municipalities of similar size, but of different complexity and centrality.

3.6.3. Population Stability

Population stability is measured by the balance of migration. The net balance of migration is computed as the difference between those who moved in the municipality and those who permanently left it. The indicator of population stability is based on the ratio of the net migration to the total population in 1990. Since both immigration and emigration refer to the lack of stability, the indicator is computed as the absolute value of the migration balance compared to the full population. The migration balance has a wide range. A municipality in the suburban area of Budapest (Telki) attracted twice as many new inhabitants as its population in 1990. In contrast, a village (Kovácsszénája), quite far from the capital, lost half of its population in a decade as a result of migration. The average absolute migration was 8.1 percent of the total population in 1990 with a standard deviation of 10.5 percent.

3.6.4. Urbanization

The urbanized character of a settlement cannot easily be quantified. For most people, the level of urbanization can be assessed by means of a simple look at the view of the municipality. I decided to use the usual measure, population density, but with some hesitation. On the one hand, municipalities of the same density may have different mentalities rooted in their historical development. In addition to its validity problems, there is some room for doubt concerning the reliability of the density indicator. Geographical conditions (e.g. islands) and special historical circumstances (e. g. secession from a larger municipality) can lead to high density without a really urbanized look. In fact, the most dense municipality (Budapest was left out) is a village (Petőfibánya). The ninth on the list is a village (Erdőkertes) which seceded from a larger municipality (Veresegyház) with a limited amount of territory. Population density was computed as the quotient of the number of inhabitants and the official territory of the local government. The mean density in the database is 70 inhabitants per squared kilometer with a sizable range (108 inhabitants per km^2).

3.6.5. Age composition

The age structure of the local society is a variable with many potential effects. The aging of the Hungarian society makes this variable especially interesting. I have two measures of the age of local society. One is simply computed as the proportion of inhabitants who are sixty or more years old according to the census data. There are already villages where every citizen is old (e.g. Tornakápolna). The mean is 23 percent with a standard deviation of 7 percent. The other indicator is the average age of the local society. Obviously, no access is possible to individual level survey data.

Thus, my computation was based on the aggregate data by age groups. I weighted each group with its central value (e.g. everybody in the group 50–59 years was regarded as 55 years old). Since all of these groups cover a range of age, I had to assume that people's age is distributed evenly within the groups. This seems a slight problem in age groups that aggregate only one year (e.g. children between five and six years). However, the measurement may not be that precise in large age groups. (For example, fewer people were born during the Second World War than after it, in all probability making the 56–59 years old subgroup less 'vast' than the 50–55 years old one.) A special problem was caused by the group over 60 years, as no natural central value could be counted. I attributed 70 years to this group. The youngest municipality is a village (Csenyéte) where the mean age of the 396 inhabitants is only 24 years. The other extreme is the already mentioned Tornakápolna where all the 12 inhabitants are older than 60 years (as a consequence, the municipality received the maximal 70 years as mean age). The average age of municipalities on the country level is 39 years with a standard deviation of 3,6 years. (This is obviously not the average age of the population of Hungary, the mean of the municipality involves giving equal weight to small and large local governments.) As the empirical analysis will show, the choice of age indicator does not influence the results.

3.6.6. Citizens' Resources

The variables of education and standard of living are combined into the variable of citizens' resources because of their conceptual closeness and empirical association. The correlation between the two variables is high enough to endanger multivariate analyses. However, they cover the same theoretical problem: citizens' individual resources. Thus, the high correlation provides the opportunity to form an indicator that can be conceptualized. First, I discuss the components of the new variable, then the way in which the combined variable was constructed.

In an ideal world, the level of education could be measured by the mean level of education based on a refined scale, e.g. the number of classes completed by inhabitants. Unfortunately, even the census does not provide data of such quality. What is available is the number of people who reached a certain level of education (completed primary school, secondary school or received a diploma from an institution of higher education). While getting a secondary school certificate is no longer a challenge, it is a respectable level of education in older generations; the number of graduates would not distinguish between more and less educated local societies. Consequently, the level of education in municipality is measured by the proportion of university and secondary school graduates in the population of 18 years or more. People with any diploma and higher education degree were counted—including trade school and 'gimnázium' ('lycé')—, and university and high school ('főiskola') degrees.

The level of standard of living is indicated by the mean personal income in a municipality. The mean personal income is computed by dividing the total personal income filed in the municipality by the number of those who submitted a tax return. The indicator ranges from 218,000 forint (Gagyapáti) to 2,152,000 forint (Telki) per capita. Unfortunately, this indicator is only a proxy measure of a highly sensitive variable. The problem is not tax evasion itself, but the fact that hidden income is distributed unevenly among occupations and economic sectors. While the self-employed and the owners and employees of small businesses can evade taxes effectively, the employees of big enterprises and government agencies are not able to defraud their revenue. Tax evasion is more widespread in certain occupations (dentists, construction workers, waiters) than in others. Thus, the aggregate personal income is likely to be higher in municipalities where a large proportion of citizens work for the government (administration, universities, etc.) or big enterprises than in municipalities where small businesses play a major role in the local economy (e.g. tourism areas), even if the mean income in reality is the same. An additional specific problem is related to pensioners, as pensions are exempt from tax. Moreover, in areas that were economically depressed in the 1990s, disability was a socially accepted way to leave the job market. Many people receive a pension based on disability, not age. As pensions are typically low (especially for those who retired many years ago or retired as disabled), the indicator of the mean personal income overestimates the actual standard of living in municipalities where disproportionally high number of pensioners live. Therefore, the use of this indicator depends on the quite unrealistic assumption; namely that the level of tax evasion and the share of inactive people are the same in each local government.

The variable of citizens' resources was constructed as the sum of the component indicators of education and standard of living. The components were standardized before the summation.

3.6.7. Societal Heterogeneity

Societal heterogeneity is indicated by two measures. First, socioeconomic heterogeneity is measured by the heterogeneity of the local employment. The municipal-level census data contains information about the number of inhabitants employed in twelve categories:

- agriculture (including forestry and fishery)
- industry (mining, manufacturing, and energy)
- construction
- commerce and repairs services
- tourism
- transportation (including postal services)
- finance
- public administration (including defense and social security too)
- education
- health care and welfare
- other community service.

As it can be seen, the last nine branches form the broader category of the service sector, while the first three are traditional economic sectors. The homogeneity of socioeconomic heterogeneity was computed by adding up the squared proportion of the individual sectors in the local job market (Herfindahl-index). The socioeconomic heterogeneity index was then calculated as 1 minus the homogeneity measure. For example, if there are only two sectors in a municipality with a proportion of 60 and 40 percent, respectively, the heterogeneity index is computed as $1-(0.6^2+0.4^2)=0.4$. In a five-sector municipality with 40, 30, 10, 10, 10 percent proportions, the index is $1-(0.4^2+0.3^2\ 0.1^2+0.1^2+0.1^2)=0.72$. Clearly, the second municipality is more heterogeneous in terms of employment distribution than the first one. The index ranged from 0 to 0.9 with a mean of 0.8 and standard deviation of 0.08.

I also measured socioeconomic heterogeneity by the occupational diversity of local societies. It was constructed as a Herfindahl-index from the following categories:

1. Managers
2. Other white collars
3. Employed in service sector
4. Employed in agriculture
5. Employed in industry and construction
6. Other.

These have been central occupational categories of the Statistical Office since the 1960s. The two indices correlate very well and, as can be seen the following chapters, produce the same results in multivariate analyses.

3.6.8. Ethnic Heterogeneity

The other indicator of societal heterogeneity refers to ethnic diversity. Measuring this kind of diversity is far from easy. The simplist source of data, the census, is in all probability unreliable. First, minority people often have a double identity in Hungary. While many of them do not speak their minority language (this is typical among Germans and Slovaks), they still preserve a certain level of separate identity. At the same time, they also feel that they belong to the Hungarian nation. In everyday life, this double identity does not cause many problems. The dispersed nature of minorities and the lack of clearly bounded ethnic subcultures result in imprecise answers to ethnic identity questions. Second and more importantly, the Roma in Hungary have a low prestige and are often treated in a prejudiced manner. No small wonder that few Roma are proud of being labeled as one belonging to this ethnic group. Therefore, they prefer to identify themselves as Hungarians in public opinion polls and censuses.

I used a more political measure of ethnic diversity here. The indicator of ethnic diversity is calculated in this research as the number of votes cast for candidates who registered themselves as minority candidates. Both independents and organizations can request this, so all the votes were counted independently of the affiliation of candidates. As the electoral law treat minority candidates in a preferential manner, ethnic entrepreneurs have an incentive to try to acquire the votes of ethnic groups.

That measure indicates at the same time more and less than the usual statistical categorization. It is less as it does not capture the precise number of people belonging to minority groups. However, it is also more than the usual categorization because it refers to the degree to which a separate identity exists. As mentioned, it is computed as the number of the votes gained by registered minority candidates in the total votes. I separately counted the proportion of votes Roma candidates obtained to see the effect of the presence of this minority. The minority vote variable ranges from 0 to 100 percent. While the mean value is only 4 percent, the standard deviation is quite large (13.2%), indicating the uneven spread and organizational level of minority people. Within that, the maximum of Roma votes was 96 percent, the mean of all municipalities 1.4 percent with a standard deviation of 0.4 percent.

The two indicators of societal heterogeneity, socioeconomic and ethnic diversity, should not correlate in theory. Still, some correlation is not unlikely because of the correspondence of social and ethnic cleavages in the case of the Roma population. The Roma are on average less educated, have lower income and more often preserve mentalities which are not always compatible with the requirements of the modern job market. Thus, a larger Roma population may mean more homogeneous socioeconomic diversity, but the overall correlation cannot expected to be high.

3.6.9. Electoral Systems

The variable of electoral systems is very simple. Its definition is legal, as presented in the section on the local electoral systems in Hungary. The indicator is a dummy variable giving 0 to the electoral system of 'short tickets' (employed in municipalities of 10,000 or less inhabitants) and 1 to the 'mixed system' (applied in municipalities of 10,000 or more inhabitants). Most local governments (2995 or 95.5%) belong to the short ticket system and only a minority (142 or 4.5%) apply the mixed system. The electoral system, as we will see, is a highly powerful predictor. Nonetheless, it is strongly related to size and, consequently, correlates very well with other variables as well. To detect the problems stemming from those natural associations and deepen our knowledge about the differences between urban and rural areas, I will study the statistical models for the two electoral categories separately.

3.6.10. Proximity to Centers

The intensive multilevel relationship of municipalities with large regional centers and each other may have important political effects. Proximity to centers is indicated here by the degree of attachment to a metropolitan area. The underlying idea is that forming part of a metropolitan area implies many contacts, both on the institutional and individual level, with a large central city and with other communities in the metropolitan area. (For more discussion on the metropolitan areas in

Hungary see Soós and Ignits 2005.) Metropolitan areas were defined by functional criteria. The intensity of contacts was indicated by the level of commuting. A community was regarded as suburban if more than half of the employed inhabitants commuted every day and 40 percent of them commute to the central city. In addition, subcenters (e.g. Gödöllő or Vác) were identified; subcenters are characterized by close functional connection with the central city, but a more independent job market, which makes the percentage of commuters to the central city less than 40 percent. Subcenters were identified based on the existing transportation (bus, rail, suburban train) links with the central city. Every social/economic phenomenon has a spatial manifestation, which is faithfully documented by the transportation links (Mokos 1998). The assumption was that proximate two-way connections exist in all those cases where these transportation links had a high density. Those communities were regarded as subcenters where the number of daily direct services with the central city was above 60. These subcenters themselves have a considerable number of transportation links with the surrounding settlements, and attract a large number of commuters in their own right. Thus, those communities were also defined as metropolitan suburbs where the percentage of commuters was above 50%, but the majority of them commuted not to the central city but to one of the subcenters. It is primarily the Budapest suburban area where the number of suburbs included has grown in consequence of the involvement of subcenters.

On the basis of the above described functional approach, six metropolitan areas with considerable size (around or over 200,000 inhabitants) were found in Hungary. These are as follows: Budapest, Debrecen, Miskolc, Szeged, Győr and Pécs. There are other agglomerations in Hungary (e. g. the one around the lake Balaton), but none of them included both a large city and a significant suburban area. According to this definition, more than one third (36,9%) of the population of Hungary live in metropolitan areas, formed by 253 local governments (8% of all municipalities).

Table 3.1. Metropolitan areas in Hungary

Metropolitan Areas	**Population (2001)**	**Ratio of the central city in the population of the metropolitan area (2001)**	**Number of local governments (2001)**
Budapest	2,557,681	69.5%	98
Miskolc	267,762	68.7%	38
Debrecen	265,097	80.0%	12
Szeged	199,647	84.0%	11
Pécs	192,106	85.0%	38
Győr	208,315	62.1%	56

The indicator of belonging to a metropolitan area is a simple dummy variable. In addition to the metropolitan indicator, I also used an alternative one, measuring the distance of the municipalities from the closest regional center (the same six cities: Budapest, Debrecen, Győr, Miskolc, Pécs, and Szeged). Distance was measured by the number of kilometers between the regional center and the municipality on road. The largest distance is 153 kilometers. The mean is 61 kilometers with a standard deviation of 34 kilometers. This indicator is more detailed, but does not include the qualitative dimension of metropolitan relationships.

3.6.11. The Organizational Strength of Civil Society

The variable of the organizational strength of local civil society in fact refers to the level of local civil society institutionalization. It is measured by the number of nonprofit organizations per 1,000 inhabitants. The usual problem with civil society measures is that they do not cover informal relationships, an important component of horizontal societal links that make up civil society. As the research design of my project explicitly requires an indicator of organizational strength, the available statistical measure covers only the precise group of social phenomena. Nonetheless, the indicators have three other, though more minor, problems. First, there is no such thing in the law in Hungary as a compulsory 'de-registration'. As a result, a certain proportion of the organizations do not actually function. If there is a high variance in the ratio of 'dead' organizations among municipalities, the measure does not reflect the actual level of organizational strength. Unfortunately, there is no survey that could give data on non-functioning nonprofit organizations on the local level. Second, the functioning organizations are different in terms of membership size, profile and activity. Certain organizations have relatively many members, while others depend on only a few individuals or only one enthusiastic prime mover. Certain organizations can maintain a high profile, while others rarely appear in media. Certain organizations are very active, while others rarely show any activity. Those differences are not reflected by the simple sum of the number of organizations. Third, not all organizations registered in a municipality actually act there. More central cities, especially Budapest, are the home of regional or country-level organizations, which are active in other municipalities as well. The exclusion of Budapest from the dataset makes this problem less significant.

In sum, I use nonprofit density as an indicator of the organizational strength of civil society with three assumptions: the ratio of non-functioning organizations is the same in every municipality; the size, profile, and activity distribution of nonprofits is the same in every municipality; and the ratio of locally active nonprofit organizations to all organizations is the same in every municipality.

The range of the density of nonprofit organizations is quite large. There are no such organizations in many (302 or 10%) local governments and there are only one or two in many others (610 municipalities or 19%). The average is 6 social organizations per 1,000 inhabitants with a large standard deviation of 5. The maximum density is 105 organizations per 1,000 inhabitants.

Nonetheless, this maximum value sheds light on the problem of this measurement: the highest scoring village (Sima) has only 19 inhabitants, but two organizations happen to be registered in that small local government (one is a hunting association – hardly the sign of a self-organized civil society in the community). From another perspective, a village of 500 or a village of 1500 may need only one sport club, but that means a huge difference in organizational density.

A possible solution is to exclude deviant cases from the analysis. Conforming to the conventions of statistical analysis, I regard a case statistically deviant if its value deviates from the mean with more than two standard deviation units. To translate that into concrete data, the municipalities with more than 16.7 social organizations per 1,000 inhabitants are statistically deviant. All of them are very small (only two have more than 1,000 inhabitants and the maximum size is 1594 inhabitants). Since there are many small local governments in the dataset, the exclusion of these 85 cases (or 2.7 % of the population) does not seem to be a high price for a cleaner dataset.

3.6.12. Electoral Participation

Political participation has different dimensions and different forms. For the purpose of the research, only one indicator conforming to the requirements is available. This is electoral participation or turnout at local elections. One must not forget that the level of turnout does not necessarily indicate the level of nonelectoral participation or the degree of political interest in local affairs. Still, turnout is a very reliable indicator, which can effectively be used in multivariate models. As usual, I calculated turnout as the ratio between the number who actually voted to the total number of citizens with voting rights in the local government. I computed the turnout rate for both 1998 and 2002. To level out fluctuations due to idiosyncratic reasons (e.g. an one-time extreme level of competition which attracted many voters), the turnout variable was computer using the means of the two elections. The overall turnout was somewhat higher in 2002 (64%) than in 1998 (61%). As turnout is higher in small municipalities than in the more populous ones; in 2002, slightly more than 50 percent of the electorate turned out altogether in Hungary. An interesting finding is the large standard deviation (11%) of the difference in turnout at two consecutive local elections. That also indicates that the political stability is relatively low in Hungary. The wide range of the turnout variable is also illuminating; it calls attention to how the success of local mobilization at local electoral campaigns is different.

Table 3.2. Characteristics of turnout at local elections in 1998 and 2002

	1998	2002	Mean	Difference
Mean	61.2%	63.7%	62.5%	+2.5%
Standard deviation	14.9%	14.0%	13.5%	10.6%
Minimum	21.0%	21.0%	28%	–48.2%
Maximum	100.0%	100.0%	98%	+47.5%

3.7. Summary

This chapter has operationalized the dependent and explanatory variables, informed by the specificities of the local government system in Hungary and the requirements made by multivariate causal analysis. The two major indicators of local party institutionalization, discussed in the next two chapters, are the level of party government and the degree of loyalty to nominating parties. An important step has been the identification and operationalization of the 12 independent variables that are used in this research, and the hypotheses that are actually tested (see Appendix A).

Chapter 4: Local Party Government

This chapter and the following three test the effect of the variables on local party institutionalization, as formulated and operationalized in the previous chapter. The present chapter uses party government as an indicator of local party institutionalization.

The degree to which parties rule local governments is an indicator of the level of local party institutionalization, especially its external legitimacy aspect: the local party government index is measured by the proportion of votes party organizations obtained at local elections. The chapter begins with an overview of the electoral results of non-independent candidates at municipal elections. This provides an opportunity to test the hypotheses about the potential relationship between the organizational form of local parties and their level of institutionalization. Then I characterize the bivariate associations between the measure of local party government and its potential determinants.

The multiple regression will be carried out for electoral systems separately, in order to avoid the problem stemming from the nonnormal distribution of the dependent variable. The final section assesses the findings from the viewpoint of the hypotheses to be tested.

4.1. Local Party Government in Hungary

In this section, I provide an overview of the dynamics of local party government and test the hypotheses about the importance of time and organizational type. As a first sensitizing step, I draw some conclusions from the general electoral data. Table 4.1 shows the frequency of organizational nominations in the four local elections that have taken place since the beginning of democracy.

A first observation may be that independents constitute a large majority. In most small local governments organizations do not run candidates. As the number of small local governments is very high (95% of all municipalities), local party organizations play a prominent role only in a few municipalities. The average level of local party rule is low in Hungary.

A second point is that the proportion of independent local representatives tends to increase. In twelve years, the ratio of independent mayors has increased from 80 to 85 percent and the proportion of independent councilors from 71 to 73 percent (with a small oscillation in 1994). In other words, the organization-nominated candidates have lost ground since the inception of local democracy. This observation diametrically contradicts the hypothesis claiming that the organizations penetrate more and more local governments as democracy becomes more consolidated. The evidence actually suggests that certain local governments that had been (at least partially) dominated by parties in the beginning of the consolidation process became unorganized or less organized by the time of third or fourth election.

A third point is that the proportion of party-nominated councilors and mayors has been decreasing since 1990. This may not necessarily be related to the ever stronger anti-party feeling in Hungary (and elsewhere in the contemporary democracies). The explanation may lie in the increasing trend of Hungarian politics towards a two-bloc system, in which the two big parties (ex-Communists and rightists) and their allies run only two candidates. As a consequence, parties nominate fewer candidates but they are nominated by more than one party (often three or four).

Fourth, civic organizations, alone or in coalition with political parties, nominate more and more candidates. This process is not parallel with the decline of party nominations; it is probably not former party candidates who change their political color (though this is not uncommon either).

Fifth, it is clear that mayors are less dependent on the electoral support of organizations. This may partly be explained by their higher name recognition (especially incumbents enjoy this advantage). Participation in local political life has accumulated the political capital of some local politicians since 1990 and, consequently, they stand in less need of the orientating labels of political parties or civic organizations. Another reason for this phenomenon maybe the different character of mayoral elections. The political 'trade marks' of organizations often suggest the representation of particular interests and a 'quarrelsome' political culture. The organizational life is usually weak in smaller local governments and the issues are rather nonpartisan, so such negative associations do not help would-be mayors, who must represent the whole municipality. The more general conclusion here is that the direct election of mayors seems to have a negative impact on party government. This potential effect will not be further discussed in this research because the effect is constant (mayors have been directly elected in all local governments since 1994).

Table 4.1. Nominations at local elections 1990–2002

Nominating organization	Mayors				Councilors			
	1990	1994	1998	2002	1990	1994	1998	2002
Independent	79.7	83.7	84.8	85.1	71.2%	68.9	73.7	73.3
Party	13.0	9.1	7.2	6.7	21.4	18.3	13.0	10.6
Civic organization	1.6	2.0	3.1	4.0	3.2	5.4	6.5	8.1

Nominating organization	Mayors				Councilors			
	1990	1994	1998	2002	1990	1994	1998	2002
Party and civic organization	5.7	5.2	4.9	4.2	4.2	7.4	6.8	8.0
Total	100	100	100	100	100	100	100	100
Party nominated	18.7	14.3	12.1	10.9	25.6	25.7	19.8	18.6
Civic nominated	7.3	7.2	8.0	8.2	7.4	12.8	13.5	16.1

Source: Central Statistical Office (2003). Bőhm and Szoboszlai (1992).

Unfortunately, the frequency of the nomination of local candidates is not a satisfactory measure of local party rule because it does not weigh the importance of candidates and is a crude measure of the level of local government institutionalization (especially in small municipalities where the number of candidates is limited). The local party government index that I will use in the rest of the chapter is a better measure as it attributes a more precise value to candidates and counts votes, a more continuous measure, not simply candidates or councilors.

The local party government index refers to the degree to which the local political life is institutionalized around local party organizations as central players. On the level of local governments, it is measured by the number of votes obtained by candidates nominated by one or more local political organizations against the total number of votes cast at the local election. To level out the fluctuations, the actual indicator is a mean of the results of two elections, 1998 and 2002. The aggregations are the means of the means of all local governments or their subsets. Unlike the introductory example, the local party government index used here does not weigh local governments by size (as the number of candidates implicitly did in the aggregation of nominations). In the means presented below, all local governments have an equal weight.

The level of local party government ranges from 0 to 100 percent. 1238 local governments or almost 40 percent (39.46%) are fully exempt from nominating organizations. There is one municipality (Szentkirály) where all the votes were collected by organization-nominated candidates both in 1998 and 2002 and 58 other municipalities where organizations obtained more than 90 percent of the votes (e.g. Paks, Pápa, Pécs, Győr, Nyíregyháza). The stem-and-leaf plot of the distribution of organizational votes leads to an interesting observation: the low and high values are more frequent than the medium level values (around 60%). I will return to this phenomenon later.

The extreme differences are indicated by the large standard deviation (20.9%) on the aggregated country level. The overall mean is 11.5 percent. The general descriptive conclusion is that the average level of local party government is low in Hungary and that the differences are large: certain municipalities are totally ruled by parties, while organizations have no influence whatsoever in many other localities. Parties obtained more than 50 percent of the votes in only 6.4 percent of local governments.

The data on the temporal change of the index of local party government points to the same conclusion as was previously drawn. While the mean level of party local government was 12.4 percent in 1998, that fell to 10.5 percent in 2002. A decline in the degree to which political life is organized around organizations characterizes both parties (from 10.6 to 8.2%) and civil society organizations (from 2.6 to 1.6%). A different angle is the proportion of local governments where a party nominated at least one candidate. This ratio plummeted from 51 percent to 45 percent between 1998 and 2002. These findings fit in the trend presented above. Again, the data do not support the hypothesis about the increasing role of local party organizations in the consolidation process. Reality is that local politics in some municipalities are becoming less and less institutionalized around parties. In all probability, personal clientelism is gaining ground in a certain category of municipalities. In this field, party government is faced with other forms of political institutionalization.

Data on fluctuation provides evidence for this inquiry too. The fluctuation index shows the difference in the total votes of local party organizations between 1998 and 2002. The larger the difference, the less likely party government is well-established in the municipalities. The oscillation of votes reached surprisingly high levels in some municipality. In three villages (Nemespátró, Nemesgulács, Felsőpáhok) the party government index increased from 0 to more than 80 percent between 1998 and 2002. In contrast, local party organizations lost more than 60 percent of their votes in three municipalities (Beret, Heréd, Ráckeresztúr). The mean level of fluctuation is 6.5 percent in the country, but higher (10.8%) if one takes only those local governments into account where organizations actually had candidates. Compared to their mean, the fluctuation is about the same among the local chapters of national parties and civil society organizations.

Summing up, the degree to which parties are major players in local governments varies to a large extent. A conclusion can already be drawn concerning Hypothesis 15: the level of local party government has not increased since 1990, so this hypothesis is not confirmed. Time does not work for local parties. There is somewhat more evidence for the reverse process in the grey zone where the competition between independents and candidates of organizations is open.

Table 4.2. Stem-and-leaf plot of the votes gained by local party organizations

0%	000000000000000000000000000000000000000000000000000000000000000000000000000000000000000000000000000000000000+2066
10%	0000000000000000000000000000000000000000000000000011111111111111111111111111111111111111111111111222+281
20%	000000000000000000000000000000011111111111111111111111111112222222222222222222222222223333333333333333333344444444+65
30%	0000000000111111111111122223333333333344444445555555666666666677788888999999999
40%	0000000001111222222333333333444445555555666667778889999
50%	000111112234444446677888889
60%	0001222333444556677899
70%	00011222333666667777778889
80%	000000111111112223333333344445555666666667777777888888888999999999
90%	000000000111111111122222223333333333334444444444455555555556666667789
100%	0

4.2. Bivariate Associations With Local Party Government

In this section, I examine the relationship of the level of party government with the explanatory variables one by one. In addition to simple correlations, I also try to include other relevant variables to gain a deeper knowledge on the more complex associations.

4.2.1. Population Size

Population size is the theoretically central variable in this research, as it is expected to associate with local party institutionalization in various ways. Table 4.3 shows a clear correlation of population size, measured as the number of inhabitants, with the local party government index. While local party organizations obviously play a huge role in large local governments, they do not make much difference in small villages. The Pearson-moment product correlation is quite large. If one defines a local government as party-dominated when local party organizations gain more than 50 percent of the votes, the data becomes very illuminating. Under 5,000 inhabitants, only a small fraction of local governments have a consistent party government (lasting more than two electoral cycles). In most small municipalities, parties play a minor role or are nonexistent. The situation changes in the category between 5,000 and 10,000, in which every sixth local government is ruled by parties. Above the 10,000 threshold, there is no municipality in which parties are not the major players.

Table 4.3. Population size and local party government[6]

Size category	All Organizations	National Parties	Social Organizations	Fluctu-ation	Party-dominated
1,000 or less	3.6%	3.0%	0.6%	4.4%	0.3%
1,001–2,000	8.7%	7.2%	1.5%	8.0%	1.1%
2,001–5,000	15.0%	12.3%	2.5%	9.5%	4.6%
5,001–10,000	32.0%	27.1%	5.8%	13.3%	18.7%
10,001–50,000	85.7%	67.6%	17.3%	7.7%	100.0%
50,001 or more	93.5%	81.7%	21.1%	3.4%	100.0%
Total	11.5%	9.4%	2.1%	6.5%	6.4
Correlation with size	.575	.578	.373	.023	.550

Dependent variable: Local Party Government Index (proportion of votes cast on local party organizations)

6 The data refer to the mean performance of local political parties in local governments by population categories.

The consistency of parties' role is also important and leads to the same conclusion: party votes do not fluctuate much in the cities of more than 10,000 inhabitants, where they gained most of the votes. Compared to the mean, the instability of parties is much higher in the 5,000–10,000 category and it reaches a very high level in the villages of 5,000 or less inhabitants. Size seems to matter.

4.2.2. Functional Size

A crucial indicator of this research is the functional size of municipalities. The hypothesis is that the more significant the municipality, the stronger its political parties. The data support this hypothesis. While the huge coefficient becomes more moderate when size and the electoral system are also included the impact of functional centrality and complexity remains remarkable. It seems to distinguish among municipalities especially in the mixed electoral system. The analysis of other variables reveals a strong indirect effect of functional size, which is mediated by several other variables.

Table 4.4. Functional size and local party government

Variables	Regression 1	Regression 2	Regression 3	Regression 4	Regression 6	Regression 7
Functional size	.70	.55	.37	.36	.16	.37
Population size		.30		.04	.40	.23
Electoral system			.58	.56		
Cases	all	all	all	all	short	mixed

Dependent variable: Local Party Government Index (proportion of votes cast on local party organizations)

4.2.3. Population Stability

Citizens who are not rooted in the local society are less likely to join and support parties or maintain contacts with them. Municipalities characterized with population instability are more likely to stabilize their political organizations. Here the level of migration, that is, the net balance of local immigration and emigration measures population instability. The result, shown in Table 4.4, is a small, but consistent effect. The more the composition of local society changes, the less likely local political parties play an important role in local political life. This effect is especially manifest in urban communities.

Table 4.5. Population instability and party government

Variables	Regr. 1	Regr. 2	Regr. 3	Regr. 4	Regr. 5	Regr. 6	Regr. 7
Population change (abs. of net migration balance)	–.05	–.03	–.02	–.02	–.03	–.04	–.30
population size		.57		.13	.08	.53	.32
electoral system			.79	.71	.67		
Urbanization					.12		
Cases	all	all	all	all	all	short	mixed

Dependent variable: Local Party Government Index (proportion of votes cast on local party organizations)

4.2.4. Urbanization

Urban people are often more ready to organize themselves and defend their interests in non-governmental organizations. The impact of urbanization is quite large, though it decreases when population size is also taken into account, reflecting the obvious fact that the larger the community, the more urban. The effect is largely independent of the size category.

Table 4.6. Urbanization and party government

Variables	Regression 1	Regression 2	Regression 3	Regression 4
urbanization (population density)	.50	.27	.22	.21
population size		.43		
Cases	all	all	short	mixed

Dependent variable: Local Party Government Index (proportion of votes cast on local party organizations)

4.2.5. Age composition

Older people often have more time to commit and participate in politics. That may affect the organizational level of local politics as well. The models that contain all the cases display a different picture, as the coefficient of the indicator of the age of local society is negative. However, the relationship between the local party government index and that of age is not linear. Local party organizations are the most successful where the age of local society is around the country average. Both young and old local societies are less characterized by party rule. The reason for that is the curvilinear association of population age with size. While larger local governments are all around the country average, there is a high variance in the category of smallest municipalities. Both very young and very old societies can be found in this category, which may partially be due simply to their small size. In a very small village, the movement of one large family in or out the locality may significantly change the age of the local society. The conclusion is that the age variable must be used with caution and it may not be included in certain linear regression models.

Table 4.7. Age and party government

Variables	Regression 1	Regression 2	Regression 3	Regression 4
% of senior citizens	–.19	–.12	–.09	–.08
population size		.56		.12
electoral system			.78	.70
Cases	all	all	all	All

Dependent variable: Local Party Government Index (proportion of votes cast on local party organizations)

4.2.6. Citizens' Resources

Education and standard of living played an important role in the conceptual models. Organizations need agents who build up and keep them activated. Agents can be characterized by free time, personal independence and a certain level of the understanding of what is going in the world. Time and independence largely depend on the level of the standard of living, while the comprehension of complex problems mostly depends on the level of education. Thus, the best approximation of the potential size of agency is a combination of education and income, a combination because agency needs both types of resources. Dependent intellectuals and the uneducated wealthy do not effectively contribute to horizontal societal organization.

The indicator of citizens' resources was constructed by adding up the standardized measures of income and education. While it is not possible to include both measures in a regression analysis at the same time, a separate inquiry of their bivariate effects is instructive.

Cultural capital is frequently shown to influence the level and type of societal organization. The simple correlation seems to confirm this belief with its relatively high coefficient. This decreases when population size and electoral system are also taken into account. What makes a drastic change is the inclusion of the variable of functional size: the coefficient becomes not only small, but alters its direction. The separate analysis by electoral types demonstrates that the effect of education is ambiguous. While an increase in education results in more institutionalized party rule in the mixed system, a larger pool of educated people decreases the chances of party government in the short ticket system.

Table 4.8. Level of education and local party government

Variables	Regr. 1	Regr. 2	Regr. 3	Regr. 4	Regr. 5	Regr. 6	Regr. 7
Education (% of post-secondary)	.45	.26	.15	.13	–.03	–.06	.10
Population size		.47		.10	.05	.41	.18
Electoral system			.73	.67	.56		
Functional size					.37	.18	.36
Cases	all	all	all	all	all	short	mixed

Dependent variable: Local Party Government Index (proportion of votes cast on local party organizations)

The better the local citizens live (and the larger the local middle class is), the more time and money they can devote to local politics, the more they are inclined to organize themselves, and the more diverse interests they have to be defended. All of these are hypothesized to strengthen the position of local party organizations. The simple correlation between the local party government index and that of income is significantly large and is in the expected direction. Nonetheless, the magnitude of the coefficient markedly decreases when the electoral system is included in the analysis.

The separate analysis by electoral systems produces a strange result: citizens' income seem to have a negative impact on local party government in the short ticket system, while the outcome is opposite in the large municipalities of the mixed system.

Table 4.9. Income and local party government

Variables	Regr. 1	Regr. 2	Regr. 3	Regr. 4	Regr. 5	Regr. 6	Regr. 7	Regr. 8	Regr. 9
Personal income	.26	.12	.05	.04	−.05	−.09	.02	−.10	.11
Population size		.54		.12	.05	.56	.36	.18	.19
Functional size					.35			.42	.40
Electoral system			.78	.70	.56				
Cases	all	all	all	all	all	short	mixed	short	mixed

Dependent variable: Local Party Government Index (proportion of votes cast on local party organizations)

In fact, the correlation between local party government and income is negative in all population categories but the last one. In cities, the average income of the citizenry (in all probability, the size of the middle class) positively contributes to the level of party government. The impact of income is negative in all other categories. Not only does this finding not support the original hypothesis, but it is simply antithetical to it.

Table 4.10. Correlation of income and party government by population categories

Population categories	Correlation of income and party government
0–1,000	−.06
1,001–2,000	−.14
2,001–5,000	−.06
5,001–10,000	−.12
10,001–20,000	−.10
20,000+	+.18

The interaction of income and education seems to affect the level of party government. In municipalities where both the level of education and income are above the mean party organizations gained 20 percent of the votes on average. This ratio is only 14 percent where only education is high, and half of that where only income level is high or both education and income are low. The initial high correlation diminishes to almost insignificant when the measure of functional size is included and becomes negative when population size is also in the equation. However, the regression analysis levels out a nonlinear effect. While citizens' resources have a negative impact on the level of party government in small communities, it plays a positive role in the mixed electoral system.

As it was shown, both components have a negative influence on party government in the short ticket system. That can be explained by the incentives of the electoral system, which provide ample opportunity to able individuals, typically well-equipped with personal resources, to run as independent candidates. Such incentives do not exist in the mixed electoral system. On the contrary, well-resourced and ambitious individuals are encouraged to cooperate and gain organizational support. Educated persons with enough personal income to invest into a campaign are more likely to successfully form such organizations.

What makes this argument less compelling is the fact, already observed in the analysis of income, that the correlation of citizens' resources with party government in the category of 10,000–20,000 is still negative (–.03), while it becomes largely positive (.09) in the category of 20,000–50,000. This problem cannot be solved without further research, which is beyond the scope of this study.

Table 4.11. Citizens' resources and party government

Variables	**Regression 1**	**Regression 2**	**Regression 3**	**Regression 4**	**Regression 5**	**Regression 6**
Citizens' resources	.38	–.04	.16	.21	–.10	.11
Population size		.05			.42	.18
Functional size		.56			.19	.38
Electoral system		.38				
Cases	all	all	short	mixed	short	mixed

Dependent variable: Local Party Government Index (proportion of votes cast on local party organizations)

4.2.7. Socioeconomic Heterogeneity

Socioeconomic heterogeneity is indicated by the sectoral diversity of the local job market. Large heterogeneity is expected to induce a larger role of local party organizations. The simple correlation shows a relatively significant association between party government and sectoral heterogeneity, the indicator of socioeconomic diversity. This effect decreases but does not disappear when size and electoral system are taken into account. However, the inclusion of a potential common cause, the functional complexity (in a sense, functional diversity), makes the impact of sectoral heterogeneity insignificant. The coefficients do not change if occupational heterogeneity is replaced with sectoral heterogeneity.

Table 4.12. Socioeconomic heterogeneity and local party government

Variables	Regr. 1	Regr. 2	Regr. 3	Regr. 4	Regr. 5	Regr. 6	Regr. 7	Regr. 8
Sectoral heterogeneity	.20	.12	−.03	−.02				
Occupational heterogeneity					.23	.15	−.03	−.02
Population size		.56		.30		.55		.30
Functional size			.71	.56			.71	.55
Cases	all	all	all	all	all	all	short	mixed

Dependent variable: Local Party Government Index (proportion of votes cast on local party organizations)

4.2.8. Ethnic Heterogeneity

The other dimension of societal heterogeneity included in this research is ethnic diversity. Again, larger heterogeneity is expected to lead to stronger party government. Nonetheless, the results fall short of what is expected. The simple association is very weak (0.01) and the coefficient does not change with the inclusion of other variables. The specific indicator of the political strength of the Roma minority has the same relationship with party government. Ethnic diversity does not seem to influence the level of party government at the local level.

4.2.9. Civil Society

Civil society organizations may produce the skilled activists necessary for political action and embed political organizations in a stable network. Thus, a larger and more organized civil society is expected to have a relatively large impact on the level of local party government. Interpreting the strength of the local civil society as the density of civil society organizations, the impact of the organized civil sector on local party government is minimal. Even this small effect appears when the level of urbanization is also taken into account. Nonetheless, The organizational density of civil society becomes a significant factor among large communities.

Indicating the organizational capabilities of the local civil society by the number of civil society organizations leads to a different conclusion. The extensiveness of civil society goes hand in hand with the power of local political parties. This expresses the close association of different forms of non-governmental organizations.

Table 4.13. The density of civil society organizations and party government

Variables	Regr. 1	Regr. 2	Regr. 3	Regr. 4	Regr. 5	Regr. 6	Regr. 7	Regr. 8
Density of civil society organizations	−.02	−.00	−.03	.32				
Number of civil society organizations					.50	.34	.50	.35
Urbanization (population density)		.50	.22	.15		.34	.03	.06
Cases	all	all	short	mixed	all	all	short	mixed

Dependent variable: Local Party Government Index (proportion of votes cast on local party organizations)

4.2.10. Political Participation

Party government presupposes a certain level of political participation of the citizenry. In fact, party government is a form of political participation. The indicator of political participation used in this research (and in many others), turnout, should positively affect the level of local party government, measured by the proportion of votes gained by non-independent candidates. Nonetheless, the simple correlation is negative: the higher the turnout, the less the degree of institutionalized party rule in the municipality. The direction of the participation indicator becomes 'correct' when functional size, an indicator of size, is added to the model. The larger the municipality in terms of functions provided by them, the more likely the party rule. In other words, municipalities of the same (functional) size have different levels of party government according to their citizens' willingness to participate in local affairs.

Table 4.14. Turnout and local party government

Variables	Regr. 1	Regr. 2	Regr. 3	Regr. 4	Regr. 5	Regr. 6	Regr. 7	Regr. 8
Participation (turnout)	–.38	.14	.12	.06	–.25	.10	–.14	.14
Functional size		.79	.63	.40		.56		.46
Electoral system				.55				
Cases	all	all	all	all	short	short	mixed	mixed

Dependent variable: Local Party Government Index (proportion of votes cast on local party organizations)

4.2.11. Electoral System

Based on Table 4.15, one may arrive at another conclusion. The threshold of 10,000, which divides the two electoral systems, is a clear border for local party institutionalization. In the mixed system, all local governments without exception are ruled by party organizations, while in the short ticket system only 2 percent of the municipalities are dominated by them.

The breakdown of the candidate nominations by electoral system (in Table 4.15) provides another view. The importance of the electoral support of parties and civic organizations is minimal in local governments of 10,000 or less inhabitants. Neither the level of organization of local civil society nor the electoral system encourage organizational support. The situation is completely different in larger municipalities. The ratio of independent representatives is very low in towns and cities, while nine out of ten representatives were nominated by at least one political party and half of them by at least one civic organization in 2002. In this category, the significance of both parties and civic organizations has been growing since the establishment of the local government system. More and more civic organizations are running compensation lists on the local elections.

One might argue that the big difference in the level of party government between electoral systems is actually due to a curvilinear effect of size and appears only in aggregate data. The simplest way to dispel this doubt is to compare the local governments around the threshold. If the parties' role is significantly different between the municipalities just under the threshold and the ones just above it, one can observe the impact of the electoral rules. So I compared two categories of local governments: municipalities of more than 8,000 but less than 10,000 inhabitants (44 local governments) and municipalities of more than 10,000 but less than 12,000 inhabitants (35 local governments).

Table 4.15. Nominations at local elections by electoral systems 1994–2002

Nominating organization	'Short ticket' (less than 10,000 inhabitants)			Electoral districts			Compensation list		
	1994	1998	2002	1994	1998	2002	1994	1998	2002
Independent	81.8%	86.8%	86.8%	8.7%	9.3%	5.9%	–	–	–
Party	10.1%	6.1%	4.7%	48.2%	43.0%	42.8%	64.8%	52.8%	38.2%
Civic organization	4.5%	4.9%	6.5%	7.8%	9.7%	9.1%	13.8%	22.7%	29.1%
Party and civic organization	3.6%	2.2%	2.0%	35.3%	38.0%	42.2%	21.4%	24.5%	32.7%
Total	100.0%	100.0%	100%	100.0%	100.0%	100.0%	100.0%	100.0%	100.0%
Party nominated	13.7%	8.3%	6.7%	83.5%	81.0%	89.0%	86.2%	77.3%	70.9%
Civic nominated	8.1%	8.3%	8.5%	43.1%	47.7%	51.3%	35.2%	67.2%	61.8%

Source: Central Statistical Office (2003).

The results speak for themselves, while only 29 percent of the local governments just under the threshold are dominated by parties, this ratio is as high as 100 percent in the category of the municipalities just above the threshold. On average, local party organizations gain twice as many votes (80%) above the threshold than below it (40%). No significance test is needed to show how effective the electoral system is in providing incentives for local politicians to form permanent representative organizations.

4.2.12. Proximity to Centers

Party government is expected to be stronger in centers and municipalities close to centers. I measure this variable by two indicators: being part in a metropolitan area (dummy variable) and the distance from the nearest regional center (in kilometers). The association of both proximity measures with the indicator of party government is in the right direction. The more distant the municipality is from a central city, the less institutionalized its party government. Correspondingly, municipalities belonging to metropolitan areas have a higher level of party government.

The effect of the distance is not very impressive, but not insignificant either. Nonetheless, this effect becomes very small when population size or the electoral system is controlled for. In fact, central cities and municipalities close to them are simply larger than more distant local governments and more often use the mixed electoral system. The remaining effect is still interesting, but does not lend much support the hypotheses about the impact of geographical proximity.

Table 4.16. Distance from centers and party government

Variables	Regression 1	Regression 2	Regression 3	Regression 4	Regression 5	Regression 6
Belonging to a metropolitan area	.10		.02		.02	
Distance from nearest regional center		−.07		−.02		−.02
Population size			.57	.57		
Electoral system					.79	.79
Cases	all	all				

Dependent variable: Local Party Government Index (proportion of votes cast on local party organizations)

4.3. Multivariate Analysis

4.3.1. Determinants of Party Government

I tried to involve variables that may potentially intervene in the bivariate analyses. Still, a full picture can be seen only by a complete multivariate regression, which implies all the independent variables. Regression 1 in Table 4.17 demonstrates that two variables are really important: the type of the electoral system and the functional size of the municipality. These two factors account for 71 percent of the variance in local party government. The ten other variables explain a further 1 percent. The level of urbanization and political participation contributes positively, while the availability of activists affects negatively the level of party government. I will return to the negative effect of agency during the analysis by electoral types. The step-by-step backward procedure stresses the importance of eight variables (see Regression 9).

A restriction of cases to the local governments of 1,000 or more inhabitants (Regression 10) does not bring about much change in the coefficients. Tiny municipalities do not seriously distort the results.

The use of alternative indicators does not alter the results either. The indicator of average age causes the same effect as the proportion of seniors in the local society (Regression 2). Sectoral heterogeneity as the indicator of socioeconomic diversity has practically the same effect as the index of occupational diversity (Regression 3). The interval measure of the distance from the regionally central city does not produce results different from those of the dummy variable of metropolitan area (Regression 4). The alternative measure of the organizational strength of the local civil society as the number of such organizations has the same effect as the density measure (Regression 6).

The only real difference can be seen when the indicator of the overall proportion of minority support is replaced with the more specific measure of Roma support (Regression 5). The practically nonexistent effect becomes somewhat larger. The presence and political activity of the Roma minority contributes to the formation and institutionalization of local party organizations.

Table 4.17. A multivariate analysis of local party government

Variables	**Regr. 1**	**Regr. 2**	**Regr. 3**	**Regr. 4**	**Regr. 5**	**Regr. 6**	**Regr. 8**	**Regr. 9**	**Regr. 10**
Electoral system	**.54**	.54	.54	.54	.54	.55		.54	.57
Population size	.03	.03	.03	.03	.03		.24	.13	.02
Functional size	**.41**	.41	.42	.40	.40	.41	.61	.41	.34
Urbanization (population density)	**.06**	.06	.06	.06	.06	.06	.14	.06	.06
Population instability (migration)	.00	.00	.00	.00	.01	.01	–.01		.01
Age (mean age of inhabitants)		.01							
Age (% of 60+)	.01		.01	.00	.02	.00	.03		.01
Citizens' resources	**–.06**	–.06	–.06	–.06	–.05	–.07	–.06	.06	–.05
Socioeconomic heterogeneity (occupations)	.02	.02		.01	.02	.01	–.01	.02	.04
Socioeconomic heterogeneity (sectors)			.00						

Variables	Regr. 1	Regr. 2	Regr. 3	Regr. 4	Regr. 5	Regr. 6	Regr. 8	Regr. 9	Regr. 10
Ethnic heterogeneity (minority votes)	.00	.00	.01	.00		.00	.00		–.02
Roma (Roma minority votes)					.03				
Civil society (density)	–.01	–.02	–.02	–.02	–.02		–.01	–.01	–.01
Civil society (size)						.02			
Participation (turnout)	**.06**	.06	.06	.06	.05	.05	.12	.06	.04
Proximity to centers (metropolitan area)	.01	.01	.01		.01	.01	.02		.02
Proximity to centers (distance from center)				.02					
Cases	all	all	all	all	all	all	all	all	1,000+
Adjusted R^2	.72	.72	.72	.72	.72	.72	.57	.72	

Dependent variable: Local Party Government Index (proportion of votes cast on local party organizations)

4.3.2. Party Government In the Short Ticket Electoral System

The electoral system seems to provide powerful incentives to political agents. As a result, the curve of the variable of party government is not fully linear. To satisfy the criteria of linear regression analysis, it is advisable to split the dataset by electoral system.

Three immediate observations can be made. First, the variance explained by the model is lower than in the previous regression on the full population. The electoral system accounts for a large part of the variance in party government. Second, there are more powerful variables now than in the full model, in which only two factors dominated. Third, the narrowing of the studied population to the local governments that have 1,000 or more inhabitants (Regression 2) eliminated the problem of measurement and produced a relatively significant coefficient for the density of social organizations.

The most important variable is the size of the local population. The more people, the more chance (and need) for functioning party organizations. The second most important variable, the significance of local government, is also an indicator of size. As predicted, size matters a great deal.

At least in the municipalities with a population of 1,000 or more inhabitants, both social and political participation influence the level of local party institutionalization positively. More organized and participatory local societies are more likely to maintain permanent political organizations.

As it was hypothesized, older populations have more of a crucial resource, time, to organize local party organizations. The positive effect of socioeconomic heterogeneity also conforms to the initial expectations.

The only surprising coefficient is that of the agency. A larger pool of potential political agents was associated with more organized and institutionalized local party organizations. In other words, more affluent and educated societies would provide more opportunity and resources to independent candidates. A possible explanation is that independents can be more viable in municipalities with larger resources due to their enhanced capability to independently influence the local political agenda and transform their own name into a brand name. In poorer municipalities, the concentrated resources of organizations give more advantage to party candidates. This effect can be expected only in local governments where there are no positions that can be gained only by organizations; in the short ticket system, candidates run for themselves. According to this logic, the influence of agency cannot be predicted to be negative in the mixed electoral system.

The only replacement with an alternative indicator that results in some change is the ethnic diversity measure. While ethnic diversity in general does not exert any effect, the specific Roma variable positively contributes to the level of party government.

Table 4.18. Determinants of local party government: short list electoral system

Variables	Regression 1	Regression 2	Regression 3	Regression 4
Population size	.45	**.43**	.45	.43
Functional size	.22	**.15**	.22	.15
Urbanization (population density)	.02	.03	.02	.03
Population instability (migration)	–.01	.02	–.01	.02
Age (% of 60+)	.01	**.06**	.03	.06
Citizens' resources	–.08	**–.10**	–.07	–.09
Socioeconomic heterogeneity (occupations)	.05	**.05**	.04	.04

Variables	Regression 1	Regression 2	Regression 3	Regression 4
Ethnic heterogeneity (minority votes)	.00	–.03		
Roma (Roma minority votes)			.04	.03
Civil society (density)	–.00	**.06**	.00	.05
Participation (turnout)	.13	**.13**	.12	.12
Proximity to centers (metropolitan area)	–.02	–.02	–.02	–.02
Cases	short	short 1,000+	short	short 1,000+
Adjusted R^2	.31	.25	.31	.25

Dependent variable: Local Party Government Index (proportion of votes cast on local party organizations)

4.3.3. Party Government In the Mixed Electoral System

The multivariate analysis of local party government in the population of the municipalities that apply the mixed electoral system produces more significant variables. The most important one, a bit surprisingly, is the net migration balance. The sign of the coefficient is as predicted, only the degree of the effect is unexpected. Party government is sensitive to the change of population.

Functional size exerts a relatively large influence again. Among cities, the level of urbanization also makes a difference, as it was hypothesized. Parties are more significant in older societies, as the hypothesis claims.

The indicator of ethnic diversity has a relatively sizeable negative impact on party government. Nonetheless, the coefficient is insignificant in the case of the indicator of the Roma minority (Regression 2). Non-Roma minorities probably like to be independent. Perhaps the size of the non-Roma minorities, which are quite dispersed in the country and form small subcultures in larger communities, does not hold out of much hope of gaining a position from a compensation list.

The coefficient of the agency variable support the argument put forward in the discussion of the results of the short ticket system. It is positive and quite large. Citizens' resources clearly contribute to the rule of parties in local governments applying the mixed electoral system.

There is also an agglomeration effect. Suburbs have significantly stronger parties than other municipalities of the same size and urbanization. This finding supports the hypothesized impact of the central city on the surrounding environment.

There are two unpredicted relationships in the results. First, the effect of the organizational strength of civil society is negligible. The organization of civil and political societies is not parallel. The second surprising finding is the considerable negative effect of electoral participation even if other variables are controlled for. A likely explanation is that, in the electoral districts, a high turnout gives independents the advantage of attracting voters outside the base of organizations. In other words, institutionalized local party organizations have a more or less stable voting base, which always turn out even if few other citizens bother to vote. By contrast, a high turnout is favorable to party candidates in municipalities where the short ticket system gives independents a head start. An alternative explanation could claim that the relationship is reversed: more voters turn out if powerful independent candidates also run in addition to party candidates. Such a relationship cannot be included in the causal analysis performed in this research.

Table 4.19. Determinants of local party government: mixed electoral system

Variables	**Regression 1**	**Regression 2**
Population size	.03	.03
Functional size	**.28**	.29
Urbanization (population density)	**.19**	.17
Population instability (migration)	**–.33**	–.32
Age (mean age of inhabitants)		
Age (% of 60+)	**.08**	.09
Citizens' resources	**.15**	.18
Socioeconomic heterogeneity (occupations)	.03	.02
Socioeconomic heterogeneity (sectors)		
Ethnic heterogeneity (minority votes)	**–.08**	
Roma (Roma minority votes)		.00
Civil society (density)	.01	.00
Civil society (size)		

Variables	Regression 1	Regression 2
Participation (turnout)	**–.13**	–.15
Proximity to centers (metropolitan area)	**.11**	.11
Proximity to centers (distance from center)		
Cases	mixed	mixed
Adjusted R^2	.29	.29

Dependent variable: Local Party Government Index (proportion of votes cast on local party organizations)

4.4. Conclusion

As a conclusion, I overview the hypotheses of this research. One of the specific hypotheses, which claimed that local party institutionalization is increasing with time, was not supported at all. National parties do not seem to extend their penetration in local governments. Actually, the ratio of municipalities without parties has climbed.

Two hypotheses were strongly supported by the data. The electoral system has a large effect on local party institutionalization. The incentives built in the electoral rules do matter. The other important variable was functional size. More complexity and centrality make municipalities more likely to have strong party organizations.

The importance of some variables depend on the electoral system. Population size is one that has an interaction with electoral rules. Its effect was clearly confirmed in the short ticket system, while disappeared in the mixed system. Similarly, the importance of social and political participations was confirmed only in the case of the short ticket system.

On the other hand, there are hypotheses confirmed only in the case of the mixed electoral system. Population stability and citizens' resources powerfully contribute to the level of local party institutionalization in this category. Urbanization and metropolitan position also seem to matter.

The hypothesis concerning societal diversity (both socioeconomic and ethnic heterogeneity) was the only one that could not be supported in either of the two electoral systems. Functional size and age were the only two factors whose hypothesized effects were proved in both electoral systems.

Table 4.20. The hypotheses and the indicator of local party government

Hypothesis	All cases	Short ticket	Mixed
H1. Electoral system	+ +	n.a.	n.a.
H2. Population size	–	+ +	–
H3. Functional size	+ +	+	+ +
H4. Urbanization	+	–	+
H5. Population stability	–	–	+ +
H6a. Socioeconomic diversity	–	–	–
H6b. Ethnic diversity	–	–	–
H7. Citizens' resources	–	– –	+ +
H8. Age	–	+	+
H9. Civil society	–	+	–
H10. Electoral participation	–	+	– –
H11. Closeness to centers	–	–	+
H15. Age of democracy	–	–	–

++ Strongly confirmed; + Confirmed; – Not confirmed; – – Rejected

Chapter 5: Local Party Loyalty

This chapter concentrates on another indicator of local party institutionalization, the loyalty of candidates to their nominating organizations. While local party government, which the previous chapter focused on, mainly covers the dimension of external importance, local party loyalty captures the internal strength of local parties, both its value infusion dimension and, to a certain degree, its systemness aspect. The level of candidates' continued faithfulness to their nominating political organizations evinces, on the one hand, the degree to which the party has been able to inculcate the party's superiority to any alternatives and, on the other hand, the degree to which the party organization has the empowered techniques to discipline their most prominent members. In this chapter, I first present data on the average level of party loyalty on the local level in Hungary. This section gives the opportunity to test some hypotheses concerning organizational types. Then, the relationships of the independent variables to party loyalty are portrayed one by one. The next section analyzes the effect of all variables on local party loyalty. Finally, the level of association between two indicators of local party institutionalization, party government and party loyalty is measured.

5.1. Loyalty to Local Party Organization

The measurement of party loyalty is based on the tracking of candidates between two elections, in 1998 and 2002. This comparison process took place with certain difficulties, as it was presented in the methodology chapter.

Only one third of the candidates in 1998 were identified in 2002. As mentioned, there are many uncertainties in the identification process, which results in two consequences. From the viewpoint of a country-level assessment, the overall ratio may be somewhat higher due to technical problems. There may be more candidates who stood as candidate both in 1998 and 2002. Since this research concentrates on the determinants of local party institutionalization rather than on its general evaluation, the probable underestimation of party loyalty does not cause major difficulties.

From a methodological point of view, however, the consequence of the low level of precision is more severe. The dataset contains much 'noise', which limits the possibility of finding strong relationships. High coefficients and large proportions of explained variance cannot be expected. The possibility to build causal paths is also limited. Therefore, the findings of this chapter cannot be more than additional information on the level of party institutionalization, which increases the validity of the findings of the previous chapter.

The comparison between more than 63,000 names in 1998 and more than 66,000 names in 2002 resulted in a dataset of almost 25,000 persons who were local candidates in both elections. Among them, more than 6000 were candidates of one or more political organizations. Their overall loyalty rate just exceeds 50 percent. In other words, more than half of the candidates who ran again were nominated by at least one organization that was the same in 1998 and 2002.

The low rate of those who run again (37%) shows that there are always new people who are willing to stand as a candidate. Nevertheless, it also demonstrates that most candidates are not would-be professional politicians resolved on a political career.

Table 5.1. Local party loyalty in Hungary

Electoral system	Candidates in 1998	Candidates in 2002	No. of the persons identified at both elections	% of the identified persons	No. of identified organizational candidates in 1998	No. of loyal candidates	% of loyal candidates
Short list	47,839	52,207	20,742	40%	2,546	1,087	42,7%
Mixed	15,320	14,303	4,054	28%	3,560	2,334	65,6%
Total	63,159	66,507	24,796	37%	6,106	3,421	56,0%

An analysis of loyalty to individual national parties tests some hypotheses formulated in Chapter 2. One of the hypothesis (H13) predicted a higher level of party institutionalization among parties of a national relevance than among other local party organizations. Table 5.2 supports this hypothesis. All the parties but one that had representatives in the Parliament between 1998 and 2002 (the first six parties in the table) had a higher loyalty rate than the country-level average (see Table 5.1). The local chapters of parliamentary parties are more institutionalized than other local party organizations.

The only exception is the Smallholders' Party (FKGP). Its low loyalty rate supports another hypothesis (H14), which claims that the electoral performance of the senior party levels, especially the national party, influences the level of institutionalization of its local chapters. FKGP obtained more than 13 percent of the votes in 1998, but received less than 1 percent in 2002. The reason for this big loss was mainly the character of the party. The FKGP worked as a one man show of a powerful populist politician, who was forced to resign before the elections.

The collapse of the charismatic leadership lead to the electoral catastrophe. Charismatic leadership is by definition against institutionalization. The lack of institutionalization led to disorder and panic, which became only more intense after the disastrous parliamentary elections. The under-institutionalization of the party led to the flight of its local politicians.

Nonetheless, the fate of a party that lost the national elections is not necessarily doomed on the local level. MIÉP, the extreme right party that won MP seats in 1998 (to the surprise of many commentators), fell out of the Parliament in 2002. Still, it could maintain a high loyalty rate on the local level. The reason probably lies in the ideological character of the party. Ideological incentives provide a high level of value infusion, which helps to keep the soldiers of the party. The electoral loss is not what matters, but the overall level of institutionalization of the party.

Table 5.2. Candidates' loyalty to nationally relevant parties

Party	**No. of candidates both in 1998 and 2002**	**Loyalty rate**	**No. of candidates both in 1998 and 2002**	**Loyalty rate**	**Overall loyalty rate**
MSZP	403	78%	642	88%	84%
FIDESZ-MPSZ	323	52%	552	78%	65%
SZDSZ	65	54%	327	81%	75%
MDF	206	52%	389	76%	65%
FKGP	149	18%	217	46%	29%
MIÉP	43	48%	208	75%	69%
KDNP	54	25%	173	60%	45%
Munkáspárt	91	57%	187	87%	74%
Lungo Drom	50	63%	10	71%	65%

The last hypothesis (H12) that can be tested by means of aggregate data proposes that civil society organizations acting as local parties are less institutionalized than the local chapters of national parties. The first evidence of the validity of this hypothesis is the conspicuous volatility of civil society organizations. The local chapters of national parties are more durable. Actually, two hypotheses (H11 and H12) are related, as most local organizations belong to parliamentary parties. Thus, the durability of parties is partly due to the higher level of institutionalization of parliamentary parties. Furthermore, the aggregate loyalty data also support the hypothesis about a difference between parties and associations.

In the mixed electoral system, national party-nominated candidates showed a high loyalty (74%), while only half of the candidates of civil society organizations (more precisely 48%, if mixed candidates are left out) maintained their organizational affiliation. The same difference can be observed in the smaller municipalities of the short ticket system (47% and 22%, respectively). The hypothesis H12 is largely confirmed by the data.

Table 5.3. Local party loyalty in Hungary by organizational types

Electoral system	**Local chapters of national parties**	**Civil society organizations**	**Total**
Short list	47%	22%	43%
Mixed	74%	48%	58%
Total	62%	42%	52%

Two interesting questions remain. (1) Are incumbents more loyal? In other words, do those who failed at previous elections tend to turn to another party for nomination? (2) What is the status of the independent's position? Does this status differ in the two electoral systems?

A very intuitive idea is to suppose that those who unsuccessfully bid for a councilor seat at one election are more active to find another local party or form a new one to increase their chances at the next election. Only the strong, well-established organizations with much ideological, solidity or material incentives can keep disappointed members. And even they are more likely to hold winners than losers. Nevertheless, a counter-hypothesis is also possible. Incumbents may reach such a level of name recognition and popularity that they are better off with an independent candidacy or a nomination by an association formed as their personal local party. The arguments lead to the statement that well-known, respected personalities jeopardize the institutionalization of local parties. This may especially apply to powerful mayoral candidates and incumbents who have a very good position in a certain part of the town.

In the mixed electoral system, the data provides more evidence for the logic of disappointment than the logic of the independent political businesses. 1665 candidates won a seat in council in 1998 (13% of candidates; an average of 7 candidates per district). Three in four (74% or 1225) made an attempt to get reelected in 2002. (Actually, two thirds of them were successful, which demonstrates the significance of incumbency.) Their loyalty was above average (65%). Electoral loss, however, encourages change. Almost half (46%) of those who failed in 1998 ran under a different flag in 2002. Interestingly enough, incumbents' loyalty to their nominating organization is only marginally higher than the faithfulness of those who failed at the previous election. Although this does not support the idea that strong incumbents tend to defect, it does not reject it either. Such a tendency would not be against the endogenous logic of the short ticket system.

Table 5.4. Local party loyalty in Hungary by incumbency

Electoral system	Incumbents	Challengers	Total
Short list	43%	42%	42%
Mixed	74%	46%	58%
Total	61%	44%	56%

Is there a passage-way between independents and organizational candidates? In the mixed electoral system, the independent status is transitory. More than half of those who stood as independent candidates in 1998 agreed with an organization (or formed one for themselves) by 2002. On the other hand, almost half (274 of 555) of those who ran as independents in 2002 had an organizational nomination in 1998. Most independents were or will be a candidate of an organization. Incumbents leaving their organization become independent or form a local association for themselves more frequently than they simply change their background organization. More than 70 percent of incumbents leaving a party become either independent or join a civil society organization.

In the short ticket system, the situation seems to be reversed: most organizational candidates were or will be independent. 44 percent of those who were nominated by a loyal party organization in 1998 ran as independents in 2002. Three quarters of the rest remained loyal to at least one of their nominating organizations and one quarter made an attempt with another logo after their name. On the other hand, one third of the organizational candidates in 2002 were independent at the previous election. The commuting between the independent status and organizational nomination seems quite easy in the electoral system based on short tickets.

The general conclusion is that the electoral system has a great effect on the strategies would-be councilors choose. More can be learned about that in the following bivariate and multivariate analyses.

5.2. Bivariate Associations With Local Party Loyalty

This section examines the relationship between local party loyalty and the same potentially explanatory variables as in the previous chapter on local party government. Not only are the simple correlations studied, but also the other variables that may show the spurious nature of the relationship. As in the previous chapter, the full population (all local governments, all candidates) is analyzed, so only coefficients (without significance levels) are presented.

5.2.1. Electoral System

Already Table 5.1 and 5.3 showed how significant the difference between the two electoral systems is. While two-third of those who were not independent candidates in the mixed system in 1998 remained loyal to at least one of their nominating organizations in 2002, more than half of the organizational candidates in the short list system became independent or were supported by another party. The value infusion of party leaders is in all probability lower and the personification of local party organizations is higher in the local governments of the short system than those in the mixed one. The existence of compensation lists for nominating organizations offers incentives for local politicians to deepen their cooperation and make it permanent.

Table 5.5. Number of representatives by legal categories

Population categories	'Short tickets'	Districts	Compensation lists
0–100	3		
101–600	5		
601–1,300	7		
1,301–3,000	9		
3,001–5,000	11		
5,001–10,000	13		
10,001–25,000	5,001–10,000	10	7
25,001–50,000		14	9
50,001–60,000		15	10
60,001–70,000		16	11
More than 70,000		+1 per additional 10,000 inhabitants	+1 per additional 15,000 inhabitants

Source: Bőhm and Szoboszlai 1996: 917.

But how strong are those incentives? While the size of municipality population does not modify the influence of the electoral system, the inclusion of the indicator of functional size in the multivariate analysis makes the effect of electoral rules much less important. In other words, the average level of party institutionalization is only a little different in municipalities of the same functional significance but in different electoral systems.

Table 5.6. Electoral system and party loyalty

Variables	Regression 1	Regression 2	Regression 3	Regression 4
Electoral system	.28	.25	.06	.07
Population size		.06		–.01
Functional size			.33	.33

Dependent variable: Party Loyalty Index (the proportion of candidates maintaining the same party nomination)

5.2.2. Proximity to Centers

Party loyalty may be higher in municipalities that are close to central cities where the national or regional headquarters of country-level parties are located. The proximity to centers is indicated by two variables: belonging to a metropolitan area (a dummy variable) and the distance from the nearest regional center (in kilometers). The coefficients are in the expected direction, but they are very small. The level of party loyalty does not seem to depend on the proximity of municipalities to political centers.

Table 5.7. Proximity to centers and party loyalty

Variables	Regr. 1	Regr. 2	Regr. 3	Regr. 4	Regr. 5	Regr. 6	Regr. 7	Regr. 8	Regr. 9	Regr. 10
Agglomeration	.03	.02	.02	.01	–.02					
Distance from the nearest center						–.05	–.02	–.02	–.02	.03
Population size			–.01					–.02		
Electoral system			.06					.07		
Functional size		.37	.33	.26	.19		.37	.33	.26	.19
Cases	all	all	all	short	mixed	all	all	all	short	mixed

Dependent variable: Party Loyalty Index (the proportion of candidates maintaining the same party nomination)

5.2.3. Population Size

Population seems to be a good predictor of party loyalty with a relatively high correlation to the aggregate loyalty indicator. The impact of population size is especially high in the short list system of elections, though it is not particularly low in the mixed system either. Still, its effect becomes insignificant when the indicator of the competing size variable, functional significance, is also taken into account. The effect of the electoral system has the same diminishing effect, but, as it has been shown above, this is also a spurious influence of functional size.

Table 5.8. Population size and party loyalty

Variables	Regr. 1	Regr. 2	Regr. 3	Regr. 4	Regr. 5	Regr. 6	Regr. 7	Regr. 8
Population size	.21	.02	.04	–.01	.23	.05	.10	.03
Functional size		.36		.33		.22		.19
Electoral system			.30	.07				
Cases	all	all	all	all	short	short	mixed	mixed

Dependent variable: Party Loyalty Index (the proportion of candidates maintaining the same party nomination)

5.2.4. Municipality Significance

The discussion above has already demonstrated the explanatory power of functional size. This effect is not really changed with the inclusion of the size of population. The electoral system has only a small influence, as the effect of functional size is somewhat higher in the short list system than in the mixed one.

Table 5.9. Functional size and party loyalty

Variables	Regr. 1	Regr. 2	Regr. 3	Regr. 4	Regr. 5	Regr. 6	Regr. 7	Regr. 8
Functional size	.37	.36	.33	.33	.26	.22	.20	.19
Population size		.02		–.01		.05		.03
Electoral system			.06	.07				
Cases	all	all	all	all	short	short	mixed	mixed

Dependent variable: Party Loyalty Index (the proportion of candidates maintaining the same party nomination)

5.2.5. Urbanization

The more urban the municipality, the more likely that local politicians remain loyal to their organizations, and their organizations do not disappear between two elections. The urban effect seems to be a threshold-like one, as it makes a much larger difference in smaller than larger local governments (see Regression 5 and 7 in Table 5.8.). The urban effect seems to largely depend on the functional significance of urban settlements, which can be seen by the drop in the coefficient of urbanization when functional size is also taken into account.

Table 5.10. Functional size and party loyalty

Variables	Regr. 1	Regr. 2	Regr. 3	Regr. 4	Regr. 5	Regr. 6	Regr. 7	Regr. 8
Urbanization (population density)	.22	.16	.08	.07	.13	.08	.01	.03
Functional size			.34	.32		.24		.21
Population size		.12						
Electoral system			.06	.04				
Cases	all	all	all	all	short	short	mixed	mixed

Dependent variable: Party Loyalty Index (the proportion of candidates maintaining the same party nomination)

5.2.6. Population Stability

As in the analysis of party government, the stability of the local population seems to have a positive impact on local party loyalty (see Table 5.9). Citizens who are more embedded in the local society are more likely to hold parties accountable. A change in affiliation has a more serious consequence in a more stable electorate than in an unstable one. The influence of population instability, measured by the net balance of local immigration and emigration, somewhat decreases when functional size is controlled for, but keeps most of its explanatory power.

Table 5.11. Population instability and local party loyalty

Variables	Regr. 1	Regr. 2	Regr. 3	Regr. 4	Regr. 5	Regr. 6	Regr. 7
Population change (abs. of net migration balance)	–.09	–.08	–.07	–.07	–.05	–.07	–.05
Population size		.20		.05	–.01		
Electoral system			.28	.24	.07		
Functional size					.32		
Cases	all	all	all	all	all	short	mixed

Dependent variable: Party Loyalty Index (the proportion of candidates maintaining the same party nomination)

5.2.7. Age composition

The hypothesis of this research says that local populations with more senior citizens are more likely to produce institutionalized local parties. From the viewpoint of party loyalty, one may argue that older people tend to pay more attention to local politicians' political maneuvers. Thus, a change in affiliation or the dissolution of a local party organization require more credible justification in older than younger societies. The data, presented in Table 5.10, seems to reject the hypothesis outright. However, the addition of functional size to the analysis shows a different picture. The effect of age disappears in the smaller communities of the short ticket system, while it shows a positive value, the right direction from the perspective of the hypothesis, in the mixed system. The multivariate analysis will tell more about the impact of age.

Table 5.12. Age and local party loyalty

Variables	Regr. 1	Regr. 2	Regr. 3	Regr. 4	Regr. 5	Regr. 6	Regr. 7
Age (% of 60+)	–.10	–.07	–.05	.00	.00	.00	.06
Population size		.20			–.01		

Variables	Regr. 1	Regr. 2	Regr. 3	Regr. 4	Regr. 5	Regr. 6	Regr. 7
Electoral system			.27		.07		
Functional size				.37	.33	.26	.19
Cases	all	all	all	all	All	short	mixed

Dependent variable: Party Loyalty Index (the proportion of candidates maintaining the same party nomination)

5.2.8. Citizens' Resources

The resources of the citizenry, both education and income, is conceptualized as an important contributor to the explanation of the variance in local party institutionalization. More resourceful citizens have more time and skills to follow what is happening in the local political theater. Moreover, they can support local parties by means of voluntary work and monetary and in-kind donations, and better understand the importance of this support. As a result, local politicians have to act more carefully and responsibly, as they can lose valuable contributions.

Indeed, the simple correlation (see Table 5.11) shows a high impact of citizens' resources on party loyalty on the local level. However, it implies a spurious size effect as well. Functional complexity especially reduces the influence of citizens' resources. Still, it seems to preserve a non-mediated, direct effect, which supports the hypothesis.

Table 5.13. Citizens' resources and local party loyalty

Variables	Regr. 1	Regr. 2	Regr. 3	Regr. 4	Regr. 5	Regr. 6	Regr. 7
Citizens' resources	.25	.19	.14	.05	.05	.04	.09
Population size		.12			–.01		
Electoral system			.21		.06		
Functional size				.34	.31	.24	.20
Cases	all	all	all	all	all	short	mixed

Dependent variable: Party Loyalty Index (the proportion of candidates maintaining the same party nomination)

5.2.9. Socioeconomic Heterogeneity

Socioeconomic diversity is predicted to boost the chances of local party institutionalization in at least two ways: (1) more diverse, i.e. more complex, local society is in need of more coordination, and (2) more distinct societal groups are more likely to maintain local party organizations that represent their interests. In general, the data confirms the validity of this logic. Cleaned of the spurious effect of (functional) size, socioeconomic heterogeneity has a significant positive effect on the level of loyalty to local party organizations. Nonetheless, the effect seems to be the reverse in the case of the municipalities that vote according to the mixed system.

Table 5.14. Socioeconomic heterogeneity and local party loyalty

Variables	**Regr. 1**	**Regr. 2**	**Regr. 3**	**Regr. 4**	**Regr. 5**	**Regr. 6**	**Regr. 7**
Socio-economic hetero-geneity	.15	.12	.11	.06	.06	.06	–.13
Population size		.19			–.01		
Electoral system			.26		.07		
Functional size				.36	.31	.24	.19
Cases	all	all	all	all	all	short	mixed

Dependent variable: Party Loyalty Index (the proportion of candidates maintaining the same party nomination)

5.2.10. Ethnic Heterogeneity

The other aspect of societal heterogeneity, ethnic diversity, is expected to have the same effect as socioeconomic diversity. The argument behind the hypothesis is similar. When controlled for functional size, the association between ethnic heterogeneity and local party loyalty turns in the right direction. The relationship of the Roma minority is similar. However, as in the case of socioeconomic diversity, there is a negative association in the mixed electoral system and a positive one in the short ticket system. This applies to minority representation in general and the presence of an active Roma minority in particular. I return to this question when discussing the results of the multivariate analysis.

Table 5.15. Ethnic heterogeneity and local party loyalty

Variables	Regr. 1	Regr. 2	Regr. 3	Regr. 4	Regr. 5	Regr. 6	Regr. 7	Regr. 8
Ethnic minority	.00	.04	.05	−.14				
Roma minority					−.04	.04	.04	−.19
Electoral system								
Functional size		.38	.26	.17		.38	.27	.18
Cases	all	all	short	mixed	all	all	short	mixed

Dependent variable: Party Loyalty Index (the proportion of candidates maintaining the same party nomination)

5.2.11. Civil Society

A dense civil society is more likely to provide both the resources that embed local parties and to be able to hold local party organizations accountable. On the other hand, more civic groups may produce more activists who may contribute to the existence of political organizations, but who also may increase the chances of mushrooming short-lived parties. As Table 5.14 demonstrates, the actual effect of the strength of local civil society on party loyalty is negligible. No relationship could be confirmed.

Table 5.16. Density of local civil society and party loyalty

Variables	Regr. 1	Regr. 2	Regr. 3	Regr. 4	Regr. 5	Regr. 6	Regr. 7
Civil society density	.01	−.02	−.02	−.01	−.02	−.01	−.01
Population size		.21			−.01		
Electoral system			.28		.07		
Functional size				.37	.33	.26	.21
Cases	all	all	all	all	all	short	mixed

Dependent variable: Party Loyalty Index (the proportion of candidates maintaining the same party nomination)

5.2.12. Political Participation

A more active local society is more likely to embed party organizations in local society, provide activists and hold local politicians more accountable. Politicians are forced to remain faithful to their nominating organization, as party organizations are stronger (e.g. they have more volunteers) and can offer more incentives, there is more competition for the candidacy, and more politically active and capable citizens demand a credible justification for the change of party color. Moreover, party loyalty is higher simply because local parties that are more embedded and have enough activists are less likely to fall apart.

Unlike local party government, the data do not provide much evidence for the effect of electoral participation on party loyalty. Turnout has a large coefficient in the simple correlation between participation and party loyalty, but it is negative. When size (especially functional size) is controlled for, the sign of the coefficient becomes correct, but its magnitude is small. What is more, there is a difference in the direction of the effect between large and small municipalities. One of the plausible explanations for the lack of effect is that electoral activity is only a segment of political participation. The specific nature of the electoral participation also offers an explanation for the difference in direction. Conforming with the requirements of multivariate models, the research design required a decision about the direction of the suspected causation before the analysis. Since the research has a dependent variable, electoral participation was naturally regarded as an independent variable. However, as it was mentioned in Chapter 3, the relationship may be reciprocal. Thus, the secession of a wing of a well-known local party certainly lessens the overall level of loyalty rate in the municipality, but may at the same time increase electoral participation by mobilizing voters. A change may involve a new segment of the local society into politics, reactivate passive voters, attract the attention of the local media that like spectacular events, and make the competition more open.

All of these effects may result in higher mobilization at the election in the mixed electoral system where the political life is organized around party organizations. As the introductory section of this section has demonstrated, the lack of loyalty is not extraordinary in the small ticket system, which does not encourage parties as much as the mixed system. The reciprocal nature of the relationship and the different status of parties may explain the difference between the two electoral systems.

Table 5.17. Electoral participation and party loyalty

Variables	**Regression 1**	**Regression 2**	**Regression 3**	**Regression 4**	**Regression 5**
Electoral participation	−.23	.04	.03	.04	−.08
Population size			−.01		

Variables	Regression 1	Regression 2	Regression 3	Regression 4	Regression 5
Electoral system			.06		
Functional size		.40	.36	.29	.20
Cases	all	all	all	short	mixed

Dependent variable: Party Loyalty Index (the proportion of candidates maintaining the same party nomination)

5.3. Multivariate Analysis

After the exploration of the bivariate associations, a multivariate regression analysis produces the actual weight and significance of the factors listed above. The independent variables are the same as in the previous chapter. The results can be seen in Table 5.17. Unfortunately, the number of cases is quite low, so some of the relationships with a relatively high coefficient did not prove significant.

The first, quite surprising finding is that the electoral system became insignificant when all other factors are also included. As the analysis above already showed, it is the functional size that decreases the effect of the variables of population size and electoral system. In the multivariate analysis the centrality and significance of municipalities became by far the most important factor that determines the level of the loyalty of party members to their organizations. The more resources available for distribution and influence and the more attention representatives enjoy, the more loyalty the local parties can expect from their members. Population size does not directly affect this indicator of local party institutionalization; its influence is mediated by functional size and urbanization. The urban effect may be related to the existence of a competitive media market, which is not measured in this research.

As in the case of party government, the stability of local population increases the probability of stable parties. The more the composition of the local society changes, the less loyal the candidates are. Heterogeneity has an influence similar to its effect on party government. Both societal and ethnic heterogeneity increase the likeliness of party loyalty. That suggests the existence of local parties that are to a certain degree tied to socioeconomic and ethnic groups. Candidates who publicly identified themselves with the representation of a societal group may lose more credibility if they leave the local party that labels itself as the organizational representative of the group. This stabilizes the relationship between local party organizations and their most ambitious members.

Citizens' resources are a powerful determinant of local party loyalty. More educated citizenry with more income are more likely to result in an empowered local society, which is able to defend its interests. More attention to local parties responsible for representation makes the organizations more embedded and controlled. Changing affiliation would cause a loss of credibility and campaign support in a society that has the individual resources to hold local politicians accountable by the direction of resources and voting.

Neither the aging nor the average age of the local society significantly affects the level of local party institutionalization, indicated by party loyalty. Social and political participation have no significant effect, though they operate in the same direction as in the analysis of party government and their level of significance is close to what is conventionally accepted. Neither the belonging to a metropolitan area nor the more detailed measurement of distance from a center are significant.

Given the small size of the sample and the normal shape of the distribution of the party loyalty variable, a separate treatment of the electoral system is hardly feasible and necessary. The most relevant finding of the separate regressions (Table 5.17) is that agency becomes more important in larger municipalities as in the analysis of party government.

Table 5.18. Multivariate analysis of local party loyalty

Variables	**Regression 1**	**Regression 2**	**Regression 3**	**Regression 4**	**Regression 5**
Electoral system	.04	.07	n.a.	n.a.	n.a.
Population size	–.04	–.02	.04	.07	–.05
Functional size	**.30**	**.32**	**.20**	**.18**	**.15**
Urbanization (population density)	.07	.08	.07	.08	**–.11**
Population instability (migration)	–.09	–.08	**–.10**	–.08	**–.16**
Age (% of 60+)	.02	.03	.02	.04	**.13**
Citizens' resources	.08	.06	.07	.04	**.35**
Socioeconomic heterogeneity (occupations)	.06	.02	.06	.02	–.06

Variables	Regression 1	Regression 2	Regression 3	Regression 4	Regression 5
Ethnic heterogeneity (minority votes)	.05	.06	.05	.07	−.08
Civil society (density)	−.05	−.09	−.04	−.08	**−.11**
Participation (turnout)	.04	**.10**	.05	**.12**	**−.10**
Proximity to centers (metropolitan area)	.01	.05	.00	.04	**−.26**
Cases	all	1,000+	short	short 1,000+	mixed system
Adjusted R^2	.15	.14	.08	.14	.04

Dependent variable: Party Loyalty Index (proportion of votes cast on local party organizations)

5.4. The Association of Party Government and Party Loyalty

In Chapter 1, I defined local party institutionalization as a multidimensional concept. Every multidimensional concept faces the methodological challenge of a weak or nonexistent correlation between the indicators of its dimensions. Thus, this research also has to address the problem of the association between party government, measuring mainly the centrality of parties in a loyal community and party loyalty, assessing primarily the value infusion in local party organizations.

The best way to measure the association of the two indicators is to observe the results of a Pearson-moment correlation. Given the amount of probable imprecision in the measurement of party loyalty, the two variables have a moderately high coefficient (.41) and the level of significance is very high (less than 0.0001). This does not change at all if population size is controlled for. However, a control for functional size decreases the coefficient (to.29), though it remains very significant (still less than 0.0001). Thus, the interconnection between party loyalty and party government is not spurious (even if functional size adds to the strength of the association).

Summing up, the two dimensions of local party institutionalization, indicated by party government and party loyalty, do 'hang together'. Nevertheless, their correlation is not very high. This is a clear sign of an independent life of these dimensions. Their interdependence is only partial.

5.5. Conclusion

This chapter has examined the systematic factors that account for the preference of loyalty to exit. Three specific hypotheses were overwhelmingly supported. There is indeed a difference in the local chapters of national parties and social organizations acting as parties in terms of their level of institutionalization. Within the category of national parties, parliamentary parties proved to be much more stable than other organizations. The electoral performance on the country level also affects the level of institutionalization on the local level.

The effect of the electoral system points in the expected direction, but is much weaker than in the case of party government. Functional size and population stability had large impact on the level of party loyalty, clearly supporting their respective hypotheses. Citizens' resources play a minor role in the short ticket system and a really major one in the mixed system. Age also has a consistent expected effect.

The hypotheses concerning population size, societal heterogeneity, and electoral participation are supported only in the short ticket system, but not in the mixed system. The case of turnout is especially interesting, as it has a large effect in both systems – but in different directions.

Unlike party government, the variable of civil society strength proved to have a consistent negative effect on party loyalty. This was the only factor that had a totally unconfirmed hypothesized effect.

Table 5.19. The hypotheses and the index of local party loyalty

Hypothesis	All cases	Short ticket	Mixed
H1. Electoral system	+	n.a.	n.a.
H2. Population size	–	+	–
H3. Functional size	+ +	+ +	+ +
H4. Urbanization	+	+	– –
H5. Population stability	+ +	+ +	+ +
H6a. Socioeconomic diversity	+	+	–
H6b. Ethnic diversity	+	+	–
H7. Citizens' resources	+	+	+ + +
H8. Age	+	+	+ +

Hypothesis	All cases	Short ticket	Mixed
H9. Civil society	–	–	– –
H10. Electoral participation	+	+ +	– –
H11. Closeness to centers	+	+	– – –
H12. Legal difference	+ +	+ +	+ +
H13. Parliamentary parties	+ +	+ +	+ +
H14. Country-level performance	+	+	+

++ Strongly confirmed; + Confirmed; – Not confirmed; – – Rejected

The final conclusion that can be drawn from this chapter is that the two indicators of local party government analyzed so far, party government and party loyalty, do 'hang together'. Nevertheless, their association is not extremely high, which emphasizes the differences between the dimensions of the concept of party institutionalization.

Chapter 6: Causal Models

As a last step, a causal analysis presents the indirect effect of more distant variables on local party government. The analysis is repeated for the two electoral systems separately.

6.1. Indirect Effects

The causal model can be simplified by focusing only on those variables that have a significant impact on the level of local party institutionalization. It is not worth investigating the variables that have only a small impact on the dependent variable. The weight of an indirect route from variable A via variable B to the dependent variable is computed as the multiplication of the effects of the relationships between A and B and between B and the dependent variable (see Section 3.4 for more discussion of causal modeling). If any of the two relationships is very small, the indirect effect will be necessarily tiny. For example, the relationship between A and B may be relatively important, say 0.4, but a low coefficient, say 0.03, between B and the dependent variable leads to an indirect effect of (0.4x0.03)=0.012. Partial coefficients close to zero make the indirect effect also close to zero.

Consequently, it is enough to concentrate on the following variables: population size, functional size, urbanization, migration, citizens' resources, and social and political participation. Other variables will be included into the models explaining the variance of the selected variables close to local party institutionalization, but their direct impact on the dependent variable will not be examined.

6.1.1. Political Participation

Political participation is the most politically independent variable and is the closest to the dependent variable, local party institutionalization. The literature on the indicator of political participation, turnout, is immense. The aim of this project is not to contribute to this literature, but to identify the magnitude and direction of the relationships of certain factors with turnout within a wider causal model.

Some of the findings, presented in Table 6.1, are unsurprising. More educated, stable and horizontally organized citizenry are more willing to turnout to vote. The functional significance of municipalities has a major negative impact. Interpreting this variable as a dimension of size makes this effect compatible with the most frequent (though not absolutely universal) observation of the literature: the larger the municipality, the lower the turnout. The effect of population size is similar.

Nonetheless, there are some unexpected results. The most peculiar one is the negative sign of the combined variable of citizens' income and education (though the coefficient itself is small). However, the separate analysis of the two electoral systems (Regression 4 and 5 in Table 6.1) points to the importance of empowered agency in the case of the mixed electoral system, while citizens' resources have no significance in the smaller municipalities. Both resources are needed to reach a high level of turnout. It is tempting to draw individual-level conclusions, but this is hardly possible without risking ecological fallacy.

Table 6.1. Determinants of political participation (electoral turnout)

Variable	Regression 1	Regression 2	Regression 3	Regression 4	Regression 5
Mixed electoral system	**.11**	–.01	n. a.	n.a.	n. a.
Population size	–.01	–.09	**–.15**	**–.32**	**–.38**
Functional size	**–.65**	**–.50**	**–.45**	**–.17**	**–.12**
Urbanization (population density)	.03	.05	.06	**.11**	**–.28**
Population instability (migration)	.01	–.08	.02	–.06	**–.12**
Age (% of 60+)	.08	–.03	.09	–.06	**–.12**
Citizens' resources	**–.12**	–.01	**–.14**	–.03	**.46**
Socioeconomic heterogeneity	.06	**.14**	.05	**.15**	.04
Ethnic heterogeneity	.01	.04	.01	.04	**.14**
Civil society density (nonprofits)	**.13**	**.21**	**.12**	**.15**	**.20**
Proximity to centers: (Metropolitan area)	–.04	–.07	–.01	–.03	**–.11**
Adjusted R^2	.48	.27	.44	.23	.28
Cases	All	1,000+	Short ticket	1,000–10,000	Mixed system

6.1.2. Social Participation

The strength of civil society is also a variable relatively close to local party institutionalization. As Chapter 3 indicated, the measurement of the density of civil society organizations leads to misleading conclusions if very small communities are also included. The large difference between Regression 1 and 2 in Table 6.2 clearly corroborates the modifying effect of tiny local governments.

The two most important determinants of civil society density are citizens' resources and functional size. It is not surprising that the extent of formal social participation largely depends on the level of education and income. Those individual resources are crucial to a successful organization of civil groups. Interpreted in functional terms, size is a major factor in both electoral systems. The influence of population size is negative in the short ticket system when functional size is also controlled for. The positive effect of socioeconomic heterogeneity was also predictable. More heterogeneous local societies imply more distinct interests, which, in turn, tends to produce more civic groups. Suburbs have less civil society groups on average because their inhabitants usually join organizations in the central cities. A replacement of the metropolitan dummy with the continuous measure of the distance from the nearest regional center does not alter the result either.

Table 6.2. Determinants of the density of civil society

Variable	Regression 1	Regression 2	Regression 3	Regression 4	Regression 5
Population size	.04	.04	**–.20**	**–.47**	–.01
Functional size	–.06	–.06	**.11**	**.30**	**.16**
Urbanization (population density)	–.08	**–.14**	–.05	–.07	–.09
Population instability (migration)	.04	**–.11**	.05	–.08	**–.19**
Age (% of 60+)	**.25**	**.10**	**.24**	.04	.04
Citizens' resources	**.21**	**.50**	**.18**	**.41**	**.74**
Socioeconomic heterogeneity	.06	**.15**	.05	**.14**	**.12**

Variable	Regression 1	Regression 2	Regression 3	Regression 4	Regression 5
Ethnic heterogeneity	.03	.01	.03	.01	.05
Proximity to centers: (Metropolitan area)	–.07	**–.19**	–.04	**–.10**	**–.26**
Adjusted R^2	.09	.18	.10	.22	.61
Cases	All	1,000+	Short	1,000–10,000	Mixed

6.1.3. Functional Size

The significance of municipalities proved to be a powerful determinant of loyal party institutionalization. In general, it is a fertile variable, which influences the level of several other factors. As an indicator of size, it correlates very well with another measure of size, the population. However, the association between them is far from being perfect (the Pearson correlation coefficient is only 0.5). There may be some other factors that influence the level of functional size. One candidate is the level of urbanization. Indeed, it has a large impact on functional size, even if population size is also included. Another potential predictor may be the belonging to a metropolitan area. Suburbs may lose administrative competence and economic functions to the regional center. Indeed, the variable of agglomeration positively correlates with functional size.

The association of the index of functional size and population is not fully linear. Thus, it is important to divide the dataset to find more fitting lines. To be compatible with the research design the cut-off point is 10,000 inhabitants, which is the borderline between the two electoral systems. The findings are quite different from the results of the regression on all cases. The importance of urbanization becomes much less significant in both size categories. Population size is the main predictor in the subset of small communities, while it is less important in the group of large municipalities. As expected, the sign of the agglomeration variable became negative and quite large in the case of the large municipality subset. Local governments in the shadow of a central city have much less significance. The division into two subsets resulted in much better explanation of the variance.

Table 6.3. Determinants of functional size

Variable	Regression 1	Regression 2	Regression 3	Regression 4	Regression 5
Population size	**.34**	**.45**	**.84**	**.78**	**.25**
Urbanization (population density)	**.30**	**.18**	.00	–.06	.06
Proximity to centers: (Metropolitan area)	.00	**–.10**	–.07	**–.17**	**–.68**
Adjusted R^2	.32	.31	.69	.59	.56
Cases	All	1,000+	Short ticket	1,000–10,000	Mixed system

6.1.4. Urbanization

The two variables in the model that may affect the level of urbanization, measured as the density of population, are population size and suburban areas. As expected, the effect of population size is quite large and the association is positive. The impact remains practically the same when the subsets of the two electoral systems are analyzed separately. It is not surprising that municipalities in metropolitan areas are also more urbanized than other communities of the same size but of different location.

Table 6.4. Determinants of urbanization

Variable	Regression 1	Regression 2	Regression 3	Regression 4	Regression 5
Population size	**.52**	**.50**	**.41**	**.27**	**.50**
Proximity to centers: (Metropolitan area)	**.23**	**.25**	**.17**	**.21**	**.44**
Adjusted R^2	.34	.31	.22	.13	.36
Cases	All	1,000+	Short ticket	1,000–10,000	Mixed system

6.1.5. Population Instability

Population instability is measured by the ratio of the absolute value of migration to the total population in 1990. The hypothesis that population is more stable in smaller communities than in larger ones was not entirely proved. In the category of small municipalities, the hypothesis does not hold (which can be the effect of the high loss of population of the very small communities). The underlying idea of the hypothesis seems to be true if urbanization is taken into account. Denser communities are more unstable than more rural ones. Interpreting size as the importance of municipality, the results consistently show that more central and complex communities can retain their population more than other municipalities of the same size and urbanization. Finally, metropolitan areas are clearly less stable than other parts of the country. Moving in and out is a more usual phenomenon in suburbs than in more remote areas.

Table 6.5. Determinants of population instability

Variable	**Regression 1**	**Regression 2**	**Regression 3**	**Regression 4**	**Regression 5**
Population size	–.07	–.07	.09	.04	–.06
Functional size	**–.15**	**–.18**	**–.20**	**–.16**	**–.24**
Urbanization (population density)	**.15**	**.15**	**.13**	**.13**	**.12**
Socioeconomic heterogeneity	.07	**.11**	.07	**.11**	.08
Age (% of 60+)	–.01	**–.16**	.00	**–.16**	–.07
Proximity to centers: (Metropolitan area)	**.21**	**.24**	**.19**	**.21**	**.50**
Adjusted R^2	.08	.18	.07	.16	.57
Cases	All	1,000+	Short ticket	1,000–10,000	Mixed system

6.1.6. Citizens' Resources

The variable of citizens' resources is a combination of the level of education and the local standard of living. It aims to indicate the degree to which individuals with a potential of political effectiveness are available locally. As the results demonstrate, functional size and level of urbanization and metropolitan location are the three crucial determinants. Moreover, the age of the local society also has a significant impact. This effect is negative, as young and middle-age people tend to have more resources: they are more educated and earn more.

Table 6.6. Determinants of citizens' resources

Variable	Regression 1	Regression 2	Regression 3	Regression 4	Regression 5
Population size	.01	.07	–.08	–.04	**.13**
Functional size	**.35**	**.21**	**.36**	**.17**	**.39**
Urbanization (population density)	**.30**	**.34**	**.28**	**.32**	**.37**
Age (% of 60+)	–.03	**–.15**	–.03	**–.16**	**–.22**
Socioeconomic heterogeneity	.04	.01	.04	.02	.06
Minority	–.01	–.01	–.01	–.01	–.06
Proximity to centers: (Metropolitan area)	**.20**	**.23**	**.21**	**.25**	**.44**
Adjusted R^2	.43	.42	.33	.29	.53
Cases	All	1,000+	Short ticket	1,000–10,000	Mixed system

6.1.7. Socioeconomic Heterogeneity

Socioeconomic heterogeneity is measured here as an index of the proportion of occupational groups in the local job market. The most important determinant included in the model is functional size. The more functions the municipality fulfills, the more diverse its local society. In addition, it seems that metropolitan areas are also more colorful places. Heterogeneity must have other determinants too, as the four variables used here explain only a low proportion of the variance.

Table 6.7. Determinants of socioeconomic heterogeneity

Variable	Regression 1	Regression 2	Regression 3	Regression 4	Regression 5
Population size	–.04	**.02**	**–.13**	–.04	**.20**
Functional size	**.41**	**.32**	**.46**	**.28**	**.36**

Variable	**Regression 1**	**Regression 2**	**Regression 3**	**Regression 4**	**Regression 5**
Urbanization (population density)	−.05	**−.10**	−.02	−.07	**−.28**
Proximity to centers: (Metropolitan area)	.08	**.13**	.08	**.13**	**.32**
Adjusted R^2	.14	.10	.13	.07	.10
Cases	All	1,000+	Short ticket	1,000–10,000	Mixed system

6.1.8. Age

Three variables within the model shed some light on what determines the age of municipalities. Depopulation and aging characterize rural rather than urban areas. Suburbs are also relatively young, as they attract both the young and middle aged population of the central cities and the surrounding countryside. Nonetheless, these factors explain only a small part of the variance.

Table 6.8. Determinants of the age of municipality population

Variable	**Regression 1**	**Regression 2**	**Regression 3**	**Regression 4**	**Regression 5**
Population size	−.02	−.02	**−.23**	−.07	.07
Urbanization (population density)	**−.20**	**−.17**	**−.12**	**−.13**	**−.26**
Proximity to centers: (Metropolitan area)	**−.15**	**−.25**	**−.12**	**−.24**	**−.24**
Adjusted R^2	.08	.12	.12	.11	.15
Cases	All	1,000+	Short ticket	1,000–10,000	Mixed system

6.2. Causal Models of Party Government

The hypotheses of the research require a careful examination of not only the direct effects, but also the indirect effects of variables. Certain hypotheses may hold even if the predictors have no direct impact on the level of local party institutionalization. In actuality, the foregoing discussion presents a few cases when the indirect paths are more important than the direct effects.

6.2.1. Municipalities in the Short Ticket Electoral System

To avoid the problems created by tiny local governments, the analysis of the municipalities belonging to the short ticket electoral system focuses on the municipalities of 1,000 or more inhabitants. The variables that do not significantly affect anything else (e.g. population instability in certain models) were left out, even if they had good predictors.

The organizational strength of civil society positively influences the degree to which local politics are characterized by institutionalized parties. In addition, it has a positive indirect effect through electoral participation (0.02) (not shown in the diagram). The impact of civil society density is positive on turnout and turnout also has a positive association with party institutionalization.

The more senior the population, the stronger local party organizations are. To this direct effect three indirect effects are added. The age of the local population associates positively with the organizational density of the local civil society, which, in turn, has a positive impact on party government (0.02). The second path also goes through civil society strength first, then the variable indicating political participation (not shown in the diagram). This chain results in a path with a positive coefficient (0.02): older societies tend to have more social organizations, which increases the likeliness of more institutionalized local party organizations. Finally, another positive path goes through the variable of citizens' resources (0.02) (not shown in the diagram). Older populations are less wealthy and educated, which increases the chances of party government, as a larger pool of agency seems to translate in stronger independent candidates.

The variable indicating citizens' resources influences the dependent variable negatively. In two other ways, however, it has positive impacts. As empowered citizens are also needed for civil society organization, the amount of citizens' resources exerts a positive influence on the organizational strength of local civil society, which, in turn, affects party government positively in a direct way and, via the encouragement of electoral turnout, in an indirect way (not shown in the diagram). Both paths are positive (the coefficients are 0.02 and 0.01, respectively), while the direct effect is negative. This is not necessarily contradictory.

More educated citizens with more money, free time and independence may be more successful as independents. At the same time, a counter–tendency is not excluded, based on the same resources. Other citizens may devote their energies to maintain organizations that defend their economic interests or cultural values. Thus a stronger civil society may contribute to the stabilization of party organizations by embedding them in their local organizational networks.

Population size proved to be the most important factor in the multivariate analysis. It also indirectly affects the dependent variable via functional size. This path has a relatively strong coefficient (0.12). The other two, less important, paths through functional size are negative (–0.02 and –0.01), as both turnout and citizens' resources have a negative association with functional complexity. The route through the strength of local civil society also has a negative coefficient (–0.03). It is less clear in this case how the counter-tendencies should be interpreted.

Proximity to centers (metropolitan area) had no impact on the level of local party government in the multivariate regression model. Still it has three consistently negative, indirect effects. As suburban local governments are less significant in terms of the functions they provide, there is a path with a negative coefficient via the variable of functional size (–0.02) (not shown in the diagram). The variable of citizens' resources has a negative impact on party institutionalization, so the positive association between the proximity variable and citizens' resources produces a negative path (–.03). Finally, suburbs have a younger population, while age is a positive factor of party government. Thus, the third path also has a negative coefficient (–0.01).

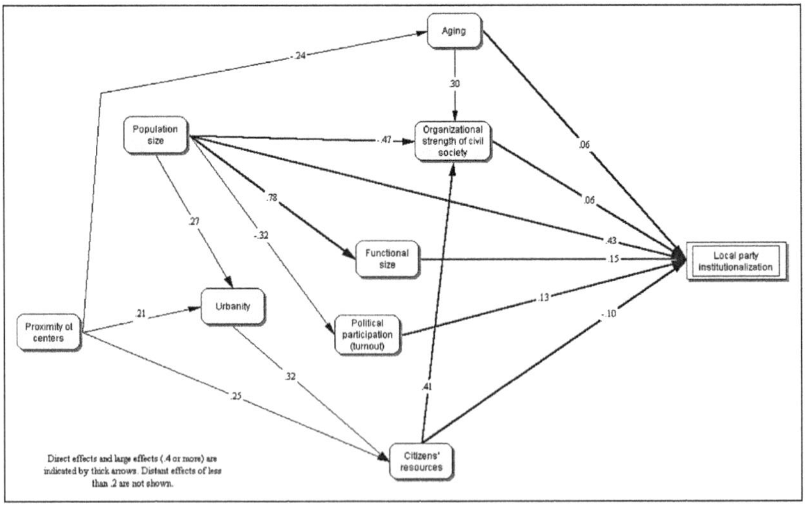

Direct effects and large effects (.4 or more) are indicated by thick arrows. Distant effects of less than .2 are not shown.

6.2.2. Municipalities in the Mixed Electoral System

In the multiple regression model in which party government was the dependent variable, six variables proved to have a direct impact: migration, functional size, urbanization, citizens' resources, electoral participation and age (in the order of the magnitude of their effect).

One surprise was the unimportance of the density of civil society organizations. Indirectly, however, it has a small effect via the participation variable (path coefficient is –.02). This effect is negative: the stronger the civil society, the higher the turnout, but the higher the turnout, the lower the level of party government. Such an effect does not obviously exclude a positive effect through other (non-electoral) forms of participation, which may exert a positive influence on the level of party institutionalization.

The instability of the local population (the degree of net migration) has a large negative direct impact on party government. In addition to that, an indirect effect goes through social and electoral participation with a negative coefficient (–.03, not shown in the diagram).

The availability of political agency (Citizens' Resources) has a direct negative influence on party government. The negative indirect impact of civil society density causes an anomaly, as the citizens' resources variable positively affects the strength of local civil society, which, in turn, has a further negative effect on local party institutionalization. A similar anomaly is the negative indirect connection of socioeconomic heterogeneity (variable not shown in the diagram) with party government via the variables of social and political participation.

Functional size influences the level of local party institutionalization in a relatively large manner. Not only is functional size a powerful direct determinant, it is also a fertile variable with important indirect effects. A relatively strong indirect path (0.08) goes through population instability. The more significant the municipality, the less unstable its population, and more stable local societies are characterized by more institutionalized party organizations. A second path goes via the variable of citizens' resources (0.06). The more functions the municipality has the larger the pool of potential activists, which, in turn, increases the likelihood of a strong party government. A third indirect path is also positive (0.02) through social and political participation.

The population size of municipalities lost its importance when other variables were included in the model. Nonetheless, it has four important indirect effects on the dependent variable. All the four are positive. First, it associates very well with the level of urbanization, which, in turn, has a positive effect on party institutionalization (the path coefficient is 0.08). The high correlation of population size and functional size also matters, as functional size has a direct impact on the dependent variable (0.07). The path via electoral turnout also creates an indirect link (0.04). Since the availability of citizens' resources depends on the amount of people living together, a fourth indirect path (0.02) also can be found. Summing up, the size of the local population is not indifferent at all.

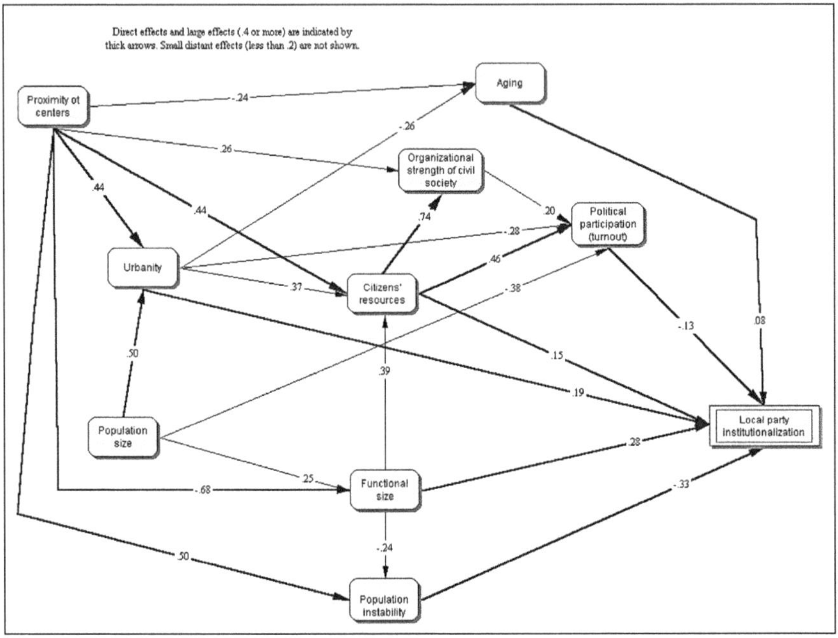

6.3. Causal Models of Party Loyalty

Following the order of the previous section, I analyze the causal models of party loyalty as indicators of local party institutionalization. After the discussion, the most important causal routes are visualized in both subsections.

6.3.1. Municipalities in the Short Ticket Electoral System

One of the small surprises of the multivariate analysis in Chapter 5 was the small effect of population size on the level of party loyalty. To the small direct influence (.04), three positive indirect effects are added. The more significant (.16!) is through functional size, which largely correlates with population size and has a sizeable direct effect on party loyalty. The other two go through the strength of civil society (.02) and urbanization and citizens' resources (.01). There is a small counter-effect (.016) through political participation, as turnout negatively associates with population size, but positively with party loyalty.

The direct influence of proximity to centers (metropolitan areas) was similar to that of population (.04). Still, it proved to be efficacious in five indirect ways. As in all the analyses here, its influence is mixed. Two indirect effects are positive: The society of municipalities close to a large city is more urban, more heterogeneous and has more citizens with more resources. These intervening factors have a positive impact on party loyalty. On the other hand, such municipalities have a younger, but less stable population, which, in turn, have a negative association with party loyalty.

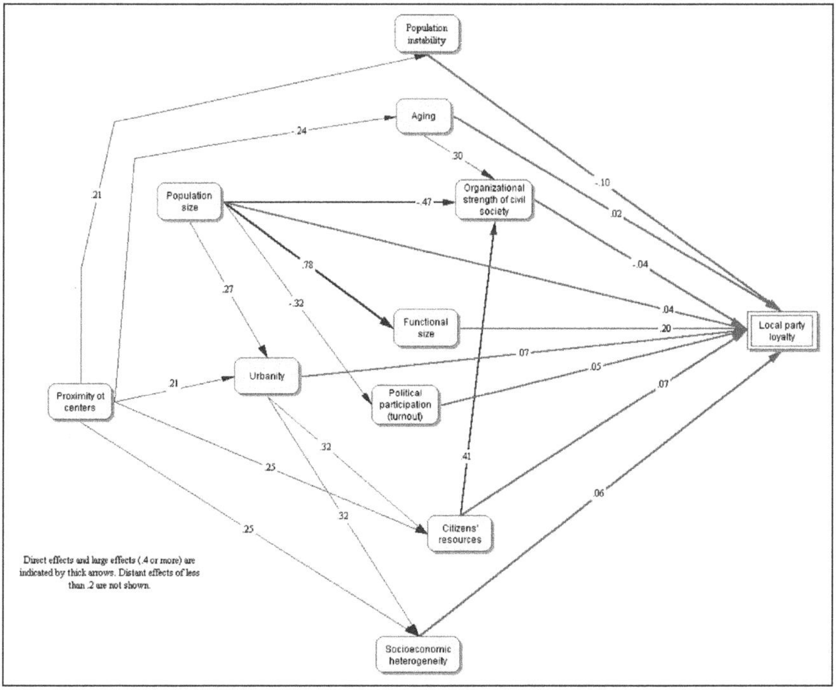

6.3.2. Municipalities in the Mixed Electoral System

The multivariate analysis (see Section 6.2.2) highlighted a number of factors that may influence the level of party loyalty in the mixed electoral system. Some of them also have an indirect effect. A prominent case is functional size, which indirectly influences the dependent variable through citizens' resources (.14!) and population stability (.04). Population size, which counter-intuitively had a negative impact on loyalty in the simple multivariate analysis, has now three positive routes to party loyalty through functional size, citizens' resources, and turnout. However, it also has a negative indirect connection through urbanization.

The proximity to centers (metropolitan area) variable had a large negative impact on local party loyalty in the simple multivariate model. In addition to that, it also has three other negative effects through functional size, the age of local population, and the strength of civil society. However, as in the previous causal analyses, it also has a (quite large) positive effect: citizens in municipalities close to centers have more individual resources and the education and income of citizens has a positive effect on party loyalty.

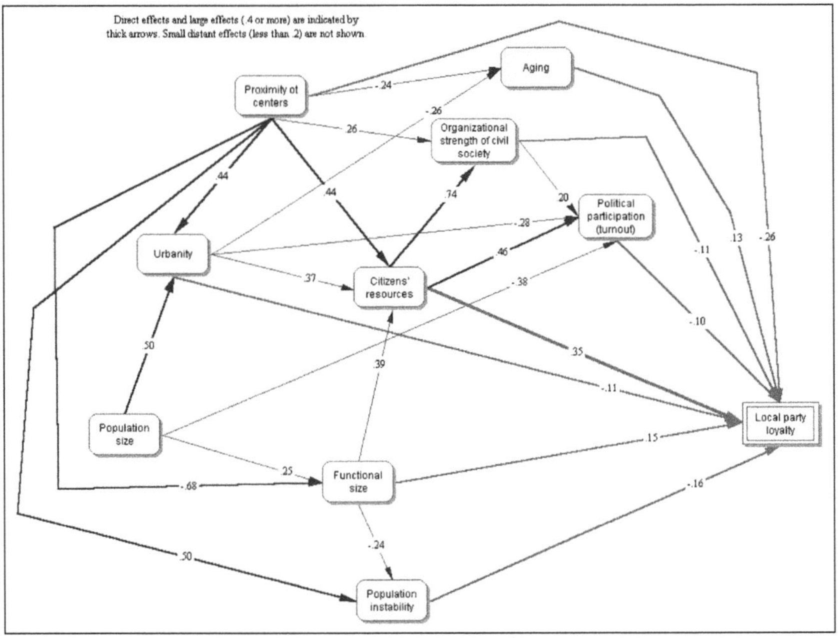

6.4. Conclusion

Following the procedure of the previous two chapters, I summarize the findings of this chapter from the point of view of the hypotheses to be tested in this research. Concerning the exogenous variables, some indirect effects can be added to their direct influence. Both types of size have strong paths through intervening variables such as the amount of resources local people possess, the stability of local population, and the level of social participation. However, these indirect effects are clearly present only in the mixed system. Municipality size has a larger direct influence, unexplained by intervening variables, on local party institutionalization in the short ticket system.

The proximity to centers variable consistently has an inconsistent indirect effect. In all cases, there are positive as well as negative paths to the two indicators of local party institutionalization. What is more, few of the intervening variables provide paths with consistently positive or negative coefficients. While routes through functional size are always positive and the paths through age are always negative, urbanization or citizens' resources contribute with negative effects in one analysis and positive in another.

In general, the causal analysis did not offer consistent, electoral-system-independent conclusions about the indirect paths between the explanatory variables and local party institutionalization.

Table 6.9. Hypotheses confirmed by indirect paths

Hypothesis	Short ticket		Mixed	
	Party government	Party loyalty	Party government	Party loyalty
H2. Population size	+/–	+	++	+
H3. Functional size			++	+ +
H4. Urbanization	–	+	+/–	+
H7. Citizens' resources	+	–	–	–
H8. Age	+	–		
H9. Civil society			–	
H11. Closeness to centers	+/–	+/–	+/–	+/–

++ hypothesis clearly supported; + hypothesis mostly supported; – hypothesis not confirmed; – – hypothesis clearly unsupported +/– mixed indirect effects

Chapter 7: Further Evidence

As Chapter 1 emphasized, local party institutionalization is a multi-dimensional concept. The indicators of party government and party loyalty primarily captured the attitudinal aspect (value infusion and reification) of local party institutionalization. This chapter discusses data about the structural aspect (systemness and autonomy) of local party institutionalization and provides additional evidence about the attitudinal facet.

The foregoing analysis is based on survey data. One of the datasets is the result of a multinational survey of local representatives. The other one is a survey of local organizations that successfully ran candidates in the 2002 local elections in Hungary. Unfortunately, the quality of the data used in this chapter do not come close to that of the electoral data analyzed in the previous two chapters. They are far from covering all municipalities. Moreover, the survey responses can be aggregated to the municipality level only with some caution, as not all representatives and organizations filled out the questionnaires. All these limitations have three consequences for the analysis. First, the small sample size does not allow any kind of causal analysis. Second, an examination of the relationships of the dimensions of local party institutionalization is hardly possible. Third, the 'noise', which characterizes most surveys, results in low statistical significance of the results. Still, even the survey data are able to reveal the major tendencies and relationships.

The chapter begins with a review of the sporadic data on the level of systemness in local party organizations in Hungary. Then, the degree of autonomy is scrutinized. The next section presents the survey evidence on the internal and external sides of the attitudinal aspect. Finally, the evidence of the existence of institutionalized governance based on direct democracy means is examined.

7.1. Local Party Survey

The Local Party Survey dataset contains survey data of 271 organizations from 147 municipalities. The questionnaire collected considerable information about the level of internal routinization and the relationship of local parties with external organizations and senior-level party organs. Unfortunately, as it was mentioned in Chapter 3, the return of the questionnaire is a clear sign of organizational strength itself. Thus, the survey data does not allow the estimation of the average level of local party institutionalization in Hungary. Nonetheless, the data makes a comparison between the local chapters of national parties and party-like social organizations possible.

Huntington (1968: 13–15) points to the importance of organizational age as an indicator of institutionalization. One of the questions of the Local Party Survey requested information about the year when the organization was founded. The perceived continuity of parties is expressed by the fact that some respondents indicated a very old date of birth (1888, 1925, etc.). Several local chapters of the Socialist party and some social organizations reported foundation during Communist times. Altogether 8 percent of the sampled organizations were founded before democracy. As Table 7.1 demonstrates, the two most important periods of party foundation correlate with the formative years of the establishment of democracy in Hungary, and the transformation of the party system from a multi-party configuration to a system in which two big parties dominate the political scene and actively mobilize all levels of politics including the local government level.

The cyclical nature of politics can clearly be seen from the fact that most organizations (76.0%!) were founded in the election years or one year before (1989–1990, 1993–1994, 1997–1998, 2001–2002) and only one quarter of them were founded in 'peace time'.

In all the cases when the organization was reported to be established in Communist or pre-Communist times, I computed a founding year in 1989, i.e. one year before the first free elections. Since the survey started in 2004, these organizations were regarded as 15 years old. Computing this way, the average age of the surveyed local parties was almost exactly 10 years with a medium of 12 years. Conforming with hypothesis H12, the local organizations of national parties are older (13.4 years) than civil society organizations (7.5 years).

Table 7.1. The foundation years of local parties in Hungary

Foundation year (by electoral cycles)	**Number of cases**	**Proportion of cases**
Before 1989	21	8.0%
1989–1990	95	36.3%
1991–1994	46	17.5%
1995–1998	27	10.3%
After 1998	73	27.9%
Total	262	100.0%

The age of organizations associates with what Huntington calls 'generational age'. The older the organization, the less likely that the founders and first leaders still participate actively in its life. The negative correlation of organizational age is higher with the survival of the first leaders (Kendall's tau b is –.41) than with the continuous membership of the founding fathers and mothers (–.29).

The difference between parties and party-like social organizations is still clear. On a four point (ordinal) scale parties reported a continuity of founders of 2.6 on average, while civil society organizations had a higher score (3.1). Similarly, the survival of first leaders is higher in social organizations (2.8) than in the local sections of national parties (2.1).

The data indicate a certain level of rotation *and* continuity of leaders. The total change and the full continuity of leadership are equally rare (see Table 7.2).

Table 7.2. Generational age of local party organizations

	How many of the founders have a membership in the organization?	How many of the first leaders have a leading position in the organization?
None of them	3.0%	12.5%
Their minority	30.8%	38.1%
Their majority	40.6%	36.2%
All of them	24.4%	13.2%
Total	100.0%	100.0%

The circumstances of the foundation process also tells much about the local parties in Hungary. Parties quite often send envoys to form local chapters in municipalities where their presence entertains hopes of strategical advantages. One quarter of the surveyed local parties were initiated by the representative of a national party.

Unifications are rare, but secessions are quite often. One quarter of the organizations were formed by former members of another organization. The internal opposition becomes external rivalary in many occasions.

From the viewpoint of general impressions, a surprisingly low proportion of the organizations claimed that they formed the organizations to increase the chances of mayoral candidates. This low percentage may be attributed to three causes. First, even mayoral parties attempt to make the impression of a programmatic or ideological organization. Overt personalism is rarely appealing in Hungary. Second, mayoral parties are often of an ephemeral character. If the candidacy fails, the leader cannot offer incentives to their followers. If the candidacy succeeds the mayor often tries to make the image of an all-municipality leader who does not divide the local community. In addition to this intention, the mayor's higher name recognition and better access to media where he or she can communicate his or her vision leads to a situation in which the mayoral party is not needed any more. That does not mean that the mayor's followers are not paid off individually or that the organization formally ceases to exist. Third, mayoral parties often have only one active member between elections: the mayoral candidate himself or herself. Nevertheless, he or she be the mayor or have a high position. Consequently, his or her capacity may not be enough to fill out a questionnaire. The latter two reasons suggest that 'mayoral organizations' are underrepresented in the survey database.

It is also very interesting that one fifth of the surveyed organizations were born as the institutionalization of a protest movement. Unfortunately, the questionnaire does not indicate what kinds of protest actions have such a strong stimulative effect that lead to the establishment of a permanent representative organization.

Table 7.3. Circumstances of the foundation

The characteristics of the foundation of the organization	Frequency
The organization was founded by people who left another organization or party	24.3%
The organization was established as the unification of two or more organizations	3.0%
A demonstration or protest action encouraged the foundation	19.8%
The founders were already candidates at local elections	26.0%
The organization was primarily established to support a mayoral candidate	9.3%
A call of the representative of a national party resulted in the foundation	25.4%

Source: Local Party Survey (Tocqueville Research Center)
Note: Respondents might choose more than one response category.

The founders of new political organizations are often experienced local politicians. One quarter of the organizations were founded by people who had already gained experience in another organization and the founders of one quarter of the surveyed organizations had run as local candidates. In two thirds of the cases (64.9%), the founders had already cooperated with each other before the establishment of the organization (see Table 7.4). It is amazing how often the foundation of an apparently value-driven association relies on friendship. Every third organization was based on friendship. This is especially interesting because Hungarians, even politicians, usually share the German-like conception of friendship, which involves much deeper emotion than, e.g., the North American conception of friendship.

The hypothesis of a spillover from the purely social sphere to the political one is to a certain degree supported by the survey data. One third of the local parties were organized by people who had regularly met in nonpolitical civil society associations. Without further inquiry, however, one cannot tell whether the proponents of social capital theory are right or the size of the elite is simply so small that the local political and social elites are not differentiated.

Finally, previous political cooperation is naturally the prehistory of many organizations. This refers to those who left a party to form a new organization and to those who met in an organization where they found a common goal or value.

Table 7.4. Cooperation before the foundation of the organization

Cooperation of founders before the foundation of the organization	Frequency
Friendship	35.4%
Cooperation in a party	19.2%
Cooperation in a political organization	20.3%
Cooperation in a social organization of another type (e.g. sport club or cultural association)	33.0%
No cooperation before the foundation	33.6%

Source: Local Party Survey (Tocqueville Research Center)
Note: After a screening question (cooperation / no cooperation), respondents had the opportunity to choose more than one response category concerning the form of previous cooperation, so the total does not add up to 100 percent.

7.1.1. Systemness: Resources

Neither the indicator of party government, nor that of party loyalty were able to indicate the level of internal routinization or 'systemness' (although one may suppose some connection with party loyalty, as organizations that lose their front warriors *en masse* are, or become, weakly organized parties). The Local Party Survey allows the assessment of routinization in three ways: it contains data about (a) the resources of the surveyed organizations and the regularity of those resources; (b) the differentiation and control of subunits and (c) the regularity of internal party activities.

The availability of certain resources to party organizations indicates the level of systemness in an indirect manner. An organization that has a permanent office or employee is more likely to have institutionalized internal practices.

Respondents of the Local Party Survey had the opportunity to mark whether the listed 10 items are available to them. One of the conspicuous findings is that local parties in Hungary are not particularly wealthy. Only a small portion of them own their office or a car. On the other hand, many of them have smaller items such as computers and are able to rent some office space. Moreover, every fifth local party has a full-time or part-time or jointly appointed employee. It is quite clear that the size and the electoral system matter. In all categories, the municipalities in the mixed electoral system have more resources than those in the short list system. For example, only 23 percent of the organizations in the smaller municipalities have a rented or owned office, while more than half of the local parties in the mixed system have such a facility. There is also a correlation between the access to facilities and functional size, and civil society density and metropolitan status, all of them in the expected direction, but, due to the impossibility of multivariate analyses, it is unclear to what degree these relationships are spurious.

Table 7.5. Resources of local parties

Resources	**Frequency**
Own office	9.7%
Rented office	34.5%
Telephone	30.3%
Copier	27.0%
Computer	28.1%
Car	2.6%
Full-time employee	10.9%
Part-time employee	9.4%
Employee with other organizations	1.9%
Website	18.7%

Source: Local Party Survey (Tocqueville Research Center)

The survey also had questions on other types of resources (annual budget, the number of active members and supporters, and the number of activists during the last electoral campaign). I will not present them, since their level does not indicate the degree of institutionalization. Loosely organized or *ad hoc* organizations may also be able to generate much money and mobilize many people. Nevertheless, the regularity of the resources matters to large measure. One of the survey questions asked information about the importance of a number of in-kind and monetary sources. A follow-up question collected data about the degree to which the resources come from those sources in a manner that is regular and scheduled. Though there might be some effect of the question order (the two questions came one after the another), the correlation between the importance and regularity of resources can be interpreted in a meaningful way. The more reliable a source of support, the more important it is for local party organizations. Institutionalization itself is a resource. The most important and reliable source of support is the membership. Their fees and in-kind contributions such as the use of their mobile phones, cars and office facilities, are indispensable to most local party organizations. A closely related source is the payments of the local representatives nominated by the local party. It is very common that councilors have to give up a part of their salary to their party. It is usually an unwritten rule, but some parties, e.g. FIDESZ-MPSZ, have incorporated this duty in their charter.

An important source, but one that cannot well be planned, are the donations of individuals and firms. Obviously, it is absolutely unclear to what degree those contributions are made out of sympathy and to what degree they cover corrupt practices. The local sections of national parties are often supported by higher party levels, while associations often have own income from their activities. Unlike Poland (see Sczerbiak 1999), the contribution of the parliamentary representatives of parties do not play an eminent role.

Localized national parties and civil society organizations are somewhat different in terms of the regularity of the support they receive. Social organizations may rely more on support from their members, other civil society organizations, donations and their own income. The local chapters of national parties get support from their senior-level organs, MPs, and can much more effectively force their councilors to pay a part of their income to the party.

There is a difference between size categories and electoral systems too. (Unfortunately, the effect of the two cannot be separated.) Nonetheless, the direction is surprising. Apart from the contributions of councilors, the organizations functioning in smaller communities reported a higher regularity of support than those in larger municipalities. Although the difference in no case is statistically significant, the uniform trend refers to something real. Organizations in small municipalities may have less resources, as it was indicated above, but their income and in-kind contribution can be better scheduled. One the other hand, the higher reliability of the contributions of local representatives clearly shows that the electoral support of nominating organizations is much more important in the mixed electoral system than in the short ticket system.

Table 7.6. Importance and regularity of the sources of support

Source of support	Importance	Regularity
Membership fee	3.4	3.9
Members' contributions (e.g., car, mobile phone, photocopying)	3.3	3.2
Support of social organizations	1.4	1.4
Donations of private persons and companies	2.4	2.1
Local government support	1.7	1.6
The office of MPs	1.4	1.3
County or national level of the organization (if any)	1.9	1.8
Income from organizational activities	1.8	1.8
Contributions of the organization's local representatives	2.4	2.5

Source: Local Party Survey (Tocqueville Research Center)

7.1.2. Systemness: Differentiation and Control

Local parties are rarely big enough to be forced to have internal subunits. The main differentiation problem is between the party and its faction in the local council. The level of institutionalization is low when their relationship is taken to extremes. One of the extremes is the lack of differentiation between party and faction. The other one is the total independence of the councilors from their nominating organization.

The first type of problem seems quite frequent in Hungary. When the election campaign is finished, even party members become passive. The only active element of the party is constituted by those who obtained a public position. The data largely support this observation. Almost half of the organizations (48%) admitted that the party functions only in the form of its faction between two elections. Only every sixth organization has an autonomous (though interdependent and cooperating) faction and party life like the parliamentary parties do. The differentiation characterizes parties more than civil society organizations. Other significant associations cannot be found in this small database.

While the party policies are clearly made by the representatives, this does not necessarily mean the total end of party life. Just 8 percent of the respondents reported that only those members who had gained a public position are actually active outside the electoral campaigns. However, more than half (59%!) admitted that this described their organizations "to a certain degree". Only every sixth organization described the members who did not have a public duty and honorarium as active.

Table 7.7. The relationship of the party organization to its council faction

Does the functioning of the organization differ from that of the organization's faction between electoral campaigns?	Frequency
Not at all, the activities and statements of the representatives are those of the party as well	47.6%
In some questions	34.9%
Fully, the organization and its faction cooperate with each other but work independently	17.5%

Source: Local Party Survey (Tocqueville Research Center)

A very characteristic indicator of party institutionalization on the local level is the capability of local organizations to control their representatives. A systematic relationship between representatives and their nominating organization is a feature that characterizes few of the organizations. Only every fifth (22%) of the surveyed local parties have a formal rule about how and when the representatives are sanctioned if they do not follow the position of the party. Even fewer organizations, only one seventh of the surveyed (14%), have actually warned their councilors for this reason.

In most cases, the reason for the lack of control may simply be the narrowing of the party life to the group of local representatives between elections. Where the party is the faction, no institutionalized relationship between them is necessary or possible. An uncontrolled parallel functioning of the party and its faction seems quite exceptional. The formal rule of faction discipline is a party phenomenon (30% of organizations), it is much more rare in civil society organizations (15%). This difference may be due to a general requirement of party centers rather than local needs. That explains why there is not much difference between electoral systems.

Political solidarity seems to work without formal pressures. Only a very small portion (1.3% or 2 respondents) of the respondents reported that the representatives of their organizations rarely vote together. The thirds of the organizations (67%) have representatives who usually vote together. The factions of almost one third (32%) of the local parties always vote together. Even if party leaders, the actual respondents of the survey, are somewhat susceptible to wishful thinking, the evidence suggests a relatively high level of cooperation in the factions of local councils. The survey took place in the second half of the electoral period, which makes the finding especially convincing.

Size makes a clear difference: while only one fifth (20%) of the organizations in small municipalities vote always together, more than one third (35%) of the respondents from large municipalities characterized their local party organizations this way.

7.1.3. Systemness: Routinized Activities

The previous data already shed some light on the level of routinization. In addition, one question directly requested information about the regularity of the functioning of a basic organ of local parties, the members' meetings. As Table 7.8 demonstrates, only one fifth of the organizations meet once a year (which is usually the minimum requirement in statutes) or even more rarely. The members of the vast majority of the surveyed organizations meet at least a few times a year. The actual frequency naturally depends on the demands of local government policy-making. Thus, the rate of meetings is higher in larger municipalities. There is a significant difference between the local sections of national parties, which meet more frequently, and the usually local civil society organizations, which have less frequent meetings. All in all, the routinization seems relatively high.

Table 7.8. Frequency of party meetings

Frequency of members' meetings	Proportion
More rarely than once a year	1.1%
Once a year	18.1%
A few times a year	49.6%
Every month	26.7%
More than once a month	4.4%
Total	100.0%

Source: Local Party Survey (Tocqueville Research Center)

Another aspect of routinization is the regularity with which the local section maintains contact with the senior-level organs of the party. Compared to the intensity of local government politics the meetings seem to be quite frequent. More than half of the local parties belonging to a national organization contact the representatives of their supra-municipal organs monthly or even more frequently. The recurrence obviously depends on the importance and availability of municipalities. Therefore, the larger local governments and suburbs enjoy more attention of national organizations.

An additional, follow-up question collected information about the degree to which those meetings are planned. The answers show a mirror of the previous question. The meetings between the representatives of local and regional/national levels are of an accidental character only in 12 percent of the cases. Usually (63%) those meetings are reported to be more or less planned. One quarter of the respondents claimed that they had meetings on a strict schedule. Again, local parties in larger and suburban municipalities have more routinized contacts with the senior levels.

Table 7.9. Frequency of contacts with regional and national party levels

Frequency of meetings	**Proportion**
Almost never	3.4%
A few times a year	44.7%
Every month	29.9%
More than once a month	22.0%
Total	100.0%

Source: Local Party Survey (Tocqueville Research Center)

7.1.4. Autonomy

One aspect of autonomy is the financial dependence of organizations on external actors. The Local Party Survey focused on two external players: the local government and the national party center. The local government provides one quarter of the surveyed local party organizations with in-kind support. Follow-up questions clarified that the support usually meant office space. 30 percent of the organizations that obtain local government support are provided with free office space, another 29% with low-rent office space (below the market price), and 15 percent also obtain office facilities. Respondents listed various other contributions: free rooms for the organization's meetings and programs (the most frequently mentioned additional item), photocopying, and legal advice. The dependence on the in-kind support of the local government is somewhat higher in communities of less than 10,000 inhabitants (32%) than in larger municipalities (22%). (However the difference has a low significance: p=.12.) Significantly more civil society organizations (28%) receive in-kind local government support than parties (18%). On the other hand, social organizations may obtain the support to help their nonpolitical activities. From a quantitative research, it is not possible to conclude the degree to which the relationship between the local government and the organization is balanced: does the organization siphon off public resources based on its representation in council or the local government leaders keep the organization dependent?

The other kind of support that may decrease the decisional autonomy of local party organizations is the support from the higher levels of the party. A dependence on extra-municipality resources makes the local party organizations not only less responsive to local needs, but also more vulnerable to the *ad hoc* requests of other party bodies. The results of the Local Party Survey support Schlesinger's (1965) theory about the exchange of local and national party levels. Indeed, local chapters mostly receive political information, which may cover ideological and programmatic guidelines plus training in exchange for local infrastructure and mobilization capabilities. Relatively few organizations obtain financial and in-kind contributions from senior party levels. The previous discussion of local party resources already indicated that these contributions constitute only an insignificant part of the full costs of running a local party organization.

Table 7.10. Frequency of contacts with regional and national party levels

Forms of support within parties	**Proportion**
Financial help	29.8%
In-kind contribution	18.5%
Training of leaders and councilors	35.4%
Political information	71.9%

Source: Local Party Survey (Tocqueville Research Center)

As the overview of the sources of support has already demonstrated (see Table 7.6), the third form of external dependency, an overly close relationship with interest organizations (including trade unions), is not a very likely case. However, a dependence on the donations of local entrepreneurs seems a more probable danger. Nevertheless, the mechanisms and degree of the danger cannot easily be revealed in a quantitative survey.

In addition to financial dependence, an organizational one is also possible if the national level of the party directly controls the activities of its local chapters. A high level of institutionalization on the local level is very unlikely if external orders may be issued at any time. The Local Party Survey reveals a high freedom of local chapters. One of the questions requested information about the degree to which the higher levels of the party influence the public position of the local chapter. Almost two thirds of the local organizations claimed that the senior party organs never try to influence the opinion formation of local organizations. (The proportions refer to a subsample composed of the local sections of national parties, as the following questions were not asked of social organizations.) A little more than one quarter (27%) reported attempts at influencing their position only in very important questions. Importance refers to what is important to the party centers, not to local chapters. Only a minority (8%) felt consistent control, and only a very small portion (1%) a total control, i.e. a duty to ask the center before every decision.

Two other questions collected information about the freedom of local chapters to choose their mayoral and councilor candidates for local elections. The vast majority of organizations (92%!) can nominate their local candidates without any consultation of other levels of the party. In some cases, the higher level maintains the right of veto, but it is the local organization that proposes the candidates. In a few cases, the list of candidates is the result of a consultation between the local and higher levels.

The selection of mayoral candidates is more controlled by party centers. Still, more than two thirds of the local party organizations may make their decision without any pressure from the center. Only every sixth organization has to undergo a review process that may result in a veto and another sixth of the municipalities must reach an agreement with a senior-level body about the person who the party nominates as a candidate for the mayoral position. (More information about local candidate selection can be found in section 7.4, later in this chapter.)

Table 7.11. Frequency of contacts with regional and national party levels

How are candidates selected?	Mayors	Councilors
The higher levels decide	0.6%	0.6%
Through a consultation between the local and higher levels	15.3%	3.4%
The higher levels can veto the candidates proposed by the local organization	14.7%	4,5%
The local organization takes the decision	69.4%	91.9%
Total	100.0%	100.0%

Source: Local Party Survey (Tocqueville Research Center)

Moreover, another kind of relationship between the party center and local sections was revealed during the Local Party Survey. It turned out that the headquarters of the Socialist Party often give thematic guidelines to their local chapters. The local organizations must raise the given issues in the local context of their municipality. Thus, the party can send the same message at the same time on every level of politics. That is also a restriction of local autonomy, though not a very tight one. It is very unlikely that the rival parties, especially the other big party FIDESZ-MPSZ, will not or do not follow the same practice if it becomes successful.

7.2. Local Representative Survey

7.2.1. Power Positions

The Local Representative Survey was conducted in Hungary in 2002 as a part of an international series of surveys. Its informants were councilors and mayors, who revealed much about the actual functioning of local governments. One of the questions presented 16 local actors and asked the respondents to indicate the level of the actors' influence on local government decisions. Table 7.12 shows the perceptions of local representatives. For them, the most influential actors, i.e. those that have a mean influence above the central value of the seven-point scale (4), are the mayor, the CAO, the central government and the items related to the respondents: factions, committees, and individual representatives. Parties and other external actors (including local businesspersons) are regarded as of secondary importance. The subsample of party-nominated representatives attributes a higher value (4.2) to parties than the full sample.

Both the Local Government Survey and the Local Party Survey found faction names that refer to the names of nominating organizations. That suggests that factions are almost always built on local parties. While the influence of the groups of representatives in the council is not related to size, the importance of party organizations clearly increases as the size (especially the functional size) of the municipality increases. That demonstrates an increasing importance of the external party and a more independent role for the party between elections. A Multivariate analysis shows that the electoral system and the functional size of municipality make the effect of population size irrelevant.

Table 7.12. Perceived influence of political actors on local government decisions

Actors	Mean influence	Correlation with population size	Correlation with municipality significance	Correlation with electoral system	Correlation with metropolitan area
Mayor	5.9	.17***	.14***	.14***	.13***
Chief administrative officer	4.7	–.14***	–.14***	–.13***	
Local administration	3.7		.17***	.14***	–.08**
Council committees	4.9	–.15***	.09**		–.09**

Actors	Mean influence	Correlation with population size	Correlation with municipality significance	Correlation with electoral system	Correlation with metropolitan area
Council factions	5.2	–.06*			
Individual representatives	4.4	–.26***	–.20***	–.20***	–.13***
Citizens	3.3	–.21***	–.25***	–.21***	–.16***
Local business	3.4		.07*		
Civil society organizations	3.1	–.14***	.06*	–.08**	–.09**
Trade unions	2.2				
Local churches	2.9		.01	.02	–.00
Political parties	3.2	.26***	.49***	.49***	
News media	3.1	.18***	.23***	.21***	
The central government	4.7				
The county government	3.7	–.25***	–.25***	–.26***	–.09***
Minority governance	2.3	–.14**	–.08*	–.06*	–.08*

Source: Local Representative Survey (Local Government and Public Service Reform Initiative and Tocqueville Research Center). The perceived influence was measured on a seven-point scale. Only the statistically significant associations appear in the table. *** Correlation is significant at the 0.01 level (2-tailed); ** Correlation is significant at the 0.05 level (2-tailed); * Correlation is significant at the 0.10 level (2-tailed).

The perceptions of local politicians show five clear categories of actors. I grouped the items by means of factor analysis (the Kaiser-Meyer-Olkin's measure of sampling adequacy was.84 and the five groups covered 64%t of the variance). (1) The most important group contains the permanent staff of the local government as an administrative unit: the mayor, chief administrative officer, and civil servants. They are the most influential actors, but their position depends on size. CAOs are powerful in smaller municipalities, but power shifts towards mayors in parallel with the professionalization of mayors. (2) The second group is formed by the other internal actors, acting as the lay representatives of the external world (factions, committees, and individual representatives). They come from outside and do not work permanently in the administrative buildings of the local government. (3) The third category is made of the actors of the local society: individual citizens, civic groups, local business, trade unions, churches, and minority representatives. (4) Very interestingly, the evaluation of party organizations and media outlets moves together composing the fourth group. That supports the hypotheses about their interrelationship. The stronger the media, the more likely that more institutionalized and organized parties emerge. Access to the powerful media depends on the strength of parties. On the other hand, the more institutionalized the parties, the more likely they extend their influence to the media as well by establishing or encouraging the establishment and continual functioning of local media outlets. The partial correlation between the influence of news media and parties remains strong (.49 and.45, respectively) even if population size or municipality significance are controlled for. (5) Finally, the national and county governments also form a separate dimension. It is quite clear that counties have a larger influence on villages and small towns than larger municipalities.

To sum up, the influence of party organizations on the decisions of local governments are perceived by local representatives as of medium level, but increasing by the size of the municipality. The internal expression of local parties, the factions of the council, are regarded as powerful in every size category.

7.2.2. Opinion Formation

The influence of local party organizations on local government decisions sheds some light on their taken-for-grantedness. A similar question on the influence of the same actors on the opinion formation of the responding representatives may show the degree to which parties are able to make the party an authority for those they nominate. This refers primarily to the value infusion aspect, and secondarily to the systemness aspect of local party institutionalization. Politicians who are inculcated with the values of the party are more likely to accept the position of the party. Politicians who feel they will lose something are more likely to follow the official line than those who feel they have a chance to survive on their own.

I analyze a subsample in which only those respondents are included who were not elected as independents, i.e. those who were nominated by an organization. Table 7.13 presents the main results. The three most important actors are the faction, the nominating organization and "the citizens who you meet". The three actors belong to the same category in the minds of local representatives. A factor analysis (the Kaiser-Meyer-Olkin's measure of sampling adequacy:.80; the factors explain 65% of the variance) results in four factors. One of them contains the three items mentioned above with high loadings. Therefore, the group of "the citizens who you meet" in all probability are those who are close to the respondents' party and share its goals and values. The constant nature of the item's influence, which is independent from size, also renders this inference likely. My conclusion is that local parties do influence the opinion of the councilors and mayors they nominated.

Unfortunately, the small size of the subsample allows only very simple, bivariate analysis of the data. Still, it seems clear that size, especially functional size, associates with the ability of local parties to influence the opinion formation of their representatives.

Table 7.13. Perceived influence of political actors on opinion formation

Actors	**Mean influence**	**Correlation with population size**	**Correlation with municipality significance**	**Correlation with electoral system**	**Correlation with metropolitan area**
Mayor	4.2				
Chief administrative officer	3.5	−.21***	−.20***	−.19***	
Local administration	3.4				
Respondent's faction	**5.5**	.13**	.18***	.15***	
Other representatives	3.4	.10*			
Citizens	**5.6**				
Local business	3.2		.10*		
Civil society organizations	3.6				
Local churches	2.7				
News media	2.3	.20**	.27**	.25**	
Nominating organization(s)	**4.9**	.17**	.21**	.24**	.15***
Other parties	2.4	.09*	.12**		

Source: Local Representative Survey (Local Government and Public Service Reform Initiative and Tocqueville Research Center). The perceived influence was measured on a seven-point scale. Only the statistically significant associations appear in the table: *** Correlation is significant at the 0.01 level (2-tailed); ** Correlation is significant at the 0.05 level (2-tailed); * Correlation is significant at the 0.10 level (2-tailed).

7.2.3. Accountability to Local Parties

Several other questions of the Local Representative Survey also asked about the involvement of political parties in the local life. One is especially important from the perspective of this project. Respondents had to indicate how often certain actors asked them to explain their position in local government issues. A more frequent occurrence of accountability claims can be regarded as a more institutionalized relationship, at least in the case of parties. Thus, the question is an indicator of internal routinization or 'systemness'.

The following table shows the level of societal accountability as measured by the answers of local representatives. The question of the Local Representative Survey was: "How frequently are you requested by the following people to explain your position on a local public issue?" The response categories were as follows: every week, once or twice a week, a few times a year, never. I combined the first two categories in the table to simplify the presentation.

Table 7.14. Frequency of accountability claims

Actors	**Monthly or more frequently**
Friends, relatives	84%
Colleagues	70%
Neighbors	57%
Respondent's civic groups (if any)	41%
Respondent's party (if any)	77%
Businesspersons	29%
Journalists	16%
Residents of respondent's constituency	73%

Source: Local Representative Survey (Local Government and Public Service Reform Initiative and Tocqueville Research Center)

Who holds councilors and mayors accountable? First of all, their family, friends and colleagues! While local representatives claim they represent the whole or a part of the municipality, a political group, or a social group, they actually have more political communication with their inner circle. This is not a consequence of the fragmented nature of the Hungarian local government system, i.e. the large number of small municipalities. Representatives in small and large municipalities alike explain their political record to people who are very close to them. There is no difference between mayors and councilors: full-time politicians are as often (and very often) are asked by friends and family as the usually amateur councilors. A survey of urban mayors (European Mayor Survey 2003 conducted in Hungary by the Tocqueville Research Center; see Soós 2004) also confirm this: powerful leaders of cities are primarily held accountable by their closer friends and family members. This is a form of interpersonal accountability we know little about.

More than 70 percent of local representatives must respond to political questions of their constituency. However, the relatively high correlation between the frequency of accountability claims by the constituency, on the one hand, and family, friends and colleagues, on the other hand, points to a partial overlapping of these groups. What local representatives perceive as 'constituency' often means the people who they more frequently meet at home or in the workplace.

What makes the difference between small and large municipalities is the frequency of accountability claims by organizations: parties, media, and civic organizations. While local representatives in smaller local governments receive accountability claims from 3.1 types of actors, this number is 4.4 in municipalities of 10,000 or more inhabitants. This increase is due to the higher accountability to the representatives of political parties, media outlets and civic organizations.

Civic organizations relatively often ask local politicians to explain their political position. Even in local governments of less than 10,000 inhabitants, where only a few organizations exist, every fourth representative is asked questions at least once a month. This proportion is much higher (46%) in larger municipalities. Belonging to civil society organization induces more frequent accountability claims. The difference between municipality categories is not that large, though civic organizations in towns and cities seem somewhat more active. More than half of the representatives in large municipalities and a little less than half of them in small municipalities are regularly asked by civic organizations. Every sixth of those who have a position in civic organization receives accountability claims every week.

Both the position of respondents in civic organizations and the electoral support of such organizations increase the likelihood of accountability claims by civic organizations. Furthermore, the combined effect of position and support is the most significant factor in the multivariate analysis. Civic organizations that supported one of their leaders at a local election and local parties in the terminology of this research seem to impose the heaviest demands for accountability.

The local sections of parties do control their members. The frequency of accountability claims is impressive. There is a relatively high level of systemness in the local parties. The electoral system has a clear effect: parties' accountability claims are more frequent in the mixed system (85%) than in the short ticket system (55% – still a high number!).

The multivariate analysis (logistic regression) does not reveal surprising associations. The frequency of accountability claims increases by municipality size. Unlike membership and electoral support, the correlation is linear. The accountability relationship is between two parties; therefore, the willingness of politicians also matters. This is the reason why mayoral position, ambition and sophistication (cultural capital) have a significant effect.

To sum up, local politicians are most often asked by their inner circle, but accountability claims are often made by local parties too, both in their civil society organizations and national party forms.

7.3. Party Charters

The constitutions of political parties contain lots of information about the place of local party organizations within the party structure. They are especially useful to characterize the level of autonomy local chapters enjoy. The following analysis is based on Machos' (2000) collection of party charters. Therefore, it reflects the situation in 2000 with the hope that the general picture has not changed much since then.

As Table 7.15 shows, there is no general trend concerning the degree of freedom enjoyed by local party branches in Hungary. In three respects, however, Hungarian political parties are quite similar. First of all, all party constitutions mention local organizations and recognize them as important components of the party. Local branches have the right to admit candidates for party membership in all parties, although unsuccessful applicants can appeal to higher bodies of the parties. The minimum membership for the existence of a local party organization is also very similar (5–10 members). It is relatively easy to form a party organization in municipalities. The fact that the number of such organizations is limited in smaller settlements, however, shows that it is not so easy to find even a handful people who are ready to commit themselves to a political party. In other respects, there are clear differences among parties and these differences do not correspond to the usual (left-right, coalition-opposition) cleavages.

One of the best indicators of the within-party centralization is the constitutional right of central bodies to dissolve local party branches. Such a rule does not exist in the party constitution of four parliamentary parties, so dissolution is not possible from above. Three parties—none of them historical—have a regulation on dissolution. While in SZDSZ dissolution is possible only if the activity of local organization violates the law or party constitution, the highest bodies of the FIDESZ-MPSZ and the Hungarian Democratic Forum can dissolve a party organization if the latter jeopardizes the reputation or interests of its party. The regulation has been enforced a number of times when a conflict arose between a local branch and the central leadership.

Another good indicator of local autonomy is the role of local organizations in nominating candidates for local and parliamentary elections. Candidates running for local representative positions are in general nominated by local party organizations. The only exception is the Smallholders' Party, in which the Presidium proposes local candidates and the National Board has the right to nominate them for the election. Local organizations do not have even a consultative role in this process. In the FIDESZ-MPSZ, territorial organizations have the jurisdiction to veto the candidates of the local organization. A similar regulation exists in other parties' constitutions with regard to mayoral candidates. Local organizations have full jurisdiction to nominate candidates for mayor only in the Socialist Party and the Hungarian Democratic Forum. Local party branches are more limited in their right to nominate candidates for parliamentary positions. The only party in which local organizations nominate MP candidates without higher approval is the Socialist Party. In the other parties, the local organization proposes individuals, but country-level (FIDESZ-MPSZ, MIÉP, SZDSZ) or territorial (Hungarian Democratic Forum) bodies nominate. Similar to their practice in local elections, local branches of the Smallholders' Party have no role in the process of nominating MPs.

Table 7.15. Frequency of contacts with regional and national party levels

Party	**Minimum Membership of Local Organization**	**Dissolution of Local Organization**	**Admission of New Party Members**	**Local Elections**	**National Elections**
FIDESZ-MPSZ (Hungarian Civic Alliance)	10 members; 5 members in municipalities of less than 5,000 inhabitants	the main board can dissolve a local organization, if it breaks the law, acts against the party program, the party constitution, or damages the interests or reputation of the party	full right to admit	right to nominate, but territorial organization has a veto	proposes; expresses an opinion to the campaign manager in the constituency, but the chief campaign manager decides
FKGP (Smallholders' Party)	(no rule)	(no rule)	full right to admit	no right (the Presidium proposes, the Board nominates)	no right (the President proposes, the Presidium nominates)
MDF (Hungarian Democratic Forum)	5 members	can dissolve a local organization, if it violates the law, acts against the party program or the party constitution, or the interests of the party	full right to admit	full right to nominate	Proposes; territorial organization nominates
MIÉP (Party of Hungarian Justice and Life)	5 members	(no rule)	right to admit	nominates but mayors must be approved by the Presidium	local organizations belonging to the same constituency propose, but higher organs have to approve

Party	Minimum Membership of Local Organization	Dissolution of Local Organization	Admission of New Party Members	Local Elections	National Elections
MSZP (Hungarian Socialist Party)	10 members; 5 members in municipalities of less than 5,000 inhabitants	(no rule)	full right to decide (only the applicant can appeal to higher party organs)	full right to nominate	full right to nominate
SZDSZ (Alliance of Free Democrats)	20 members (more than 50,000 inhabitants); 10 members (10,000–50,000); 5 (less than 10,000)	higher party organs can dissolve local organization if it violates the constitution of the party	admits new members	nominates candidates for local representatives; proposes candidates for mayor, but country-level organ nominates	proposes, but country-level organ nominates

Source: My systematization based on Machos 2000.

7.4. Direct Democracy

Direct democracy was mentioned as a potential alternative to party institutionalization on the local level in Chapter 1. In theory, an established system of direct contact between citizens and the local government could fulfill all functional needs of an institutionalized local polity. The lack of such systems can be accounted for only by means of an empirical investigation. I divided the research problem into two questions. First, I analyze the formal rules of local referenda, the major means of direct democracy, and explain why referenda took place so rarely on the local level. Second, I focus on local solutions that were not centrally regulated. No legal constraints prohibit local governments from formally or informally institutionalizing direct channels through which decision-makers and citizen groups can govern the municipality together. Finally, I draw some conclusions.

7.4.1. The Underused Institution of Local Referendum

According to the Hungarian Constitution, local self-government is the local citizens' legal due. "Eligible voters exercise the right to local government through the representative body that they elect and by way of local referendum. (44. § 1)"

In the Constitution, local referendum is treated on par with indirect representation. From a legal-constitutional point of view, local referendum is as legitimate an institution in Hungary as the local elections in which the mayor and council of the local government are directly elected.

The Local Government Act contributes a full chapter to local referenda and initiatives. It is compulsory to call a local referendum in the case of territorial changes: unification of local governments or separation of a part of a local government. In these referenda, only those citizens living in the affected area are entitled to vote. Moreover, the representative body (municipal council) of the local government is entitled to call a compulsory local referendum at any time. The council may hold a local referendum to reinforce one of its previous decisions or to ask questions before a decision within the jurisdiction of local governments. Nevertheless, it is legally prohibited to hold a local referendum on budgetary questions, local taxes, the rules of the operation of the representative body, or the dissolution of the representative body.

It is relatively easy to officially initiate a local referendum. One quarter of the local council, a committee of the council, or the leaders of an NGO can all submit a proposition to the mayor. However, the council is not obliged to actually call a local referendum in these instances. It is compulsory to hold a referendum only if enough citizens petition for one; the proportion of citizens, required by the law, is between ten and twenty-five percent. The actual threshold is set by the local governments themselves. Local councils must adopt a decree on local referenda, in which they specify the proportion of citizens needed for holding an obligatory referendum. This local decree on referenda also sets the threshold for popular initiatives, which must be within five and ten percent. The decree must also specify the local rules for the arrangements of local referenda (e.g. the way in which signatures must be collected).

As one might guess, local governments like to set a high threshold in these decrees. Although their is no survey on the actual percentages adopted by councils, a quick overview shows that ten of the eleven randomly surveyed municipalities of different size set the limit high: either 25 percent (six local governments) or 20 percent (four local governments). Only one of them has opted for the lowest possible limit, i.e. 10%). Local representatives seem more generous concerning the non-binding popular initiatives: more than half (six municipalities) set the threshold at 5 percent, which is the lowest possible legal proportion.

The result of a local referendum is valid if more than half of the entitled citizens turn out and a majority of the actual voters vote in the same way. In villages with less than 500 inhabitants, a village meeting may replace a local referendum provided that half of the villagers participate in the meeting. The council is obliged to respect the results of local referenda. If the referendum fails, the council can decide on its own and no referendum can be held on the same question within a period of one year.

A popular initiative may propose the debate of any public issue in the jurisdiction of local governments. The council is required to discuss the question, but has no further obligations.

In sum, initiating a local referendum is not easy, but far from being impossible in Hungary. The legal status of local referenda is high and the rules are well defined. The proportion of citizens who can call an obligatory referendum is not prohibitively high if the issue is a concern of many. Since an NGO may also propose a referendum to the council, the cost of getting publicity and further support is low.

Still, the actual use of the institution of local referendum is low. Eight to nineteen local referenda were initiated annually in more than 3,200 municipalities between 1999 and 2002. (The Hungarian bureaucracy is not able to produce aggregate data for prior periods.) In the first three months of this year, only one local referendum has taken place. The small number of referenda suggests that the popularity of a local referendum is very limited in Hungary.

Referenda are used in two exceptional cases only. The law requires a referendum for territorial changes (secession from, or accession to, a municipality or an alteration of county borders); therefore this is the subject of voting in some municipalities every year. Twenty-three (or 41%) of the total fifty-six referenda in 1999–2002 dealt with territorial changes. Disregarding the number of compulsory referenda on territorial issues, one will find only one year (2000) had more than ten non-compulsory, citizen-initiated local referenda.

The other category is the strong conflict over big projects. Unwanted facilities (toxic waste dumps, shopping malls, quarries, etc.) form one group in this category (24 referenda or 43%). The other group of project referenda is fairly mixed, including the closing of schools to the selling of community property. Nine referenda (or 16%) belong to this group.

Table 7.16. Initiatives of local referenda in Hungary (1999–2002)

	1999	**2000**	**2001**	**2002**
Territorial change: Separation	8	4	7	4
Projects: Unwanted facilities	7	10	3	4
Projects: Other	2	5	2	0
Total	17	19	12	8

Since 50 percent of local voters must turn out to make the referendum legally binding, many of the initiatives fail due to a lack of interest. For example, only seven (or 37%!) and nine (75%) of all referenda were successfully implemented in 2000 and 2001, respectively. The ratio of failures is higher among the unwanted facilities group. That refers to the weakness of single-issue protest groups to mobilize local citizens.

Longitudinally, no trend can be observed. Even if data are not available from the 1990s, the low annual number of local referenda does not indicate a Post-Communist learning process.

In general, one can draw the conclusion that this important element of the local government reform of 1990, which aimed at direct democracy, is largely underused in Hungary.

Why is the institution of local referendum, with a solid legal-constitutional basis and high political potential, so neglected? There has been no research conducted on this problem. (Actually, this might also be an indicator of the status of the institution.) Speculatively, three potential causes (institutional, cultural, and societal) can be listed:

1. An obvious institutional barrier is the threshold set by local governments. It is not easy to mobilize 20–25 percent of the local society for a petition, and again mobilize half of them to turn out. In a country where the highest turnout at local elections was 51 percent, those thresholds seem very high.

That institutional explanation can at best be partial, as lower thresholds do not seem to induce more frequent use of local referenda and there are examples of successful initiatives in high-threshold municipalities. For instance, the threshold is twenty percent in a municipality where a referendum has recently taken place. Another problem with this simple explanation is that country-level referenda are not held more frequently: there was one held on the direct election of the president (failed) and another one on NATO membership (succeeded). The threshold of a country-level referendum is only 200,000 signatures (2% of the total population) and is effective if twenty-five percent of the eligible voters vote in the same way (that is why the NATO referendum was effective, though only 49% turned out).

2. In terms of political culture, local referendum has no tradition in Hungary. The institution was created in 1990. Since few cases have since crossed over the stimulus threshold of media, the awareness of the institution is limited among Hungarian citizens. It is not a part of people's mental toolkit of claim-enforcement.

3. A societal hypothesis for the underused nature of referendum on both national and local level is the low organization of civil society in Hungary (like in

other Post-Communist countries). The Communist regime systematically destroyed the spontaneous horizontal organization of the society. The dense network of Catholic, Socialist and other associations were officially regarded as a potential danger for the building of Real Socialism. In addition to a deep economic crisis, democracy inherited a weak society, largely characterized by amoral familism.

Although much has happened since the fall of Communism, the density of civil society organizations is comparatively low in Hungary: 4.7 non-profit organizations per 1000 inhabitants. Their territorial distribution is largely skewed. Almost one third of non-profit organizations are located in Budapest (where 18% of the population lives), while there are no such organizations in one sixth of the local governments. Similarly, there are no media outlets in 57 percent of the Hungarian municipalities. (Soós and Kálmán 2002: 46, 82) The societal potential for political participation is limited by the level of social participation.

A related problem is the lack of local counter-elites. First, representative institutions need to be strong and flexible to be able to cope with the emerging new leaders and movements. Second, the new democratic political institutions, especially parties, absorbed the leaders available in civil society organizations at the end of the eighties and in the beginning of the nineties. Third, the number of skilled or potential leaders in small villages is limited by the small size of the local government. The social and political societies almost fully overlap each other in smaller communities. Without leaders, the potential for political action is small.

Another related problem is the dependence of local society on local government resources. Administrative leaders of local governments reported in a survey conducted by the Tocqueville Research Center that eighty percent of the civil organizations received some financial or in-kind support from the local government.

For lack of research, the above-mentioned hypotheses can only be regarded as untested research proposals. What is certain is that the institution of local referendum is largely underused in Hungary and the causes of this situation have yet to be uncovered.

7.4.2. Inviting Citizens to Local Governance

While local governments are not participatory institutions per se, the Local Government Act, adopted in 1990, treated the inclusion of local citizens as the crucial duty of local governments. In fact, the Hungarian name of local governments, "önkormányzat" means "self-government": government by the people. Hungarian local governments are freely elected. Nonetheless, the local democracy dreamed of by the designers of the administrative system requires the inclusion of citizens into the decision-making process between elections. This chapter of the paper addresses the question as to what degree local governments operate as participatory institutions.

Legally speaking, the only requirement set by the Local Government Act is that local governments must hold one public hearing per year. There are no rules for the organization of public hearings, e.g. their deliberative or informative nature or the way in which they are advertised to the citizenry. Formally, public hearings are ordinary meetings of the local representative body, in which any citizen can contribute to the discussion. Local governments are naturally free to hold as many public hearings or forums as they wish.

Administrative leaders, interviewed in the survey carried out by the Tocqueville Research Center in 2001, reported the actual number of forums and public hearings held by local government in 2000. Two percent of local governments did not fulfill even the minimum legal requirement. Two-thirds of municipalities held the minimum number of public hearings, i.e. one, while one in three local governments had more than one forum or public hearing.

There is significant positive association between the number of forums held by local governments and the level of socioeconomic development of a municipality. A similar, but negative relationship can be found between the number of forums and the position of the municipality on the West-East axis. In other words, local leaders in municipalities of similar size are more likely to engage their citizenry in settlements that are more developed and are closer to the country's Western border.

The number of forums and public hearings is also low in comparative terms. While the average number of meetings is only 1.6 in Hungary, Polish or Romanian municipalities held an average of 15 and 12 forums, respectively, in 2000 (Local Government Survey 2001).

My participatory observation and interviews with local leaders do not indicate that forums and public hearings held by local governments would realize the aspirations of participatory democracy proponents. The agenda of the meeting is set by the mayor or the council, this allows representatives to avoid uneasy questions. The advertisement of forums and public hearings are limited to some billboards or an ad in the monthly newsletter of the local government. As a result, few people attend. The style of these meetings is rarely deliberative. In most instances, local leaders play the major role by giving information on the state of affairs and responding to related questions. In some cases, the discussion is lively, but participants are not constructive and do not try to convince each other. Local governments never appoint a neutral, but skilled moderator. Many representatives cynically view forums and public hearings as safety valves through which the most annoying citizens can release their steam.

Participation in local political life can be initiated by actors other than the local government. The Local Government Survey of the Tocqueville Research Center collected information about five types of local collective political activities in the year 2000. Unfortunately due to resource limitations a citizen survey could not be carried out parallel with the survey of notaries in municipalities, thus the views of citizens cannot be added to these data.

Table 7.17. Local political activities in Hungary (2000)

	% of surveyed municipalities	**Average number of activity per municipality**
Public demonstrations	3.0%	0.05
Petitions	13.0%	0.16
Requesting meetings	24.0%	1.17
Court challenges of local government	5.0%	1.00
Civil society proposals	37.0%	1.63

Source: Local Government Survey 2001

The submission of proposals by civic organizations took place in the highest proportion of municipalities, and requests for meetings were the second most widespread tools used. Understandably, more drastic actions such as demonstrations, petitions and challenging decisions at courts were not generally employed. Although the frequency of court cases ranks third, such situations occurred in only 5 percent of the municipalities surveyed.

In almost half (49%) of the Hungarian municipalities, none of the above presented actions took place in 2000. It is not surprising that the number of initiatives to influence local government decisions is largely determined by municipality size.

In other words, citizens participate much more actively in the politics of larger cities. The differences are quite substantial, with participation about 10 times more frequent in the larger cities than in the smaller ones – obviously this is linked to the complexity of issues as well. The second most important predictor of the intensity of local collective actions is the density of civil organizations. In all population categories, citizens of more civic municipalities tend to participate more in local politics. The third significant factor is the level of socioeconomic development. People in richer municipalities are more likely to participate collectively in local political life.

The Local Government Survey shows that wherever such participatory actions took place, generally speaking individual citizens were the most active in initiating them, next in order came civil society organizations, and in last place were political parties.

In sum, local governments are not participatory institutions. Decision-making is rather exclusive than inclusive in Hungarian municipalities. It is clear from multivariate analysis that the density of civil society organizations and the extent of economic development increase the chance of participation and encourage (or press) leaders to hold more public meetings on local problems. The actual use of institutions depends on the social environment in which they exist.

7.4.3. Local Direct Democracy in Hungary

Summing up, there is no evidence about the extensive existence of local systems based on institutionalized direct democracy. Local referenda are rarely initiated and even more rarely implemented successfully. Local governments usually rely on indirect representation and infrequently involve citizen groups directly into the their decision-making.

7.5. Conclusion

This chapter has surveyed various sources of evidence in order to broaden our knowledge on all the dimensions of local party institutionalization and contribute to the testing of hypotheses of this research. The chapter has especially focused on two aspects, systemness and autonomy.

Systemness refers to the routinization and complexity of internal processes. The evidence on the level of systemness of local parties in Hungary is mixed. Local parties do not have many resources and, what is even more important, the available resources often rely on the personal contribution of party members. The ability to influence the local representatives that are nominated by organizations to contribute to the organizational resources is a sign of systemness. The representatives belonging to the same organization also vote together very frequently and local parties to a large degree attempt to hold their members accountable. Party meetings seem to be rare but well planned. The most important factors that influence the opinion of party members are also related to the nominating organization (the party itself and its faction in the council). On the other hand, the frequent lack of regularized organizational control over the representatives of local parties indicates a low systemness.

The concept of autonomy refers to the independence of the local party organization from sponsor organizations and national or other bodies of the organization. In general, Hungarian local parties, even the local chapters of national parties do not depend on external sponsors too extensively. The local party organizations mainly rely on members' fees and in-kind contributions and the contributions of the local representatives who were nominated by the organizations. What local chapters receive from their 'mother' party is usually ideological guidance and training, not material resources. Local organizations also have much opportunity to select their candidates (though some kind of veto rights concerning the mayoral candidates are often maintained by the national center). However, the donations of private persons and companies are also of some importance among the resources, which may hide the party's dependence on important supporters.

The chapter has provided evidence for some hypotheses as well. One of the counter-intuitive findings is that the Local Party Survey indicated that the institutionalization of support is higher in the short ticket system than in the mixed one. That might be explained by the somewhat self-selective nature of the survey process. Actually, there is much difference (and in the expected direction) in the level of discipline local parties can impose on their representatives. The most compelling evidence for the size effect is from the Local Representative Survey that clearly showed a positive correlation between party influence over representatives and population size. Functional size also seemed to have a large effect on party rule and the ability of parties to influence the opinions of their members.

There is some evidence for the contribution of civil society to the institutionalization of local parties, as many party organizations are based on a previous cooperation in social organizations.

The local chapters of national parties have more resources, higher discipline, and more routinized internal life than the social organizations that function as local parties. That confirms the hypotheses about the difference in legal registration.

Table 7.18. The hypotheses based on further evidence

Hypothesis	Confirmation
H1. Electoral system	+
H2. Population size	+
H3. Functional size	+
H9. Civil society	+
H12. Legal difference	+ +

++ hypothesis clearly supported; + hypothesis mostly supported; – hypothesis not confirmed; – – hypothesis clearly unsupported +/– mixed indirect effects

Chapter 8: Conclusions

This last chapter returns to the initial hypotheses and summarizes the findings. It also speculates on what kind of reform could increase the role of political parties in local governments in Hungary. The final section discusses the limitations of the research and outlines a research agenda that could go beyond those limitations in the future.

8.1. Aspects of Local Party Institutionalization

Chapter 1 defined local party institutionalization as a multidimensional concept with four components: reification, value infusion, systemness and autonomy. This section characterizes the level of institutionalization by these four aspects.

The level of reification, i.e. the degree to which parties are conceived as central actors, is best characterized by the Local Party Government index. Chapter 4, which examined this index, concluded that parties are present only in half of the municipalities in Hungary. It also found that parties become indispensable players in local politics only in the mixed electoral system. The analysis of certain questions of the Local Representative Survey in Chapter 7 arrived at the same conclusion.

Value infusion was primarily measured by the indicator of Local Party Loyalty. Chapter 5, discussing the loyalty of candidates to their nominating organizations, indicated a low general level of party loyalty: only every second candidate remained loyal. However, it must be noted that party organizations often disappear between elections. The malleability of local party organizations is also a sign of the (low) level of institutionalization, but does not refer to value infusion. The loyalty rate clearly differed by certain structural factors, first of all, population size.

Systemness, i.e. the level of internal routinization, was not measured in the same sophisticated way as party government and party loyalty, but Chapter 7 provided some evidence about its level. In some respects, the level of systemness seemed high: members are a regular source of support, party meetings are often planned, the faction of local parties usually maintain united, and representatives often have to justify their deeds to their nominating organization. On the other hand, the factions of local parties in councils often live an independent life and party meetings are rare.

Decisional autonomy, i.e. the independence from sponsor organizations, seems high in Hungary. Local parties mainly rely on the fees and in-kind contribution of their members and representatives, and sponsors play a limited role in financing their activities (though the donations of private persons and companies matter too). The local chapters of national parties gain more 'soft' resources such as coherent worldviews and policy packages with the appropriate slogans and underlying ideology than money or other material contribution. Their independence of candidate selection is also high.

To sum up, parties rule only a minority of local governments, but are often strong in them, their value infusion largely depends on the type of organization; the level of their systemness is medium, but they enjoy a relatively high autonomy.

8.2. Confirmed and Unconfirmed Hypotheses

This section assesses the direct and indirect effects of the independent variables on local party institutionalization. I begin with the specific hypotheses, continue with the size-related propositions, and finish with a report on the rest of the hypotheses.

8.2.1. Specific Hypotheses

Three of the four hypotheses that were not involved in the causal models were overwhelmingly supported. First, there is indeed a difference in institutionalization between the local chapters of national parties and social organizations that nominate candidates at local elections. On average, the local organizations of parties are more stable in every respect than civil society organizations acting as local parties. Second, the local chapters of parliamentary parties are clearly more institutionalized than other local chapters or social organizations. Third, the hypothesis about a positive relationship between the electoral performance of national-level parties and the institutionalization of their local organizations has also been confirmed. While the latter two propositions are quite intuitive, the empirical confirmation of the first one is an interesting addition to extant knowledge.

One hypothesis was not supported by the data. It claimed that the institutionalization of local parties increases as democracy becomes older. The reason for that may be the increasing penetration of national parties parallel with their organizational buildup and the general consolidation tendency of democracy with its aging. What one can see instead is a stagnation or slow decline of party penetration. This finding is quite surprising as political competition has become cut-throat on the national level for the last few years as the country moved towards a two party system. One might expect an extension of the organization of the big parties. There may be three explanations. First, the small local governments may still not offer enough voters to justify organization building. Second, the indicator of local party government, the only data for the test of this hypothesis, may be deceptive. It focuses on penetration and does not measure the internal strengthening of the existing organizations. National parties might choose a strategy of concentrating on towns and cities, which are more important for them. Third, it might be too early to test the expectation and the next election may show a trend of expansion. In any case, institutionalization will clearly not be due to a general trend of consolidation, but an intensification of the competition between political players.

8.2.2. Size-related Hypotheses

Size does matter in many ways. It is clear that functional size, the functional form of size, has a sizeable impact on the level of local party institutionalization. The municipality population also has a large effect, plus it indirectly influences party institutionalization by determining functional size to a large degree.

The direct effect of population size may signal spurious effects actually caused by other factors. Certain size-related variables have not been measured in this research or their indicator associates with size too well. For one, the number of political positions strongly correlates with size, but is conceptually different from it. The more elected and non-elected positions available, the more likely local politicians will form political organizations. The direct influence of functional size may also include this spurious effect, as the size of the political spoil depends on the number of functions provided by the municipality.

A second, probably implied effect, is the distance between local politicians and voters, this can easily be computed, but correlates so strongly with size that it is unclear to what degree the effect the population size comprises the difficulty of communication between voters and representatives/candidates.

Third, the cost of politics-making cannot be measured, but, in all probability, it associates well with size. The impact of this important aspect is likely to be implied in the direct effect of the size variables.

Fourth, population size is a proxy measure of the size of local civil society (not its density). This can be computed (at least as the number of registered civil society organizations), but it has such a strong correlation with the size of the local population that it is unclear what actually exerts the influence on local party institutionalization.

There are some indirect effects that were successfully detected in the causal analyses. Population size has a consistently positive path through functional size.

Political participation mediates negatively in the short ticket system and positively in the mixed system. Other routes are either weak or inconsistent. Functional size has two well-supported positive effects through population stability and citizens' resources in the mixed system, but no serious paths could be found in the short ticket system.

To sum up, both types of size have direct and indirect impact on local party institutionalization. Therefore, H2 and H3 were confirmed.

8.2.3. Other Hypotheses

The single most important factor that influences the level of local party institutionalization is the electoral system. In the mixed electoral system, where there are also party lists, parties dominate the political field. In the so-called short ticket system, few local governments are fully based on party politics. The drastic difference can especially clearly be seen by comparing the municipalities just below and above the dividing line between the two electoral systems. In the multivariate model, the electoral system accounts for 30 percent of all variance in the level of party government. In sum, the impact of the incentives created by electoral rules is immense. H1 is strongly supported.

Suburban areas form a special part of the local government system. The overall direct effect of belonging to a metropolitan area is negligible. Nonetheless, it explains the differences by electoral system. In the mixed system, the effect is direct and manifest. Organizing a local chapter in a town close to the central city is relatively easy for national parties. If there is sufficient gain, as it is the case in suburban towns, the incentive is especially high for parties. On the other hand, party loyalty is low in suburbs. Recruitment is easy, but stabilizing the organization is much more difficult. In the short ticket system, the impact is rather indirect and contradictory. On the one hand, more affluent and educated citizens, which characterize suburbs, contribute to the strength of local party organizations. On the other hand, suburban denizens are busy families with children who have less time and energy for strengthening political organizations and suburban villages have much less functional significance in the shadow of a large city than municipalities of the same size but of different location. This has a negative indirect impact on the level of local party institutionalization. The metropolitan area has a very complex effect: H11 is not supported.

Only two other hypotheses were clearly confirmed. The stability of the local population (H5) has a clear positive impact on the level of local party institutionalization. The more unstable the local society, the less likely that political organizations become stable and routinized. The other factor is the age of the local population (H8). More senior people make local parties more institutionalized.

As predicted, the amount of personal resources local citizens (H7) possess has a clear effect on the level of local party institutionalization in the mixed electoral system. More free time, political skills, and donation capacity of local people stabilize political organizations. However, the effect of personal resources on party loyalty is weak and on party government it is simply negative.

Other factors showed a weak relationship with party institutionalization in the short ticket system, but produced a nonexistent or unpredicted effect in the mixed electoral system. Their hypotheses were not clearly confirmed.

Table 8.1. Summarizing the hypotheses

Hypothesis	All cases	Short ticket	Mixed
H1. Electoral system	++	NA	NA
H2. Population size	++	++	+
H3. Functional size	++	++	++
H4. Urbanization	+	+	–
H5. Population stability	+	+	++
H6a. Socioeconomic diversity	+	+	–
H6b. Ethnic diversity	+	+	–
H7. Citizens' resources	+	–	++
H8. Age	+	+	+
H9. Civil society	–	–	–
H10. Electoral participation	+	+	–
H11. Closeness to centers	–	–	–
H12. Legal difference	++	++	++
H13. Parliamentary parties	++	++	++
H14. Country-level performance	+	+	+
H15. Age of democracy	–	NA	NA

++ Strongly confirmed; + Confirmed; – Not confirmed; – – Rejected

8.3. A Case for Amalgamation?

Policy makers have some options if they want to increase the role of political parties in local governments in Hungary. A simple change in the electoral system would alter the average level of local party institutionalization. There is a threshold around 5,000 inhabitants (see Horváth 1996) where the organizations step in. In municipalities above this threshold, the political organizations increasingly form local political life and make the role of individual politicians less and less important. A move of the dividing line between the short list and mixed systems would change the character of local politics in the category under the present 10,000 threshold.

A much more far-reaching reform could target the size of local governments. In the middle of the systemic changes in 1990, every community was entitled to become independent as a compensation for the previous merging attempts, widely perceived as illegitimate and forced. As a result, practically every single community formed their own local government. In the Hungarian language, 'settlement' and 'local government' often refer to the same concept.

Can a change in functional size increase the role local party organizations play in community life? In a sense, the answer is affirmative. Giving more resources and financial means to local governments would make local politics more interesting to national parties and attract personalities of a higher calibre. That would work especially well in the small town-large village category where parties are not yet present. Beyond a general level of devolution and decentralization, functional size cannot be changed, as it is a relative concept. The more importance a local government gains, the less important the neighboring municipalities become.

Other factors such as the level of urbanization or education cannot be changed or a reform would be extremely expensive merely to increase the institutionalization of local party organizations.

While the consequences of a reform are manifest in this research, the intention of a reform depends on the other considerations too. While the proponents of amalgamation can add a new, political argument to their (usually efficiency-based) reasoning, the expected uses of parties and the value given to the legitimacy of local communities must be clarified. First, parties may not make local life better. As Chapter 1 warned, local party organizations may have a negative role in local politics. This research focused on parties as a dependent variable and did not analyze the impact of party politics on local life. One must take those potential effects into account before any steps toward a territorial reform. Second, an open, societal-level debate should decide the rank order of values. For many, the independence of well-established communities, which often have a history of hundreds or sometimes more than one thousand years, has a priority over any kind of reforms aiming at more efficiency or transparency. For others, the local governments are public administration units that must meet the same standards as any kind of government: they must be effective, efficient, and transparent. A reform of public administration must take both arguments into account and find the best available compromise that involves both the value of autonomy and the requirements of transparent and efficient policies.

8.4. Limitations and Further Research

There are obviously a number of caveats that must be kept in mind in interpreting the results presented here. A major limitation from a technical point of view is the use of recursive models. The direction of some relationships is far from being unambiguous. A non-recursive model could reveal more interesting cross-effects. However, that would have required a more complex model in this research.

The research has been limited in the sense that the analysis of local party institutionalization was carried out in a non-comparative way. The competing channels (personal contacts through clans, networks, and patronage) have not been examined. That leaves some questions unanswered. To what degree can organizational and network-like integration co-exist? How do they compete? What are the consequences of their competition? What is the impact of personal contacts on the decisions of politicians who leave their party? Qualitative case studies would help to better understand the actual mechanisms through which local parties become institutionalized in a competitive institutional environment.

This research outlined a theory of local party institutionalization, which can be used both by qualitative and quantitative studies. Qualitative methods could add much to the understanding of local party institutionalization. Qualitative case studies may focus on the competition between rival ways of political institutionalization. As I outlined in the first chapter, party government is not the only possible form of local political organization. Personal clientelism seems an especially powerful rival of the organization-based governance. While this research has hopefully shed some light on the structural factors that affect the level of party government, further research could specify the relationship between personal clientelism and party institutionalization. The fact that the presence of powerful party organizations and personal clienteles within the same polity do not exclude each other makes the research problem particularly interesting.

Qualitative case studies may also specify the importance of the unmeasured theoretical variables that are hypothesized to affect the level of local party institutionalization directly. For example, a research specifying what kind of local conditions attract the attention of the party builders on the national level could add much to our knowledge on the vertical relationship between local and country level politics. The forms of local mobilization costs and their effect on the organization of local political life is another possibility for a qualitative inquiry.

References

Aldrich, John H. 1995. Why Parties? The Origin and Transformation of Political Parties in America. Chicago: The University of Chicago Press.

Anderson, Gordon and Ying Ge. 2003. "The Size Distribution of Chinese Cities." Online Publication, www.uibe.edu.cn/upload/up_jmxy/xscg/ywgzlw/44.pdf.

Bergman, Torbjörn and Kaare Stroem. 2004. "Shifting Dimensions of Citizen Control." Scandinavian Political Studies, vol. 27, no. 2.

Bogason, Peter. 2004. "Institutional Theory and Democracy." Roskilde, DK: Center for Democratic Network Governance. Working Paper 2004/7.

Böhm, Antal. 1993. "The Hungary National report." In: Jacob et. al. (eds.) Democracy and Local Governance. Ten Empirical Studies, Honolulu: Matsunaga Institute for Peace.

Bützer, Michael. 2004. "Continuity or innovation? Citizen engagement and Institutional reforms in Swiss cities." Conference paper: "Revolution or Renovations? Reforming Local Politics in Europe." University of Gent, Ghent: 16–17 December, 2004.

Clark, Alistair. 2004. "The Continued Relevance of Local Parties in Representative Democracies." Politics, Vol. 24, No. 1, Pp. 35–45.

Cohen, Jean L., and Andrew Arato. 1992. Civil Society and Political Theory. Cambridge: MIT.

Colton, Timothy J. and Michael McFaul. eds. 2004. Popular Choice and Managed Democracy: The Russian Elections of 1999 and 2000. Washington, D.C.: The Brookings Institution.

Cusack, Thomas R. 1997. "Social Capital, Institutional Structures, and Democratic Performance: A Comparative Study of German Local Governments" Berlin: Wissenshaftzentrum Berlin für Sozialforschung.

Dahl, Robert and E. R. Tufte. 1973. Size and Democracy. Stanford, CA: Stanford University Press.

Damgaard, Bodil. 2004. "Network Governing: A Rare Occurrence in the Network Society." Copenhagen: Roskilde University. Conference on "Democratic Network Governance", 21–22 October, 2004.

Downs, Anthony. 1957. An Economic Theory of Democracy. New York: Harper and Row.

Dugger, William M. 2003. "General Introduction." In: William M. Dugger. ed. Evolutionary Theory in the Social Sciences. Vol. 1. Early Foundations and Later Contributions. London: Routledge.

Duverger, Maurice. (1951) 1964. 2nd Revised English Edition. Political Parties: Their Organization and Activity in the Modern State. London: Methuen.

Duverger, Maurice.1964. 3rd ed. Political Parties. London: Methuen.

Edwards, Bob and Michael W. Foley. 1998. "Social Capital and Civil Society Beyond Putnam." American Behavioral Scientist, Vol. 42, No. 2.

Edwards, Bob, Michael W. Foley, and Mario Diani. eds. 2001. Beyond Tocqueville: Civil Society and the Social Capital Debate in Comparative Perspective. Hanover and London: University Press of New England / Tufts University.

Enyedi Zsolt and Körösényi András. 2004. Pártok és pártrendszerek. [Parties and Party Systems.] Budapest: Osiris.

Enyedi Zsolt. 1995. "Az ésszerűen nem-racionális párt." [The Rationally Nonrational party.] Politikatudományi Szemle, vol. 4, no. 3.

Evans, Alfred B. Jr. and Vladimir Gel'man. eds. 2004. The Politics of Local Government in Russia. Lanham, MD: Rowman & Littlefield.

Farrell, David and Paul Webb. 2000. "Political Parties as Campaign Organizations." In: Parties Without Partisans, edited by Russell J. Dalton and Martin P. Wattenberg. Oxford: Oxford University Press.

Fekete, Éva G., Mihály Lados, Edit Pfeil, Zsolt Szoboszlai. 2002. "Size of Local Governments, Local Democracy and Local Service Delivery in Hungary." In: Consolidation or Fragmentation? The Size of Local Governments in Central and Eastern Europe ed. by Pawel Swianiewicz. Budapest: Local Government and Public Service Reform Initiative.

Field, John. 2003. Social Capital. London: Routledge.

Fogarasi, József. ed. 1999. Önkormányzati kézikönyv. [Handbook of Local Governments.] Budapest: HVGOrac.

Frandsen, Annie Gaardsted. 2001. "Size and electoral participation in local elections." Paper for ESF-working conference Size and Local Democracy in Europe, Zurich, November 8–11th 2001.

Frendreis, John P., James L. Gibson, and Laura L. Vertz. 1990. "The Electoral Relevance of Local Party Organizations." American Political Science Review 84: 225–235.

Gerber, Alan S. and Donald P. Green. 2000. "The Effects of Personal Canvassing, Telephone Calls, and Direct Mail on Voter Turnout: A Field Experiment." American Political Science Review 94: 653–664.

Geser, Hans. 1999. "The Local Party as an Object of Interdisciplinary Comparative Study: Some Steps Toward Theoretical Integration." In Martin Saiz and Hans Geser. eds. Local Parties in Political and Organizational Perspective. Boulder, Colorado: Westview Press.

Goodin, Robert E. 1996. "Institutions and Their Design." In Goodin, Robert E. The Theory of Institutional Design. Cambridge: Cambridge University Press.

Hajnal, György (2001) "Hopes and Reality: The First Decade of the Hungarian Local Government System in the View of the Public" in Public Perception of Local Governments ed. by Pawel Swianiewicz. Budapest: Local Government and Public Service Reform Initiative.

Hall, Peter A. and Taylor, Rosemary C. R. 1996. "Political Science and the Three New Institutionalism." Political Studies, vol. 44, pp. 936–957.

Horváth, M. Tamás. 1996. Pártok a helyi önkormányzatokban. [Parties in Local Governments.] Budapest: Magyar Közigazgatási Intézet.

Horváth, M. Tamás. 1994. "Basic Information on Local Governments in Hungary." In: Local Governments in the CEE and CIS: An Anthology of Descriptive Papers. Budapest:Open Society Institute.

Huntington, Samuel P. 1968. Political Order in Changing Societies. New Haven: Yale University Press.

Immergut, Ellen M. 1998. The Theoretical Core of the New Institutionalism. Politics & Society Vol. 26. No.1.

Janda, Kenneth. 1980. Political Parties: A Cross-National Survey. London: Macmillan. Available also on the Internet: http://www.janda.org/ICPP/ICPP1980/

Jensen, Roger Buch. 1999. "Local Party Organizations in Denmark: Crisis or Adaptation?" In Martin Saiz and Hans Geser. eds. Local Parties in Political and Organizational Perspective. Boulder, Colorado: Westview Press.

Jin Seok Bae. 2003. "Why Not Organization? Toward a Definition of Party Institutionalization." Chicago: Annual Meeting of the Midwest Political Science Association.

John, Peter. 2001. Local Governance in Western Europe. London. SAGE.

Kákai, László. 2004. Önkormányozunk értetek, de nélkületek! Pártok és civil szervezetek a helyi társadalmakban. [We Govern For You, But Without You!

Parties and Civil Society Organizations in the Local Societies] Budapest: Századvég.

Katz, Richard and Peter Mair. 1995. "Changing Models of Party Organization and Party Democracy: The Emergence of the Cartel Party." Party Politics, Vol. 1, no. 1.

Katz, Richard S. 1987. "Party Government and Its Alternatives." In Richard S. Katz. ed. Party Governments: European and American Experiences. Berlin: Walter de Gruyter.

Keating, Michael. 1995 "Size, Efficiency and Democracy: Consolidation, Fragmentation and Public Choice". In: Judge, David, Gerry Stoker and Harold Wolman. eds. Theories of Urban Politics. London: SAGE.

Klijn, Erik-Hans. 2004. "Governance Networks and Democracy: A World to Gain." Copenhagen: Roskilde University. Conference on "Democratic Network Governance", 21–22 October, 2004.

Knight, Jack and Itai Sened. 1998. "Introduction." In: Jack Knight and Itai Sened. eds. Explaining Social Institutions. Ann Arbor: The University of Michigan Press.

Knight, Jack. 1992. Institutions and Social Conflict. Cambridge: Cambridge University Press. "Political Economy of Institutions and Decisions".

Koeble, Thomas. A. 1995. The New Institutionalism in Political Science and Sociology. Comparative Politics No. 1.

Kopstein, Jeffrey and David A. Reilly. 2000. "Geographic Diffusion and the Transformation of the Postcommunist World." World Politics Vol. 53, pp. 1–37. (October).

Központi Statisztikai Hivatal [Central Statistical Office]. 2001. Területi Statisztikai Évkönyv 2000. [Statistical Yearbook of Territorial Units.] Budapest: Központi Statisztikai Hivatal.

Kuper, Adam and Jessica Kuper. eds. 1985. The Social Science Encyclopedia. London: Routledge and Kegan.

Ladner, Andreas. 2002. "Size and Direct Democracy at the Local Level: The Case of Switzerland" Environment and Planning C: Government and Policy, Vol. 20, No. 6.

Levitsky, Steven. 1998. "Institutionalism and Peronism: The Concept, the Case and the Case for Unpacking the Concept." Party Politics, vol. 4, no. 1.

Lijphart, Arend. 1977. Democracy in Plural Societies: A Comparative Exploration. New Haven: Yale University Press.

Lin, Nan. 2001. Social Capital: A Theory of Social Structure and Action. Cambridge: Cambridge University Press.

Lipset, Seymour Martin and Stein Rokkan. 1967. "Cleavage Structures, Party Systems and Voter Alignments: Introduction." In Seymour Martin Lipset and Stein Rokkan. eds. Party Systems and Voter Alignments: Cross-National Perspectives. New York: The Free Press.

Little, Daniel. 1991. Varieties of Social Explanation: An Introduction to the Philosophy of Social Science. Boulder: Westview Press.

Lomax, Bill. 1997. "The Strange Death of Civil Society in Post-Communist Hungary." Journal of Communist Studies and Transition Politics, Vol 13, No 1.

Luther, Kurt Richard and Kris Deschouwer. eds. 1999. Party Elites In Divided Societies: Political Parties In Consociational Democracy. London: Routledge.

Machos Csilla. 2000. A magyar parlamenti pártok szervezeti felépítése (1990–1999). [The organization of the Hungarian parliamentary parties.] Budapest: Rejtjel.

Mainwaring, Scott and Timothy R. Scully. 1994. "Introduction: Party Systems in Latin America." In: Scott Mainwaring and Timothy R. Scully. eds. Building Democratic Institutions: Party Systems in Latin America. Stanford, CA: Stanford University Press.

Mainwaring, Scott. 1998. "Rethinking Party Systems Theory in the Third Wave of Democratization: The Importance of Party System Institutionalization." Working Paper #260. Notre Dame, Indiana: The Helen Kellogg Institute for International Studies, University of Notre Dame.

March, James. G. and Johan Olsen. 1989. Rediscovering Institutions. The organizational basis of politics. New York: The Free Press.

Marcusen, Martin and Jacob Torfing. 2003. Grasping Governance Networks. Roskilde: Centre for Democratic Network Governance.

Marelyin Kiss, József, Imre Kabai and Attila Dénes. 2001. "Önkormányzati rendszer és demokratikus deficit: A helyi önkormányzatok első tíz éve Magyarországon" [Local Government System and Democratic Deficit: The First Ten Years of Local Governments in Hungary] In: Magyarország Politikai Évkönyve 2000-ről [The Political Yearbook of Hungary, 2000] Budapest: Demokrácia Kutatások Magyar Központja.

Martins, M. R. 1995. Size of Municipalities, Efficiency, and Citizen's Participation: a Cross-European Perspective In: Environment and Planning C: Government and Policy, November.

McGuire, James. 1997. Peronism Without Perón: Unions, Parties and Democracy in Argentina. Sanford, CA: Stanford University Press.

Meyer, John W. and Brian Rowan. 1992. "Institutionalized Organizations: Formal Structure as Myth and Ceremony." In Meyer John W., W. Richard Scott. Organizational Environments Ritual and Rationality. London: Sage.

Michels, Robert. 1968. Political Parties: A Sociological Study of the Oligarchical Tendencies of Modern Democracy. New York: Free Press.

Milner, Henry, and Susan Ersson. 2000. "Social Capital, Civic Engagement and Institutional Performance in Sweden: An Analysis of the Swedish regions." Paper presented for the ECPR Joint Sessions of Workshops, University of Copenhagen, 14–19. April 2000, Workshop 'Voluntary Associations, Social Capital and Interest Mediation: Forging the Link.'

Miszlivetz Ferenc. 1997. "Participation and Transition: Can the Civil Society Project Survive in Hungary?" Journal of Communist Studies and Transition Politics Vol. 13, No. 1. 27–40.

Morlino, Leonardo. 1998. Democracy Between Consolidation and Crisis: Parties, Groups, and Citizens in Southern Europe. Oxford: Oxford University Press.

Mouritzen, Poul Eric. 1989. City Size and Citizens Satisfaction: Two Competing Theories Revisited. European Journal of Political Research Vol. 17. No. 6.

North, Douglass. 1990. Institutions, Institutional Change, and Economic Performance. Cambridge: Cambridge University Press.

Oliver, J. Eric. 2000. "City Size and Civic Involvement in Metropolitan America." American Political Science Review Vol. 94, No. 2.

Orozco, Wistano L. 2004. "Consolidation and the Institutional Infrastructure of Democracy." Seminario en Latinoamérica de Teoría Constitucional y Política (SELA), Oaxaca, México.

Panebianco, Angelo. 1988. Political Parties: Organization and Power. Cambridge: Cambridge University Press.

Peng, Yusheng. 2004. "Kinship Networks and Entrepreneurs in China's Traditional Economy." American Journal of Sociology, vol. 109, no. 5.

Peters, Guy. 1999. "Political Institutions: Old and New." In Goodin, Robert E. and Hans-Dieter Klingemann (eds.) The New Handbook of Political Science. Oxford: Oxford University Press.

Peters, Guy. 1999. Institutional Theory in Political Science: The 'New Institutionalism.' London: Pinter.

Peters, Guy. 1999. Institutional Theory in Political Science: The 'New Institutionalism'. London: Pinter.

Pizzorno, Alessandro. 1981. "Interests and Parties in Pluralism." In Berger, Suzanne D. ed. Organizing Interests in Western Europe: Pluralism, Corporatism, and the Transformation of Politics. Cambridge: Cambridge University Press.

Post, Robert C., and Nancy L. Rosenblum. 2002. "Introduction." In: Nancy L. Rosenblum and Robert C. Post. eds. Civil Society and Governance. Princeton and Oxford: Princeton University Press.

Powell, Walter W. and Paul J. DiMaggio. eds. 1991. The New Intitutionalism and Organizational Analysis. Chicago: The University of Chicago Press.

Putnam, Robert D. 2001. Bowling Alone: The Collapse and Revival of American Community. New York: Simon & Schuster.

Putnam, Robert. 1993. Making Democracy Work: Civic Traditions in Modern Italy. Princeton: Princeton University Press.

Putnam, Robert. 1995. "Bowling Alone: America's Declining Social Capital." Journal of Democracy, Vol. 6, No. 1.

Randall, Vicky and Lars Svåsand. 2002. "Party Institutionalization in New Democracies." Party Politics, Vol. 8, No. 1.

Rothstein, Bo. 1996. "Political Institutions: An Overview." In Goodin, Robert E. and Hans-Dieter Klingemann (eds.) The New Handbook of Political Science. Oxford: Oxford University Press.

Sartori, Giovanni. 1976. Parties and Party Systems: A Framework for Analysis. Cambridge: Cambridge University Press.

Schattschneider, Elmer E. 1942. Party Government. New York: Rinehart & Co. Reprint edition. 1977. Westport: Greenwood Press.

Schedler, Andreas. 1995. "Under- and Overinstitutionalization: Some Ideal Typical Propositions Concerning New and Old Party Systems." Working Paper #213. Notre Dame, Indiana: The Helen Kellogg Institute for International Studies, University of Notre Dame.

Schmitter P. C. 1997. "Civil Society East and West." In Larry Diamond. ed. Consolidating the Third Wave Democracies. London: The Johns Hopkins University Press.

Scott, W. Richard. 2001. Institutions and Organizations. 2nd ed. Thousand Oaks: Sage.

Schlesinger, Joseph A. 1965. "Political Party Organization." In: James G. March. ed. Handbook of Organizations. Chicago: Wiley.

Sczerbiak, Aleks. 1999. "Testing Party Models in East-Central Europe: Local Party Organization in Postcommunist Poland." Party Politics, Vol. 5, No. 4.

Smolar, Aleksander. 1996. "From Opposition to Atomization." Journal of Democracy Vol. 7. No. 1.

Soós, Gábor and Judit Kálmán. 2002. "Country Report – Hungary". In Soós Gábor, Tóka Gábor, and Glen Wright. eds. The State of Local Democracy in Central Europe." Budapest: Local Government and Public Service Reform Initiative.

Soós, Gábor. 2001. Concepts and Hypotheses: The Indicators of Local Democratic Governance Project. Budapest: Open Society Institute Local Government and Public Service Reform Initiative. LGI Documents.

Soós, Gábor. 2004. "Can Civil Society Control Politicians? A Case Study From Local Politics in Hungary." ECPR Joint Sessions of Workshops, Uppsala, 13–18 April 2004.

Sørensen, Eva and Jacob Torfing. 2004. "Network Governance and Post-Liberal Democracy." Copenhagen: Roskilde University. Conference on "Democratic Network Governance", 21–22 October, 2004.

Sørensen, Eva. 2003. "Meta-governance: The changing role of politicians in processes of democratic governance." Paper presented at the Conference on Democratic Network Governance, Copenhagen, May 22–23, 2003.

Stoner-Weiss, Kathryn. 2001. "The Limited Reach of Russia's Party System: Underinstitutionalization in Dual Transitions." Politics & Society, Vol. 29, No. 3.

Swianiewicz, Paweł. 2002a. "Size of Local Government, Local Democracy and Efficiency in Delivery of Local Services – International Context and Theoretical Framework." In: Paweł Swianiewicz. ed. Consolidation or Fragmentation? The Size of Local Governments in Central and Eastern Europe. Budapest: Local Government and Public Service Reform Initiative.

Swianiewicz, Paweł. 2002b. "Is There a Third Way Between Small yet Ineffective and Big yet Less Democratic? Comparative Conclusions and Lessons Learned." In: Paweł Swianiewicz. ed. Consolidation or Fragmentation? The Size of Local Governments in Central and Eastern Europe. Budapest: Local Government and Public Service Reform Initiative.

Temesi, István. 2000. Local Government in Hungary. In Horváth, Tamás M. ed. Decentralization: Experiments and Reforms. Vol. 1 of the Local Governments in Central and Eastern Europe. LGI Books. Budapest: Open Society Institute Local Government and Public Service Reform Initiative.

Thompson, William. R. 2001. "Evolving Toward an Evolutionary Perspective." In William. R. Thompson. ed. Evolutionary Interpretations of World Politics. New York: Routledge.

Tóka, Gábor. 1997. "Political Parties in East Central Europe". In: Consolidating the Third Wave Democracies: Themes and Perspectives. ed. by Larry Diamond, Marc F. Plattner, Yun-han Chu, and Hung-mao Tien. Baltimore and London: The Johns Hopkins University Press.

Uslaner, Eric M. 2002. The Moral Foundations of Trust. Cambridge: Cambridge University Press.

Van Deth, J. W. (2000) 'Interesting but Irrelevant: Social Capital and the Saliency of Politics in Western Europe', European Journal of Political Research 37(2), pp. 115–147.

Vatter, Adrian. 2003. "Legislative Party Fragmentation in Swiss Cantons: A Function of Cleavage Structures or Electoral Institutions." Party Politics, vol. 9, no. 4.

Verba, Sidney, Norman H. Nie and Jae-on Kim. 1978. Participation and Political Equality: A Seven Nation Comparison. Cambridge: Cambridge University Press.

Weingast, Barry R. 1996. "Political Institutions: Rational Choice Perspectives." In Goodin, Robert E. and Hans-Dieter Klingemann (eds.) The New Handbook of Political Science. Oxford: Oxford University Press.

Yishai, Yael. 2001. "Bringing Society Back In: Post-Cartel Parties in Israel." Party Politics, Vol. 7, No. 6.

Young, H. Peyton. Individual Strategy and Social Structure: An Evolutionary Theory of Institutions. Princeton, New Jersey: Princeton University Press.

Appendice

A. Research Hypotheses

The following hypotheses are tested in this research:

H1. The level of local party institutionalization is higher in the mixed electoral system than in the short ticket system.

H2. The larger the municipality population, the higher the level of local party institutionalization.

H3. The larger the municipality's functional size, the higher the level of local party institutionalization.

H4. The more urban the municipality is, the higher the level of local party institutionalization.

H5. The more stable the local population, the higher the level of local party institutionalization.

H6. The more heterogeneous the local society, the higher the level of local party institutionalization.

H6a. The higher the socioeconomic diversity, the higher the level of local party institutionalization.

H6b. The higher the ethnic diversity, the higher the level of local party institutionalization.

H7. The more resources the citizens possess, the higher the level of local party institutionalization.

H8. The older the local society, the higher the level of local party institutionalization.

H9. The more active the local society politically, the higher the level of local party institutionalization.

H10. The more organized and institutionalized the local civil society, the higher the level of local party institutionalization.

H11. The closer to political and cultural centers the local government, the higher the level of local party institutionalization.

Specific Hypotheses

H12. The local chapters of national parties are more institutionalized than grass-roots civic associations functioning as local parties.

H13. The local chapters of parliamentary parties are more institutionalized than other local party organizations.

H14. The electoral performance of the national party influences the level of institutionalization of its local chapters.

H15. The level of local party institutionalization increases with the age of democracy.

B. The Variables in the Index of Functional Size

The index of functional size is composed of the following variables:

T-STAR variable	In Hungarian	In English[7]
TAAM001	Körjegyzőség székhelye	Seat of notarial district
TAAM002	Munkaügyi központ, illetve kirendeltség léte	Labor center or branch office
TAAM100	Vasútállomás léte	Railway station
TAAM101	Távolsági autóbusz-megálló léte	Long-distance bus station
TAAM102	Postahivatal (fiókposta) léte	Post office or branch office
TAAM106	Helyi autóbuszjárat léte	Local bus line
TAAM107	Benzinkút (üzemanyagtöltő állomás) léte	Gas station
TAAM111	Bankfiók léte	Bank office
TAAM202	Piac léte	Open market
TAAM203	Kemping léte	Camp site
TAAM204	Ruházati szaküzlet léte	Shop for clothes
TAAM205	Iparcikk jellegű üzlet és áruház léte	Shop or department store with dominance of manufactured goods
TAAM300	Közüzemi vízhálózat léte	Public water conduit network
TAAM301	Zárt közcsatorna-hálózat léte	Closed public sewerage
TAAM402	Járóbeteg szakellátás léte	Outpatient service
TAAM403	Kórház léte	Hospital
TAAM404	Szülészeti ellátás léte (kórházban vagy szülőotthonban)	Obstetrical provision (either in hospitals or maternity homes)
TAAM405	Mentőállomás léte	Ambulance station
TAAM406	Gyógyszertár léte	Pharmacy
TAAM407	Bölcsőde léte	Infant nursery
TAAM410	Fogászati szakrendelés léte (községi fogászattal együtt)	Dental care

7 Official translation into English by the Central Statistical Office, see Központi Statisztikai Hivatal 2001.

T-STAR variable	In Hungarian	In English[7]
TAAM411	Központi körzeti (háziorvosi) ügyelet léte	General Practitioner's service with district attendance obligation
TAAM412	Tartós bentlakásos és átmeneti elhelyezést nyújtó szociális intézmény léte	Social institution providing permanent or temporary accommodation
TAAM413	Időskorúak otthonának léte, amely a település, több település, illetve a megye rászorultjait látja el	Homes for the aged providing for the residents of one or more settlements of of a county
TAAM414	Szállást adó idősek klubjának léte	Clubs for the aged providing accommodation
TAAM415	Nappali ellátást nyújtó idősek klubjának léte	Clubs for the aged providing day-care
TAAM416	Háziorvosi székhely léte	General Practitioner's seat
TAAM500	Óvoda léte	Kindergarten
TAAM501	Általános iskola léte	Primary school
TAAM502	Középiskola léte	Secondary school (apprentice schools are not included)
TAAM503	Települési könyvtár léte	Public library maintained by local governments
TAAM504	Filmszínház léte	Cinema
TAAM505	Művelődési otthon jellegű intézmény (telephely) léte	Cultural halls (or branches) and similar institutions
TAAM512	Működő mezőgazdasági szövetkezetek léte	Active agricultural cooperative
TAAM513	Szakiskolai és speciális szakiskolai feladatellátási hely léte	Apprentice or vocational school
TAAM514	Kollégiumi feladatellátási hely léte	Student hostel
TAAM515	Múzeum léte	Museum

www.ingramcontent.com/pod-product-compliance
Ingram Content Group UK Ltd.
Pitfield, Milton Keynes, MK11 3LW, UK
UKHW020121290926
15471UKWH00003B/206

9 783631 657348